KING ALFRED'S CO

Perspectives on inflation

Perspectives on inflation
Models and policies

Edited by
David F. Heathfield

Longman
London and New York

Longman Group Limited London

*Associated companies, branches and representatives
throughout the world*

*Published in the United States of America
by Longman Inc., New York*

© David Heathfield, J. D. Byers, S. P. Chakravarty, V. Chick,
   Phyllis Deane, J. A. Kregel, G. W. McKenzie, Alec Nove 1979

First published 1979

British Library Cataloguing in Publication Data

Perspectives on inflation.
   1. Inflation (Finance) – Mathematical models
   I. Title   II. Heathfield, David Frederick
   332.4'1   HG229   78–40186

   ISBN 0–582–44189–7
   ISBN 0–582–44190–0   Pbk.

Printed in Great Britain by Richard Clay (The Chaucer Press) Ltd, Bungay, Suffolk

Contents

Acknowledgements

We are grateful to the following for permission to reproduce copyright material:

American Economic Association and the author, George A. Hay, for tables and equations from 'Production, Price and Inventory Theory' from *American Economic Review* September 1970; Cambridge University Press for extracts from *Abstract of British Historical Statistics* by B. R. Mitchell and Deane; Cambridge University Press and the Department of Applied Economics, for extracts from *Statistical Tables of National Income, Expenditure and Output of the United Kingdom 1855–1965* by C. H. Feinstein; Chapman and Hall Ltd., for an adapted extract from *Applied Economics* Vol 3 by Heathfield and Evans 1971; International Economic Review and the author, T. Courchene, for tables from 'An Analysis of the Price-Inventory Nexus with Empirical Application to the Canadian Manufacturing Sector' from *International Economic Review* Vol 10 No. 3 October 1969; The London School of Economics and Political Science for extracts from 'Seven Centuries of Building Wage Rates' by E. H. Phelps Brown and S. V. Hopkins from *Economica* August 1955, 'Wage Rates and Prices: Evidence for Population Pressure in the Sixteenth Century' by E. H. Phelps Brown and S. V. Hopkins from *Economica* November 1957, 'The Relationship Between Unemployment and the Rate of Change of Money Wages in the United Kingdom 1862–1957: A Further Analysis' by R. G. Lipsey from *Economica* February 1960; The MIT Press for an adapted extract from *World Dynamics* by Jay Forrester; John Wiley and Sons Inc., for a table from *Price, Output and Inventory Policy* by E. S. Mills 1962.

Editor's preface

There can be no doubt that inflation is topical, but many would doubt the need for yet another volume devoted to this already well-served subject. Our reply would be that this volume treats more than inflation and treats inflation in a novel way. It is aimed at illuminating inflation, and the diversity of views held about it, by asking of a number of models, 'What is inflation and what if anything ought to be done about it?' Equally, some light is thrown on to the models themselves, but the light is directed on only one facet of each model – its treatment of inflation. This approach though restricted, does serve to highlight some of the models' differences and similarities. Our purpose dictates our choice of models and we exclude those which have little or nothing to say about inflation, no matter how powerful or popular they may otherwise be. This, then, is a volume about models as well as about inflation.

The scene is set as it were by Phyllis Deane's survey of the history of inflation and of the policies which were pursued or advocated in the past. From this it is clear that inflation is no new phenomenon and that many of the views held today are echoed down the years. Time, it seems, is unlikely to resolve those disagreements which remain.

The most persistent view has been that of the monetarists. Their central theme is that the quantity of money is the key to the problem and that the control of the money supply is at least a first step in any attempt to control inflation. Victoria Chick's chapter reveals the complexity and multiplicity of views labelled 'monetarist'.

A more recent candidate for the leading role in the inflation saga would be labour; it is the supply of, and demand for, labour rather than the supply of, and demand for, money which determines the general level of prices. Whereas the monetarist view focuses on the exchange value of goods, the labour model emphasises the supply costs of goods – i.e. it is production rather than exchange which dominates. Just as money plays a part in almost every exchange, so does labour play a part in almost all production – hence both can have an effect on the general level of prices. David Byers' chapter looks at labour not only in the narrow Phillips' curve sense but in a more (almost a modern Keynesian) model.

Apart from labour, another major unavoidable cost of the production of all goods is that associated with raw materials and fuel. There is a growing school of thought which ascribes rising costs to the increasing difficulties of extracting fuel and minerals and the increasing scarcity of that land which has 'original and indestructible properties'. This view is outlined by Shanti Chakravarty who uses two very stylised models to illustrate the possible time paths of output and prices. The rising costs of oil (and other fossil fuels) to which much of the inflation in industrialised countries has been ascribed is a case in point.

The effects of oil costs raise the question of the international transmission of inflation which is the subject of George McKenzie's chapter. He provides a critique of the standard monetary theory underlying the international transmission of inflation and suggest that real factors and the growing role of international financial intermediation need to be taken into account. Once this is done, the stable relationship between money and other economic variables is immediately called into question.

It has long been a criticism of monetarist models that they fail to specify the causal links between increasing the quantity of money and the ultimate increase in prices. The chapter by David Heathfield attempts to investigate empirically the way in which manufacturers and retailers make decisions about prices. This is perforce a rather limited investigation and, like most empirical work, is suggestive rather than conclusive.

Jan Kregel's chapter gives an account of Keynes' view of inflation taken from the *General Theory* and from elsewhere. Curiously, it summarises much of the material in foregoing chapters and deals with money, labour, raw materials, imports and institutions. The richness of the Keynesian view is surprising, since in the popular mind Keynes had little to say on inflation.

The final chapter by Alec Nove gives an account of administered prices as operated in the USSR and Poland. There is no finely drawn theoretical model of a communist economy, but he describes what happens in a real-world economy run by central planners. It is evident that inflation is not so much avoided as suppressed. Though less 'theoretical' than the other chapters, Nove's chapter does touch on a matter which is central to the whole question of inflation and yet rarely dealt with. Why is inflation supposed to be a bad thing? Unless one wants to say inflation *per se* is disliked, the answer to this question clearly depends on the model used. If one's model suggests that money is merely a 'veil' then no real variables are affected by it and hence there are no welfare implications. If, on the other hand, planning is more difficult when future prices are uncertain then it is unfulfilled expectations about the rate of inflation rather than the actual rate of inflation which causes problems. The chapters by Chakravarty and Nove suggest that inflation is a result of (or a device to obscure) the incompatibility of competing claims on the international and national cakes. On a national level if defence takes more than consumption or if labour tries to take more than capital then the loser bids for more. Rather than say there is no more, it is tempting to pretend that there is by raising money incomes (and subsequently prices). This is often the substance of Keynesian 'maintenance of demand' policies. On an international level, if the underdeveloped oil-rich states takes more then the developed oil-using states have less. This redistribution of income is moderated and obscured by maintaining or even increasing money incomes in the developed countries. Inflation may therefore be the least disruptive method of reconciling the irreconcilable, and what is being lamented is the underlying conflict rather than the inflation itself. The choice of model, it seems, influences not only one's choice of policy instruments but also has a strong bearing on one's objectives. Certainly, not all models would suggest that inflation is 'the greatest threat facing this country since Hitler'.

Perhaps a collection of models such as this is the only way to clarify and weaken prejudices about so contentious a subject as inflation. No doubt each chapter contains only part of the story, but as so often is the case it is necessary to see many facets of the problem before one's own position on it is understood.

D.F.H
Southampton 1978

Chapter 1

Inflation in history

Phyllis Deane

There are a variety of definitions of inflation current in economic literature, the differences between them often associated with implicit theories of causes of inflation or of the policies appropriate to its correction. In this chapter I shall adopt the definition which seems to be most appropriate to the long-term perspective of the economic historian rather than the short-term perspective of the policy-maker. I shall try to avoid committing myself to a specific theory of inflation on the grounds that the explanation for inflation in a historical context is unlikely to be monocausal and that different past episodes must be expected to display different patterns of causation and consequences. So I begin by defining inflation as a situation in which there exists a generalised excess demand for goods and services such that it produces a tendency for the purchasing power of money to fall. Understanding the historical experience of inflation thus involves explaining the process which maintains the excessive demand and gives rise to the fall in the value of money. It is generally possible, in principle, to measure the falling purchasing power of money by the rise in the general price level, but if prices are not fully flexible (e.g. if they are controlled in war or in planned economies) the inflation may be fully or partially repressed and will show up in shortages of goods as well as, or instead of, price changes.

So, inflation occurs when the current demand for goods and services grows faster than total output. The discrepancy between these two growth rates may arise either for monetary reasons, i.e. on account of an autonomous increase in the supply of money, or for real reasons, i.e. because of factors restraining the growth of output or raising the physical demand for it. A harvest failure (or even a succession of harvest failures) may lift the general level of prices – perhaps substantially in a pre-industrial economy – but it is not inflation in the sense I choose to define the term unless it leads to a cumulative or persistent process of price increases not reversed by return to the normal harvest pattern. Nor shall I be concerned here with the relatively modest price rises which occur in the inflationary phase of a trade cycle when an investment boom leads to a rise of prices destined to be reversed when the capital thus accumulated expands the rate of growth of output. What I propose mainly to focus on, that is to say, is the kind of inflation which is a cumulative process persisting into the long term and riding over minor short-term fluctuations in prices generated by temporary disturbances on the side of either demand or output.

In short, this is not intended to be a history of prices, or even of periods when the general level of prices was on an upward trend, but an analysis of selected episodes of inflation in British history.

If we take a very broad view of the long-run trend in the value of money in order to give some perspective to an analysis of selected episodes of inflation it is evident that the long-run trend in prices has been upward, i.e. that the value of money has shown a long-run propensity to fall. Over the whole period for which price records exist, accelerated inflation has been a side-effect of every major war and indeed of every substantial government intervention in economic life. Moreover, as Keynes [24, p. 8] pointed out, 'this progressive deterioration in the value of money through history is not an accident and has had behind it two great driving forces – the impecuniosity of governments and the superior political influence of the debtor class. The power of taxation by currency depreciation is one which has been inherent in the State since Rome discovered it'. Since Keynes wrote this passage in the early 1920s – apart from a decade or so of falling prices which characterised the interwar period for some countries – the upward trend of prices has continued without interruption in most countries and with unprecedented momentum in many. After the price rise associated with the recovery from the Depression of the 1930s came the Second World War price inflation and for the first time in world history there was no fall back in prices from the inflated levels to which they had been pushed by a major war. The fall in the value of money has continued and indeed accelerated in the post-Second World War era.

On the other hand, leaving aside the post-Second World War experience on the grounds that this may be abnormal – either in the sense that it represents the beginning of a new era in the world monetary system, or that it has contained an unusual concentration of the kind of political circumstances that are peculiarly conducive to inflation – it is not obvious that the fall in the value of money has been so persistent or so pronounced as the conventional wisdom might suggest. The record differs for different countries of course. However, a consumers' price index stretching back over seven centuries for southern England, for example, indicates an overall average trend from 1275 to 1959 of only about $\frac{1}{2}$ of 1 per cent per annum – a creeping long-term rise in the cost of living [35]. Moreover a large part of the increase since 1275 seems to have occurred in four periods of relatively rapid price change: i.e in (a) the period associated with the so-called Price Revolution of the fifteenth and early sixteenth centuries; (b) the latter part of the eighteenth and early nineteenth centuries – particularly the period associated with the French Revolutionary and Napoleonic Wars; (c) the period of the First World War and its post-war boom; and (d) the Second World War and its aftermath. Looking at it by centuries it would appear that the sixteenth, eighteenth and twentieth centuries have been characterised by a persistent (but not continuous) decline in the value of money and that prices were on the whole moving down rather than up in the fourteenth, seventeenth and nineteenth centuries.

Lipsey has expressed these differences rather vividly in terms of the probability that prices were likely to move up rather than down (or vice versa) over a succession of finite time intervals from 1275 to 1949 and concludes that, given a fifty-year time horizon, it was 'a fairly good bet that the price level would rise' except during the fourteenth and nineteenth centuries when the odds were slightly in favour of a fall [26, p. 7]. However, taking a ten-year time span, the picture changes markedly. 'If we took a bet in each year that the price level would be higher ten years from the date in question, we would be wrong more times than we would be right in the thirteenth, fourteenth, fifteenth, seventeenth and nineteenth centuries.' [26, pp. 7–8] The odds, that is to say, seem to have been heavily in favour of inflation in the sixteenth, eighteenth and twentieth centuries and modestly in favour of deflation in the fourteenth, fifteenth, seventeenth and nineteenth centuries.

The Price Revolution of the sixteenth century

The first inflationary episode to gain prominence in economic writings was the secular price rise generally referred to by historians as the sixteenth-century Price Revolution. Like the post-Second World War inflation it was an international phenomenon, though – again like the recent twentieth-century experience – the rate and timing of its incidence varied considerably as between countries. It seems to have been universal in Europe for most of the second half of the sixteenth century and early seventeenth century and for Western Europe (e.g. Spain, France, Belgium, England) it shows up in the price statistics from the early years of the sixteenth century if not from the closing years of the fifteenth century. Taken over the long period it was a rather slow rate of inflation, involving long-term price increases averaging at most about 2 per cent per annum and more often nearer 1 than 2 per cent. Even the short-period upturns aggravated by harvest failures were relatively modest compared to twentieth-century experience in less developed countries. In Spain, for example, where the inflation seems to have been sharpest, Nadal's estimates of the quinquennial rises in cereal prices for the period 1506–10 to 1596–1600 average only about 6½ per cent though periods containing particularly bad harvests registered quinquennial increases of 15 to 17 per cent [19] in [29].

In retrospect, indeed, the most remarkable feature of the Price Revolution was not the pace at which prices rose but the fact that a rising trend was sustained for so long and that the violent periodic upswings in staple foodstuff prices characteristic of a pre-industrial economy were rarely fully compensated by subsequent downswings in periods of plenty. Carlo Cipolla, for example, using price data for Florence, showed that over the half century 1552–1600 prices roughly doubled, representing an average increase of 1½ per cent per annum, and concluded that 'the rise (avoiding the term "revolution") in prices during the sixteenth century was due to the fact that they did not fall during periods of decrease' [5, p. 45]. Similarly for Spain, Nadal's price data suggest that there was only one sixteenth-century quinquennium (1511–15) when cereal prices actually fell – though not so low as to offset the previous increase – and only two when they failed to show some advance.

The traditional explanation for the persistent international inflation of the so-called Price Revolution attributes it primarily (sometimes exclusively) to an unprecedented expansion in the world supply of precious metals – beginning with an increase in the output of European silver mines at the end of the fifteenth century, developing momentum under the influx of Caribbean gold to Spain in the early sixteenth century and reaching a climax with the massive Spanish imports of South and Central American treasure (primarily silver) in the second half of the century. The monetary explanation was first given prominence by the French jurist Jean Bodin in 1568. It gained wide acceptance in the seventeenth century and had become received doctrine by the time of Adam Smith. 'The discovery of the abundant mines of America seems to have been the sole cause of this diminution in the value of silver in proportion to that of corn. It is accounted for accordingly in the same manner by everybody; and there has never been any dispute about the fact itself or about the cause of it.' [42, p. 191]

The doctrine was given a substantial statistical underpinning by the price historians, e.g. C. Wiebe and Thorold Rogers at the end of the nineteenth century and by Earl Hamilton in the 1920s. In his *Treatise on Money* J. M. Keynes [23] accepted the traditional quantity-theory view of the Price Revolution as readily as Adam Smith had done and went on to lend the weight of his authority to the theory of economic growth through inflation which Earl Hamilton built up on the basis of his research into the sixteenth-century influx of Spanish treasure. The theory was simple enough. It was that the price rise caused by the imports of Spanish-American treasure outstripped the less flexible wages and rent costs and thus generated a profit inflation which stimulated enterprise. Keynes used this interpretation of the sixteenth-century experience to support his conclusion concerning 'the extraordinary correspondence with the periods of Profit Inflation and Profit Deflation respectively with those of national rise and decline' [23, p. 16] and generalised it with characteristic rhetoric, to the whole of human history, e.g. [23, p. 150]:

> It would be a fascinating task to re-write Economic History in the light of these ideas from its remote beginnings; – to conjecture whether the civilisations of Sumeria and Egypt drew their stimulus from the gold of Arabia and the copper of Africa, which being monetary metals, left a trail of profit behind them in the course of

their distribution through the lands between the Mediterranean and the Persian Gulf, and probably, farther afield; in what degree the greatness of Athens depended on the silver mines of Laurium – not because the monetary metals are more truly wealth than other things, but because by their effect on prices they supply the spur of profit; how far the dispersal by Alexander of the bank reserves of Persia, which represented the accumulated withdrawals into the treasure of successive empires during many preceding centuries, was responsible for the outburst of economic progress in the Mediterranean basin, of which Carthage attempted and Rome ultimately succeeded to reap her fruits; whether it was a coincidence that the decline and fall of Rome was contemporaneous with the most prolonged and drastic deflation yet recorded; if the long stagnation of the Middle Ages may have been more surely and inevitably caused by Europe's meagre supply of the monetary metals than by monasticism or Gothic frenzy, and how much the Glorious Revolution owed to Mr. Phipps.[1]

However, when historians did begin to investigate the mechanics of the Price Revolution the stylised facts used to support the quantity theory and the profit inflation theory proved hard to confirm. Nef had pointed out as early as 1937 that the French inflation had not led to the industrial development which was supposed to have developed out of the contemporary but less marked English inflation.[2] Paradoxically enough, however, it was the economic historians, writing under the influence of the 'new economics' of Keynes' *General Theory*, who reopened the whole question of the orthodox explanation for the Price Revolution. In the event, attempts to explore quantitatively, for particular countries, the mechanism by which the increased imports of Spanish-American treasure could have produced the sixteenth-century price rise have failed to confirm the traditional interpretation. This failure – associated with mid-twentieth-century doubts about the ability of the quantity theory to account for all cases of inflation, and with the propensity for authors using Keynesian techniques of analysis to emphasise the 'real' causes of inflation (e.g. factors causing the demand for output to fall short of supply – has encouraged historians to focus on alternative explanations for the Price Revolution. New research has been stimulated in a number of European countries on these lines, but since both the nature of the data problems and the rate and timing of the inflation varies as between countries it is convenient to restrict ourselves here to one case for which the existing documentation, though still grossly inadequate, is relatively abundant, namely England.

Early sixteenth-century England was a primarily agrarian economy which was already climbing out of the long period of economic and demographic contraction associated with the sequence of catastrophic

---

1. Mr Phipps is reported to have recovered Spanish treasure to the value of £250,000 to £300,000 in 1688.
2. For a systematic critique of the profit inflation thesis see [31] and [11].

epidemics which characterised the century or so following the Black Death of 1349. It was, however, an increasingly commercialised economy using a bi-metallic currency (mainly consisting of gold and silver coin issued by the Royal Mint but also including a variety of Scottish and foreign coin) supplemented by a probably growing proportion of near-money assets such as inland and foreign bills of exchange. Like twentieth-century low-income agrarian economies it was subject to low elasticities of both supply and demand for its principal products, and the resulting price fluctuations were aggravated by an imperfectly integrated national market and a primitive system of communications. Accordingly, wars, harvest failures, epidemics and currency manipulations had disproportionately large effects on the price level. By the late sixteenth century there was evidence of a quickening in the pace of technical progress and industrialisation in large-scale industry (coal-mining and various manufacturing industries) developments which some writers have seen as a prelude to the Industrial Revolution of the late eighteenth and early nineteenth centuries; but these failed to sustain their promise through the seventeenth century [32].

Table 1.1   Summary of English price trends 1451–1700 (1451–75=100)

Annual averages for decade	(1) Price of a composite unit of consumables	(2) Price of a composite unit of foodstuffs	(3) Price of a composite unit of industrial products
1451–60	99	98	99
1461–70	105	105	103
1471–80	94	93	100
1481–90	115	121	103
1491–1500	100	100	97
1501–10	105	106	98
1511–20	115	116	102
1521–30	151	159	110
1531–40	154	161	110
1541–50	203	217	127
1551–60	290	315	186
1561–70	282	298	218
1571–80	322	341	223
1581–90	362	389	230
1591–1600	478	530	238
1601–10	479	527	256
1611–20	527	583	274
1621–30	527	585	264
1631–40	611	687	281
1641–50	647	723	306
1651–60	621	687	327
1661–70	636	702	343
1671–80	614	675	351
1681–90	571	631	310
1691–1700	663	737	331

Source: Col. 1. Based on annual data from E. H. Phelps-Brown and Sheila V. Hopkins [36], reprinted in E. H. Carus Wilson [4], pp. 194–5. Cols. 2 and 3. E. H. Phelps-Brown and Sheila V. Hopkins [37], p. 306.

The evidence on price movements in the sixteenth century remains incomplete, but – taking the Phelps Brown and Hopkins index of a composite unit of consumables as a rough but convenient index of the overall price trend – it would appear that the English inflation began in the 1480s and continued almost without interruption until the 1640s. The rate of increase seems to have been faster in the first sixty years or so than it was later, as can be seen from column 1 of Table 1.1. Between the trough value of the 1490s and that of the 1550s the compound rate of increase averaged about 1·8 per cent per annum compared with about 1 per cent per annum measuring between the 1558 and the 1644 troughs. By the 1640s the price of Phelps Brown and Hopkins' composite unit of consumables was roughly six and a half times that of the 1490s. Apart from a kink in the 1560s and two further slowdowns in the 1600s and 1620s it represented an erratic but otherwise remarkably sustained growth in the price level.

Informed contemporaries were aware of the fact that the sixteenth-century price trend was taking a different direction from that experienced in the fifteenth century and of the international character of the rise. But the short-term price fluctuations continued to dwarf the secular trends. According to Fisher [12, p. 122], for example;

> Tudor and Stuart Englishmen were alive to the agonies and dangers of harvest failures. But few of them spent much time looking back over their shoulders at the prices which their fathers had enjoyed, and a long upward drift of those prices at a compounded rate of little more than one per cent – or even less – per annum was insufficient to silence for long the farmer's traditional complaint that when crops do not fail corn is too cheap.

Scholars – such as Bodin – who did discuss the creeping inflation through which they were living identified a shopping list of factors tending to raise the general price level – including abundance of precious metals, monopolies, scarcities due to exports or wastage of resources, the demonstration effects of conspicuous consumption by kings and noblemen, debasement of the currency and rising rents. Of these explanations some – e.g. monopolies – were more relevant to the short-term price increases; for in an increasingly commercialised economy speculators who could raise credit were quick to see and exploit the opportunities for profit inherent in a poor harvest. Others – such as the currency manipulations – were obviously significant at certain periods. For example, the currency debasement of 1526 and the so-called 'great debasement' of 1542–51 must have contributed largely to the sharp price rises characterising the affected decades. Gould [15], for example, refers to the successive debasements of the 1540s and early 1550s as a 'shattering experience' and argues that the associated rapid inflation 'the only part of the Price Revolution comparable with twentieth-century experience – caused widespread hardship, confusion and discontent'. Similarly, the Elizabethan revaluation of 1566 must have played its part in producing the subsequent kink in the Tudor price curve. The other explanations need more analytical justification to render them plausible, but most could be fitted into a theory stressing the rise of population and diminishing returns as forcing up costs and prices.

Unfortunately, the quantitative evidence is too sketchy to permit a systematic evaluation of the alternative explanations for the Price Revolution. Monetary explanations, for example, are vitiated by the fact that there is no satisfactory indicator of changes in the quantity of money. True, the debasement periods can be presumed to have involved substantial increases in the money supply, but exactly when these increases occured is unclear. Gould [15, p. 258], for example, argues that: 'During the great debasement of 1543–51, indeed, the English Mint never really caught up with the successive debasements of the silver coinage.' Supporters of the orthodox doctrine noted that the timing of the Mint issues of silver coin in the second half of the sixteenth century matches well with the Spanish imports of treasure. But, in a country with substantial private and ecclesiastical hoards of non-monetary gold and silver, it is impossible to say whether the increases in the Mint issues reflected imports of specie rather than conversion of domestic hoards to monetary use (due perhaps to an increased demand for money). Nor indeed is the evidence on overseas trade, such as it is, always consistent with the view that Spanish treasure flowed into England in payment for a surplus on the current account balance of trade. It may be that even when the balance of overseas trade was in deficit there were imports of specie on capital account (e.g. brought in by immigrant merchants), but this hypothesis remains so far untested and possibly untestable.

On the other hand, the view that the price inflation was primarily a consequence of population pressure or inelastic supplies of staple agricultural products is likewise vitiated by the fact that there is as little hard evidence on the rate of population growth as there is on the money supply. It is generally believed that, in the century or so after 1377, the English population – already severely cut back by the Black Death – was further reduced by the incidence of 'at least 15 outbreaks of plague and/or other epidemic disease of national or extra–regional proportions' [16, p. 57], the last of these in 1485, and that in the next two centuries it began to grow again from a low of perhaps between 2 and $2\frac{1}{4}$ million in the later fifteenth century to perhaps between 5 and $5\frac{1}{2}$ million in the late seventeenth century.[3] But the timing of this growth is a matter of conjecture. Some historians would argue that most of it was concentrated in the period from the 1480s to 1630s – though as Outhwaite has noted, 'much of the evidence for this has come from a scrutiny of the relative price movements so that the argument tends to be circular running from prices to population and back again to prices' [33,

---

3. Hatcher, [16, p. 63] for example says that past medieval and modern historians 'have tended to agree that the origins of the demographic explosion of the sixteenth and early seventeenth centuries lay in the last quarter of the century, more particularly in the decade 1475 to 1483'.

p. 42 fn.]. Certainly the fact that the price indices (such as they are) for agricultural products rise so much more steeply than those for industrial products, or for wages, appeared to lend strength to the 'real' explanations stressing population pressure in a situation of diminishing returns; and at the same time to weaken the force of the profit inflation theory which associates the influx of Spanish treasure with the growth of capitalist industrial enterprise. Similarly, Phelps Brown and Hopkins' indices showing a lag between wage increases and price increases (particularly marked for foodstuffs) sits better with an interpretation based on population pressure in a context of diminishing returns than with that which hinges on the influx of Spanish silver. Kerridge's estimates of rising rents further undermine Hamilton's and Keynes' profit inflation theory [22].

In sum, the one thing that seems clear from recent researches and analyses is that neither the simple monetarist interpretation, nor the undiluted demographic interpretation, suffices to explain the Price Revolution of the sixteenth century. What seems most likely is that both sorts of factor played some part in the secular rise of the price level, but that the structure of causes varied as between countries and as between time periods. It is hard, for example, to believe that the relatively sustained rise in the English price level was unaffected by the accompanying increase in the world's supply of monetary metals and the contemporaneous increases in prices throughout Europe. On the other hand, it is important to keep the influx of Spanish treasure in perspective, for recent researchers suggest that the increase in the world's stock of precious metals was not as great as used to be supposed. According to Braudel, for example: 'The sixteenth century did not loose unprecedented riches on the world.' [1, p. 29] His estimates suggest that Hamilton's figures for arrival of bullion from America during the one and a half centuries between 1500 and 1650 represented an addition to the stock of gold and silver in circulation in Europe and the Mediterranean *before* the discovery of America, amounting to less than 4 per cent in the case of gold and 26 per cent in the case of silver. Almost certainly, moreover, stocks of gold and silver in non-monetary forms were such as to dwarf the new arrivals of treasure. On the one hand, the dissolution of the monasteries probably added more to the English stock of negotiable treasure than the booty brought back by Drake in the *Golden Hind* which Keynes [23, p. 156] suggested 'may fairly be considered the fountain and origin of British Foreign Investment'. On the other hand, much of the Spanish-American treasure that did find its way to England may have disappeared more or less at once into private hoards. As for the debasements of currency which took place in the first half of the century, it is not easy to establish whether these were consistent with a monetarist explanation of the price rise or whether they represented a response to an increase demand for money in a period of population growth, rising food prices and accelerating industrialisation, or whether it was simply a result of the 'impecuniousness of governments'.

Equally, it is hard to believe that in a low-income agricultural economy experiencing an increase in the rate of population growth there would not have been a tendency for prices to rise owing to pressure of demand on inelastic supplies; or that an acceleration in capitalist development, using exports and increased urbanisation would not have involved a disproportionate increase in the circulation of other sorts of money than gold and silver coin; or indeed that active monetary manipulation or influenza would alone be sufficient to explain the kink in the Tudor grain price curve during the late 1550s and 1560s.

We are left, therefore, with various plausible explanations for the Price Revolution, none of which can be assigned exclusive long-term significance and each of which probably played a strategic role in some stages of the long inflation. Without more detailed research into the primary data for particular countries it is impossible to go further than this and to evaluate quantitatively the role of real and monetary factors for any country or over any appreciable proportion of the century or so in question.

The war inflation of 1793–1815

The war inflation of the period of the French and Napoleonic Wars was the first major inflation in modern British history. It took off from an already rising price trend which characterised the second half of the eighteenth century. If we take the Schumpeter–Gilboy price indices [41] as our guide for the eighteenth century we find that the short-term price fluctuations were often violent, but that the peaks and troughs seem to have been drifting upwards from the mid-1740s for consumers' goods (a similar turning point shows up in the Phelps Brown and Hopkins' index of the price of a composite unit of consumables) [36] and from about a decade later for producers' goods. Measured as an average compound rate over the four decades ending in 1792, the year preceding the outbreak of the French Wars, the annual rate of inflation indicated by a combination of the indices for producers' and consumers' goods amounts to rather less than three-quarters of 1 per cent per annum.

There is no shortage of explanations for this inflationary trend – it would be straining terms to call it an inflation. A monetary economist might ascribe it to contemporary developments in the banking sector. Lipsey, for example, selects as the most likely cause 'a large expansion in the money supply caused by the rapid growth in the number of banks, particularly country banks during this period [26, p. 10]. A development economist who favoured a structuralist interpretation of the process of inflation might be inclined to point to the fact that the radical structural changes associated with the first Industrial Revolution began to gather momentum in the second half of the eighteenth century. If indeed it was true that eighteenth century prices were less flexible in a downward than in an upward direction, then the relatively high incidence of poor harvests in the second half of the century and the disruptive consequences of two long and expensive wars (the Seven Years War ending in 1763 and the War of American Independence 1776–83) might both have had an impact on the upward trend. Most economic historians would give some weight to the fact that the sustained upturn in British population growth also dates from the middle decades of the eighteenth century when explaining the increase in food prices.

In sum, the real forces pushing up the level of demand in the second half of the century were so evidently more substantial than those prevailing in the first half that what seems to need explanation is not that prices tended to rise but that the inflationary trend was so modest. The answer seems to be first that there was a sufficient degree of slack in the economy to permit output to grow rather faster than population and to prevent resource disproportionalities becoming acute in the course of structural change; and second that there was a quickening in the rate of technical progress. The rising tide of enclosure, the canal manias and the application of labour- and natural resource-saving inventions in industry all played their part in keeping output rising in response to increased demand.

However, the wartime inflation was a different story. First of all it was faster. Between 1792 – the year before war broke out – and 1813, the peak year for the wartime inflation the annual compound rate of growth of prices (domestic and imported) averaged nearly 3·2 per cent.[4] Though it must be admitted that as between 1792 and 1815, when peace was restored, the annual average works out at only 1·7 per cent – not a high rate of inflation by modern standards (see Table 1.2).

The other interesting feature of the wartime inflation was that it was associated with a shift to inconvertible paper and with important developments in contemporary monetary theories and attitudes to monetary policy. Certainly by the 1820s informed contemporary opinion was explaining the wartime inflation in terms that have a modern ring to them. Joseph Lowe, for example, writing in 1822, listed the principal causes of the wartime price increases as follows:

'The extra demand for men for government service and the consequent increase of wages and salaries.
'The inadequacy of agricultural produce, consequent on the drain of labour and capital, for the public service.
'The increase of indirect taxation; and lastly,
'The non-convertibility and consequent increase of our paper money.' [27, p. 43]

It is worth noting, moreover, that Lowe's own rather impressionistic assessment of the rate of inflation over a period through which he had

---

4. Using the Gayer-Rostow-Schwartz weighted index of monthly prices of domestic and imported commodities converted to annual averages [14, pp. 468–70].

Table 1.2 Indicators of inflation 1785–1826. Prices and money supply (price index 1821–5=100)*

Year	Domestic and imported commodities* (£m.)	Note circulation (£m.)	Bullion (£m.)	†Bank of England Securities		Yield on consols ‡ (%)
				Private (£m.)	Government (£m.)	
1785	87·3	6·2	4·1	4·1	7·0	4·8
1786	88·2	7·9	6·1	3·0	7·4	4·1
1787	86·8	9·0	6·0	3·8	7·9	4·1
1788	89·3	9·8	6·3	3·4	8·3	4·0
1789	85·8	10·5	7·9	2·4	9·0	3·9
1790	89·3	10·7	8·5	2·0	9·2	3·9
1791	89·7	11·6	8·0	2·1	10·7	3·6
1792	88·1	11·2	5·9	3·2	10·3	3·3
1793	96·6	11·4	4·7	5·4	10·0	4·0
1794	98·5	10·5	6·9	4·1	9·4	4·4
1795	114·9	12·4	5·6	3·7	13·2	4·6
1796	116·1	10·0	2·3	6·2	11·9	4·8
1797	106·2	10·4	2·6	7·3	10·2	5·9
1798	107·9	10·6	6·2	6·0	11·1	5·9
1799	124·6	13·2	7·3	6·5	10·5	5·1
1800	151·0	15·9	5·6	8·0	13·8	4·7
1801	155·7	15·4	4·5	10·4	13·9	4·9
1802	122·2	16·1	4·0	10·7	13·9	4·2
1803	123·6	15·7	3·7	14·0	11·4	5·0
1804	124·3	17·1	4·6	11·6	14·8	5·3
1805	136·2	17·1	6·8	14·1	14·2	5·0
1806	134·5	19·4	6·1	13·5	14·5	4·9
1807	131·2	18·3	6·3	15·2	13·4	4·9
1808	144·5	17·7	6·9	13·8	14·6	4·6
1809	155·0	19·1	4·1	16·3	15·0	4·6
1810	153·4	22·9	3·3	22·4	15·8	4·5
1811	145·4	23·3	3·3	17·6	19·5	4·7
1812	163·7	23·2	3·0	16·5	21·6	5·1
1813	168·9	24·0	2·8	13·7	25·3	4·9
1814	153·7	26·6	2·2	15·9	29·3	4·9
1815	129·9	27·3	2·7	18·9	25·9	4·5
1816	118·6	26·9	6·1	17·6	22·8	5·0
1817	131·9	28·5	10·7	7·1	26·3	4·1
1818	138·7	27·0	8·2	4·6	27·1	3·9
1819	128·1	25·2	3·9	4·6	23·9	4·2
1820	115·4	23·9	6·6	3·8	20·4	4·4
1821	99·7	22·1	11·6	3·8	15·9	4·1
1822	87·9	18·1	10·6	3·6	13·1	3·8
1823	97·6	18·8	11·5	5·1	12·8	3·8
1824	101·9	19·9	12·8	5·4	14·5	3·3
1825	113·0	20·1	6·2	6·6	18·4	3·5
1826	100·0	23·5	4·6	9·9	19·1	3·8

Notes

*Based on Gayer, Rostow and Schwartz monthly indices of British commodity prices 1790=1850 converted to annual averages. Source: B. R. Mitchell [28], p. 470.
†B. R. Mitchell [28], pp. 442–3.
‡B. R. Mitchell [28], p. 455.

himself lived accords quite well overall with the implications of the price indices compiled by modern investigators. He quantified his assessment as a rise of 30 per cent over the fourteen-year period 1792–1806 and a further rise of 30 per cent over the eight-year period 1806–14. Taken literally, this would give an *overall* annual rate of price increase of slightly under 2½ per cent for the period 1792–1814 compared with slightly over 2½ per cent which emerges from the Gayer–Rostow–Schwartz series.[5]

Early in the war, however, there occurred a major change in the monetary basis of the British credit structure which stimulated an active controversy on the causes and consequences of the current inflation of prices and depreciation of the foreign exchange value of the £. The break with past experience came in 1797 when the Bank of England ceased to redeem its banknotes in gold, for the Suspension of Cash Payments, as it was called, injected into the nation's money supply a large element of paper money which grew with the government's war debts.

The Bank of England, originally established in 1694 to meet the government's perennial thirst for war finance, had in the course of the eighteenth century become the central institution in the nation's credit structure. To solve the government's financial problems it raised fixed-interest loans from the public, the interest charges secured by the yield of specific taxes. To pay the government's creditors it issued banknotes which, since they were redeemable in metallic money on demand, became effective substitutes for metallic currency. It arranged the foreign currency dealings necessary to finance British military operations abroad, or to subsidise allies, and it handled the transactions in precious metals destined for the Royal Mint. At the same time it was a major banker to the private sector – discounting bills of exchange and making short-term loans to joint stock companies on a scale which it would have been difficult for a smaller or less privileged institution to undertake. So as the century wore on the circulation of Bank of England notes expanded both in value (quadrupling between 1720 and 1790) and in geographical range, becoming the most important liquid asset in the credit system, apart from the metallic coin for which it was exchangeable. Banknotes, i.e. Bank of England notes, came to constitute a substantial proportion of the liquid reserve assets against which prudent country bankers could safely issue their own notes.

Eighteenth-century writers on economic questions were well aware of the potential advantages and disadvantages of lubricating an economy with paper currency. It was obvious that a shortage of ready money

5. The Gayer–Rostow–Schwartz commodity price indices (see footnote 4 for derivation) are the most useful currently available for the period 1790–1850 and will be used in this section to indicate price movements unless otherwise stated. On the whole they are more likely to exaggerate than to understate the rate of inflation (a) because they omit services whose prices were less volatile (e.g. house rents) and (b) because they are thin in their representation of finished manufactured goods whose prices were falling as a result of technological progress.

could hinder trade and industry and that the creation of money by the banks could stimulate productive enterprise. On the other hand it was equally clear that an over-issue of paper currency, i.e. a currency of no intrinsic worth, would topple its exchange value and destroy confidence in the credit system generally. What was not clear was how to prevent a healthy expansion from turning into over-issue. Adam Smith whose views on all economic matters were regarded as authoritative in the later eighteenth century seemed to think that all would be well provided that the credit was extended to creditworthy borrowers and the notes were issued (in large denominations) by reputable bankers,[6] e.g.: 'A paper money consisting of banknotes owned by people of undoubted credit, payable on demand without any condition and in fact readily paid as soon as presented, is, in every respect equal in value to gold and silver money.' [42, p. 307] For earlier writers, John Law's spectacularly disastrous attempt to liquidate the French national debt, reflate the metropolitan economy and develop the colony of Louisiana – at a stroke – on the strength of a note issue backed by land and in principle (though not *in toto*) redeemable in specie, constituted an object lesson. David Hume, for example, thought that the Bank of Amsterdam's practice of issuing notes fully backed by bullion was the only safe rule.

Towards the end of the century it was increasingly appreciated that there was a connection between the state of the foreign exchanges (as evidenced in a tendency of gold to flow out or in) and the supply of bank money. In 1783, 1793 and 1797, for example, the Bank temporarily restricted credit in order to check a drain of gold abroad. According to Horsefield [21, p. 12]:

> From these experiences the spokesmen of the Bank in 1797 deduced that normally the circulation of the Bank affected prices and consequently the foreign exchanges; but that in times of internal crisis the effects on prices were likely to be counterbalanced in practice by changes in the velocity of circulation. They accordingly suggested that a drain of gold caused by adverse foreign exchanges could be checked by a contraction of the Bank's circulation leading to a reversal of the balance of payments; but that for an internal drain the remedy was not the contraction but the expansion of credit in order to maintain confidence.

With the outbreak of war in 1793, however, the dangers of a crisis of confidence leading to a run on gold took on a special significance. Between 1793 and 1796 annual net government expenditure went up from £19·6 million to £42·4 million and its net income from £18·6 million to £19·4 million: in effect public revenue declined in real terms for prices were already rising under the pressure of war-inflated demand. By 1796 prices were 30 per cent above 1790–2 levels. It was an inflation of a rate beyond all previous eighteenth-century experience. Poor harvests in 1795 and 1796 added to the public demand for imports while business

---

6. Until 1797 no banknotes were issued for less than £10.

confidence was highly vulnerable to war scares of one kind and another. By February 1797 the Bank's gold reserves had fallen to £1·2 million (they had been about £7 million three years earlier) in face of a panic rush to cash banknotes; and a Privy Council order was issued requiring the Bank to stop paying out cash 'until the sense of Parliament can be taken'. The sense of Parliament was expressed in May in the Bank Restriction Act, originally designed to suspend cash payments for a further two months, but destined to remain in force for twenty-four years.

The effect was to alter the rules of the monetary game by breaking the link between the supply of money and the nation's reserves of precious metals. While the Suspension was in force the Bank could expand credit without fear of a gold loss. How much money came into circulation then depended partly on government demands for war finance and partly on the discretion of the Bank's Directors in assessing the 'needs of trade'. Britain had gone from a gold standard to a paper standard.

In retrospect it is surprising that the value of money did not fall more rapidly. In fact the Gayer–Rostow–Schwartz price indices show an average for domestic prices in 1797 and 1798 which was below that for 1795 and 1796, and only about 3 per cent above the 1793–94 price level. Prices of imported commodities rose faster, it is true, but the increased transport and insurance costs and the disruptions and losses of overseas trade due to war were a sufficient explanation for that rise. Merchants, bankers and the general public adjusted rapidly to the fact that banknotes were not redeemable in gold for the 'emergency'; and when

Table 1.3   Net public income and expenditure, United Kingdom*

Year †	Total net income (£m.)	Total net expenditure (£m.)
1785	15·5	25·8
1786	15·2	17·0
1787	16·5	15·5
1788	16·8	16·3
1789	16·7	16·0
1790	17·0	16·8
1791	18·5	18·0
1792	18·6	17·0
1793	18·1	19·6
1794	18·7	28·7
1795	19·1	39·0
1796	19·4	42·4
1797	21·4	57·6
1798	26·9	47·4
1799	31·8	47·4
1800	31·6	51·0

Notes
* *Source:* B. R. Mitchell [28], pp. 388–91.
† Years ended 29 Sept. except 1800 which is year ending 6 Jan 1801.

Table 1.4   Gross public income and expenditure, United Kingdom*

Year†	Total gross income (£m.)	Total gross expenditure (£m.)
1801	39·1	65·5
1802	41·2	54·8
1803	42·4	53·0
1804	50·2	62·8
1805	55·0	71·4
1806	60·1	72·9
1807	64·8	73·3
1808	68·2	78·0
1809	69·2	81·5
1810	73·0	81·6
1811	71·0	87·3
1812	70·3	94·8
1813	74·7	111·1
1814	77·9	112·9
1815	79·1	99·5
1816	69·2	71·3
1817	57·6	58·7
1818	59·5	57·6
1819	58·1	57·5
1820	59·9	58·4
1821	61·6	58·4
1822	59·9	56·5
1823	58·5	54·3
1824	59·7	55·5
1825	57·7	54·1
1826	55·2	56·1

Notes
* *Source:* B. R. Mitchell [28], pp. 392–6.
† Years ended 6 Jan. of following year.

the acute emergency was past there appeared to be no obvious necessity to return to convertibility. Government, of course, needed to conserve the nation's gold supplies as a back-up to its own subsidies and military operations overseas and saw no reason to open the door to a possible drain – internal or external. And there was indeed no sign before 1809 of a serious discrepancy developing between the free market price of gold on the foreign exchanges and the Mint price of gold. The paper standard was sustained, in spite of the strains of war, by the confidence of the business community in the Bank of England's notes. Prices continued to rise: but between 1799 and 1809 the annual rise averaged only about 2·2 per cent overall and the real reasons associated with the diversion of resources to the war effort, plus the disruption of overseas trade, were more than enough to explain inflation on that scale.

The fact that from 1797 onwards the supply of high-powered money depended partly on government demand for war finance and partly on the discretion of the Directors of the Bank in assessing the needs of the private sector, stimulated an active debate on monetary policy. The orthodox view, supported on the whole by the teaching of Adam Smith, was that the Bank need not worry about an over-issue provided that it lent only to creditworthy borrowers against the collateral of sound trade bills, i.e. bills of exchange drawn in relation to sales of goods and services expected to materialise within a matter of months. To the extent that the bulk of bank lending was thus secured either on 'real bills' or on the yield of specific taxes this doctrine – the real bills doctrine – provided a reasonably acceptable criterion on which to base a prudent credit policy. Advances to the private sector could then be regarded as a kind of revolving fund with a turnover of a few months: and, cushioned against this background, major commercial failures could be prevented from having secondary repercussions by a deliberately unflustered policy on the part of the lender of last resort. Some thought that in times of crisis the Bank's credit policy was in practice more stringent than it should have been to shore up shaky confidence. Thus, Henry Thornton [43, p. 127], for example, writing in 1802, argued that, 'If there has been any fault in the conduct of the Bank of England, the fault, as I conceive it has been . . . on the side of too much restricting its notes in the late seasons of alarm than of too much enlarging them.'

Nevertheless, when the bulk of the banknotes issued were against government unfunded borrowing for emergency war purposes rather than against normal business transactions, the real bills doctrine had less force and the dangers of an over-issue assumed a more menacing form. In 1808 there was a speculative trade boom stimulated by the sudden opening up of Latin America to British trade and the price of gold began to rise sharply. 'Early in 1809', according to Cannan [3, p. xxi], 'the price of gold went up to 90s., or to put it the other way £1 in notes would only buy as much as 107 grams of gold instead of 123¼.' In August that year Ricardo joined the debate on the bullionist side with the first of three letters to the *Morning Chronicle* and in 1810 a Select Committee of the House of Commons was appointed 'to enquire into the cause of the high price of gold bullion'.

Opinion in the ensuing debate polarised along two main lines of argument – one of which we might now describe as 'monetarist' and was then called 'bullionist', and the other being the antibullionist or banking view. Most of the leading economists of the day (including Thornton by 1810) held bullionist views and stressed the importance of regulating the note issue by reference to the nation's reserves of bullion. The banking and political establishment shared the view of the Directors of the Bank that there was no danger of an over-issue provided that its loans went only to safe borrowers and that there was no justice in the accusation that it was the Bank's note-issuing policies which had depreciated the currency and inflated prices. The Select Committee came out strongly in favour of the view that

> there is at present an excess in the paper circulation of this country, of which the most unequivocal symptom is the very high price of Bullion, and next to that, the low state of the Continental Exchanges;

that this excess is to be ascribed to the want of a sufficient check and control in the issues of paper from the Bank of England; and originally, to the suspension of cash payments, which remove the natural and true control [3, p. 66],

and advocated a restoration of convertibility within two years (whether or not peace was restored in the interval). But full convertibility was not restored until 1821.

The fact is that subsequent events did not seem to confirm the monetarist argument and the establishment was not easily persuaded of its validity. After falling back in 1810 and 1811 prices rose 16 per cent in the two years between 1811 and 1813. But it was not at all obvious that this acceleration of inflation could be laid at the door of the Bank, for its 1813 circulation was not much above that for 1811. As Cannan, a staunch monetarist, admitted [3, p. xxvii]:

The course of events from 1810 to 1816 was unfavourable to the easy propagation and acceptance of the [bullionist] doctrine, for from August 1810 to August 1813 while the Bank of England circulation did not increase at all, the price of gold was rising and from August 1813 to October 1814, while the circulation rose 3½ millions the price of gold was falling. And the violent fluctuation in the price of gold in the year of Waterloo could certainly not be attributed to changes in the note circulation.[7]

In the event the inflation peaked in 1813 and from then on till the mid-century the trend of prices was down – each cyclical peak being markedly below its predecessor. However, the ending of inflation and the resumption of cash payments did not solve the money supply problems of the British economy, for even when the Bank of England was converted to the bullionist line of thought and when government expenditures were contracting, there was still the danger of an over-supply of money being generated by the many country banks which issued their own notes. In the share mania and financial crisis of 1825, for example, domestic prices shot up by about 11 per cent in a single year. The debate was resumed as between: (1) the Currency School, whose members took a hard monetarist line in arguing that a mixed currency ought to be operated in all essential respects as if it were a wholly metallic currency; and (2) the Banking School, the spiritual heirs of the antibullionists, who took the view that *given convertibility* an over-issue of notes would be rapidly liquidated by natural market forces and that financial stability depended on leaving the Bank with some discretion to determine its credit policy in response to the needs of trade. This round of the monetarist debate culminated in the Bank Charter Act of 1844 which was a victory for the Currency School – the hard-line monetarists. The Bank of England was given a virtual monopoly of the note issue, but its role in managing the money supply was reduced in

7. The circulation figures shown in Table 1.2 are from J. H. Clapham [6] and represent accounts drawn upon the last days of February and August each year.

principle to that of raising its rate of discount when gold flowed out of the country and of reducing it when gold flowed in. It was to be guided, in principle, exclusively by the foreign exchanges and to take no account of general business and political conditions at home and abroad.

In seeking an explanation for the relatively slow rate of wartime inflation (as seen through twentieth-century spectacles) it should be noted first that the overall weight of government expenditure – measured in terms of its ratio to national expenditure – was light in comparison with the experience of the First and Second World Wars and even in relation to recent peacetime experience in the United Kingdom. The interesting questions are first why the expansion in the banknote circulation, when freed from the discipline of the gold standard, was not much faster, and second why it did not lead to an explosion in the money supply through the increased note issues of the country banks which the additional liquidity permitted. Tooke thought that the Bank's 5 per cent rate of discount was high in the circumstances of the time and that this restrained the private sector from borrowing from the Bank [44, p. 161].[8] Five per cent may not seem high in the context of an inflation running at about 3 per cent; but given the risks and uncertainties of war, the continental blockade, the shortage of labour and the high rates of indirect taxation prevailing, the prospects for new investment must have been generally unattractive for the majority of merchants and industrialists.[9, 10] If the country bankers could have borrowed at 5 per cent and lent at some higher rate they would no doubt have been glad to do so. But the usury laws put a ceiling of 5 per cent on private loans, whereas the yield on an investment in the Funds could and often did rise above 5 per cent. From a lender's point of view 5 per cent was often too low a rate to attract long-term investment when the yield on Consols was at or above 5 per cent. On the other hand, when the climate of business expectations improved, as it did in 1808–10, there was no shortage of borrowers or lenders in the private sector. It is noticeable that the Bank's holdings of private securities expanded by over 60 per cent in these two years – exceeding its holdings of government securities. Thereafter the Bank's holdings of private securities diminished rapidly so that by 1813, at the peak of the inflation, they were back to the 1803 level in nominal terms and not much more

8. Cannan questions this theory on the grounds that there was nothing to stop the Directors lowering the rate. Cannan [3], p.xxxv.

9. There were relatively high rates of direct taxation, too, as a result of Pitt's introduction of an income tax, but the incidence of the income tax was rather uneven and fell more heavily on agriculture than on trade and industry.

10. Hoffman's index of industrial production suggests a retardation in the pace of industrial growth over the war period and there was certainly a slow-down in the expansion of overseas trade from 1799 on. In the fifteen years between 1783 and 1799 total overseas trade (imports plus domestic exports at constant values) more than doubled: in the next fifteen years, 1799–1814, the increase was of the order of 20 per cent. For the index of industrial production see W. G. Hoffman [20]. For the official values of imports and exports see B. R. Mitchell [28]. Most of the expansion in overseas trade in the second period took place in the last five years or so, i.e. after 1808.

than half the value of government securities. The post-1813 decline in the rate of inflation suggests that the credit multiplier built into the monetary system by the Suspension of Cash Payments did not have explosive implications.

However, in spite of its moderate scale the 1797–1813 inflation experience had a considerable impact on contemporary monetary ideas, and through that on the subsequent shape of British monetary institutions and policy. By 1810, for example, Henry Thornton – whose 1802 analysis explored the mechanism of the relation between the supply and demand for money in terms that modern observers have identified as containing Keynesian insights – had abandoned the view that it was appropriate to leave the Directors of the Bank any discretion to adjust the money supply to the needs of the domestic economy. (See 'Thornton's Paper Credit 1802', in [19].) When the monetarist debate was resumed in the 1820s and 1830s both sides in the controversy – Currency and Banking Schools – had shifted in the direction of the quantity-theory approach and accepted explicitly a fixed gold exchange rate for Bank of England notes as the '*sine qua non* of any sound system of currency' [44, p. 177]. The stage was then set for a monetary orthodoxy, based on quantity-theory assumptions, which effectively determined the behaviour of the world's leading central banks up to 1914; and, through the mechanism of the international gold standard, it had still wider repercussions on monetary policy among the world's major commercial nations. The fact that the nineteenth-century industrial revolutions were undertaken within the framework of the international gold standard – even if the recognised rules of the game were not universally adhered to *in toto* – was one of the reasons why they did not generate the sort of inflationary problems which have dogged the industrialising countries of the mid-twentieth century.

Twentieth-century inflation

The First World War and its aftermath

After the end of the Napoleonic Wars there was no comparable conflict until the First World War broke out in 1914 and precipitated an inflationary episode of some violence in all the leading economic powers. Keynes [24, pp. 1–2] looking back on this episode from the vantage of the early 1920s, saw it as

> one of the most significant events in the history of the modern world. The fluctuation of the standard, whether gold, silver or paper, has not only been of unprecedented violence, but has been visited on a society of which the economic organisation is more dependent than that of any earlier epoch on the assumption that the standard of value would be moderately stable.

The wholesale price indices he listed to illustrate the scale of the international inflation showed what amounted to roughly a doubling of prices in the UK, Germany, the USA and in Canada and Japan, a trebling in France and Sweden and a fourfold increase in Italy between 1914 and 1918 [24, p. 3]. In some European countries – notably in Germany, Austria, Hungary, Poland and Russia – the post-war inflations ran out of control and developed into hyper-inflations which destroyed the currency.[11]

It was the repercussions of an international financial crisis, provoked by fear of war, in late July 1914, that initially disturbed the stability of the British monetary system. Closure of the principal European stock exchanges broke the chain of credit with foreign customers of British banks, there was a run on the Bank's gold reserves and a number of the British clearing banks added to the strain by refusing to pay out sovereigns to their customers. The solution adopted to the domestic crisis of confidence was to announce a moratorium, to relieve the shortage of ready cash by a Treasury issue of small (£1 and 10*s*.) banknotes and for the Bank to break the bottleneck in the discount market by standing ready to accept all approved bills at Bank Rate. The immediate result was a massive addition to the cash stocks of the financial institutions and this continued to glut the market after the danger of an internal drain was past and when the international financial situation was producing a large influx of gold. 'The Bank was thus faced through the remainder of 1914 and into 1915 with a money market so flushed with funds that it was, for the ordinary purpose of control of rates, completely out of hand. Bank rate remained at 5 per cent but there was no chance for the Bank to make it technically effective.' [39, p. 78]

It was within this potentially inflationary context that the government began its task of financing a major war. From the start it relied heavily on borrowing rather than on extracting the necessary resources by taxation, and inevitably this borrowing led to inflationary pressures. In 1915 the central government deficit stood at 77 per cent of total current expenditure, and although taxation was progressively increased in later years, the central government deficit remained above 60 per cent of current expenditure throughout the war years as can be seen in Table 1.5. This table also illustrates the further inflationary implications of the government's borrowing programme by showing the changing structure of the national debt. Between 31 March 1914 and March 1919 the total funded debt actually fell, while the unfunded debt rose from £33½ million to a staggering £7097 million, when it exceeded the annual value of total domestic expenditure at market prices by about a fifth. The effect of running up this huge load of government short-term debt was to expand the liquid assets of the banking system out of all proportion to the national volume of transactions, i.e. to provide a system already

---

11. Phillip Cagan lists seven twentieth century hyper-inflations of which there were two in the Second World War and five after the First World War. See his article [2] in Friedman [13].

glutted with cash with an additional plethora of near-money assets. Much of the money subscribed to government long-term loans, for example, came out of the bank advances made possible by the expanding short-term debt.

Table 1.5   Central government expenditure and deficit, 1919–22 (£m.)

Years	Total current expenditure	Total current balance	Total public debt at 31 Mar. Funded	Unfunded
1914	299	−129	587	33
1915	1051	−806	583	494
1916	1403	−974	319	1789
1917	1849	−1191	318	3670
1918	2160	−1331	318	5532
1919	1408	−427	318	7097
1920	990	+49	315	7295
1921	494	+54	315	7242
1922	962	+10	581	7058

Source: First two columns from C. H Feinstein [10], Table 31; second two columns from B. R. Mitchell [28], p. 403. The total excludes borrowing for investment purposes, e.g. under the Telegraph and Telephone Acts, Naval Works Act, Barracks Act, etc.

Against this inflationary combination of circumstances – a financial system glutted with liquid funds and a government determined to finance what was expected to be a short war with a minimum commitment to increasing the burden either of taxes or of long-term debt – the stage was set for an unprecedentedly rapid bout of inflation in the United Kingdom. It was initially propelled by a rapid rise in import prices due to rising war freight and insurance costs imposed on an international inflation. For the UK, dependent as it was on overseas trade to the extent of an import bill amounting to between a fifth and a quarter of total final expenditure at market prices, the early rise in import prices inevitably set the inflationary process off at a rapid pace. Import prices rose by 24 per cent in 1915, 27 per cent in 1916 and peaked at nearly 30 per cent in 1917 before falling back to 9 per cent in 1918. As the figures in Table 1.6 show, the inflation in the general price level (as measured by the implicit price deflator of total final output) also peaked in 1917, being 14 per cent in 1915, 16 per cent in 1916 and 24 per cent in 1917. By 1917, however, the high cost of imported food and the increasing shortage of labour had brought a new pacemaker into action, i.e. rising wage rates; and when the rise in import prices dropped back to 9 per cent in 1918 the general price level still showed an increase of 16 per cent.

On the face of it – given the rapid increase in prices of imported wage goods, the shortages of essential labour, the limited range and effectiveness of either price controls (generally based on a cost-plus normal profits criterion) or distribution procedures (rationing was not introduced until 1918 and then only of certain foods) – it is surprising that wage costs did not begin to set the pace of the inflation much earlier. During the first three years of war the prices of consumers' goods and services were fast outstripping average weekly wage rates though not (as Table 1.6 shows) average weekly earnings. In the event, the rapid expansion of employment opportunities, plus the early increase in real incomes per person employed (amounting to a remarkable 16 per cent over the two years 1913–15) seems to have restrained the labour market. By 1917, however, real incomes were tending to fall rather than to rise, import prices were soaring, as were uncontrolled domestic prices under the pressure of demand released by a gradual extension of price control, and the general shortage of labour in key industries put workers into an unprecedentedly strong bargaining position. As a result, average weekly wage rates rose by 18 per cent in 1917 and 29 per cent in 1918.

Table 1.6   Price and wage indices for the United Kingdom, 1914–22 (1913=100)

Year	Price of total final output	Price of consumers' goods and services	Price of imported goods and services	Average weekly wage rates	Average weekly wage earnings
1914	100·2	99·7	101·1	101	101
1915	114·2	112·3	125·5	108	117
1916	132·8	132·5	159·1	118	133
1917	165·2	166·0	206·1	139	170
1918	192·0	202·5	224·7	179	211
1919	224·2	222·9	239·7	215	241
1920	271·4	257·2	284·8	257	278
1921	229·9	235·0	189·9	256	260
1922	196·2	202·0	152·0	198	209

Source: C. H. Feinstein [10], Tables 132.3 and 140.

State intervention in the UK economy was extended unwillingly and pragmatically through the First World War. Price control was introduced as a by-product of the requisitioning and licensing of supplies permitted under the Defence Regulations. By 1917 supplies (and hence prices) of most raw materials were directly controlled by government, and distributions to manufacturers were made in accordance with a schedule of priorities and in consideration of a controlled rate of profit. Import prices were further restrained by bulk purchase agreements, by requisitioning shipping, and by the government taking over the business of war risks insurance. So by 1918 the patchwork of price controls was beginning to bite. Only the labour market remained relatively free. Compulsory military service had been introduced in 1916, but there was no compulsory direction of civilian labour, only a series of voluntary agreements with the trade unions or *ad hoc* enactments designed to keep up the supply of labour to the munitions industries. In a situation of excess demand, with interest rates low, and with a banking system ready and able to extend virtually unlimited credit, private industries could still poach skilled female or juvenile (and hence exempt) labour from the public sector, and luxury industries could still take labour from essential war industries.

When the Armistice came in 1918 the rate of inflation went into brief reverse. Pigou characterised the period between November 1918 and April 1919 as the Breathing Space [38]. It was certainly very short and was followed by a rapid post-war boom stimulated by a hasty bonfire of controls and a sudden upsurge of business optimism. Most of the controls over supply had been scrapped before the end of 1919. 'Within eight months of the end of the war munition work had ceased, some 6 million soldiers and war workers had been released and nearly 90 per cent of them had either voluntarily withdrawn from the labour market or been reabsorbed into peacetime industry.' [29, p. 65] In March 1919 the government freed from control all new Stock Exchange issues for investment within the United Kingdom. The contraction of government expenditures was cushioned by a sharp increase in subsidies and grants to the personal sector. By April 1919 the Ministry of Labour cost of living index was 9 per cent below its October 1918 value. By October, however, it had reverted to the level of a year earlier and by October 1920 it had risen a further 23 per cent – representing a rate of inflation comparable to that reached in the war peak of 1917.

The post-war boom accorded with expectations. It had been predicted by the Cunliffe Committee on Financial Facilities which reported in November 1918 and which recommended keeping some control over new issues in the immediate post-war period. But opinion in Whitehall and the City was overwhelmingly in favour of relaxing all constraints on the operation of private enterprise as rapidly as possible. So although some controls lasted into late 1920 (sugar rationing, for example, was maintained until November 1920) the abandonment of all significant restrictions on the free market economy was either completed or actively in hand by the middle of 1919. At the same time the legacy of partially suppressed inflation in the last year of the war, associated with a sharp rise in personal incomes plus a growing shortage of consumer goods, had given consumers an abnormally high pent-up level of purchasing power awaiting a suitable outlet.

It is not hard, therefore, to explain the post-war boom. It was essentially a restocking boom in which both consumers and producers were buying things they had been frustrated from acquiring during the war. Consumers' goods led the way:[12] while business men – encouraged by the low bank rate, the relaxation of controls and a worldwide pressure of demand on the one hand, and driven by the need to replace rundown stocks and worn-out capital equipment on the other – found credit wonderfully easy to come by in a money market still flush with liquid assets and no longer obliged to lend heavily to government. In

12. E. V. Morgan [29, p. 297] notes that 'This reversal of the normal course of events in a peace-time cycle is quite reasonable in the aftermath of a war' when both consumers and dealers urgently need to restock consumers' goods.

view of what happened in some other European countries – e.g. in France where the 1920 level of wholesale prices was 43 per cent above the 1919 level or in Italy where it was 71 per cent above, to say nothing of countries like Germany, Russia and Austria in each of which a post-war boom crossed the threshold into hyper-inflation and destroyed the currency – what seems to need explanation is not so much the strength of the post-war boom in the UK as the speed with which inflation turned into deflation.

In one sense the boom was self-cancelling, of course. To the extent that it was financed out of consumers' or producers' involuntary saving it must run out of steam as soon as these limited resources were exhausted. To the extent that it rested on business optimism generated by the restocking demand, the restoration of stocks to a more normal level must be associated with a reduced pressure of demand. According to Pigou [38, p. 188], for example:

> It was as though the public had in a short once-for-all rush stocked itself with some new kind of durable commodity, such as motor cars or radio sets, and, thereafter, only called for the much smaller rate of output needed for replacements and for the small annual increment of new customers. In conditions such as these, at all events with industry organised as it was at that time, with no large scheme of public works to intervene and take up the slack, entrepreneurs would find their opportunity for using money to advantage cut down.

At the same time, the 20 per cent rise in weekly wage rates which took place in 1920, in a year when total real incomes from employment were falling, was more likely to squeeze profits than to support domestic demand.

However, the significant factor which distinguishes the UK experience in the 1920s from either those contemporary countries whose post-war booms deteriorated into hyper-inflation, or from the UK experience in the post-Second World War era was the criteria and objectives of official policy. Government current expenditure fell by 30 per cent between 1919 and 1920 and a budget deficit of £427 million was transformed into a budget surplus of £49 million. The current take of taxes was more than enough to cover current expenditure, and government deliberately set about reducing the weight of the short-term debt with all possible speed.

In short, fiscal policy was once more predicated on pre-war criteria of sound finance, involving a balanced budget and a systematic funding of the short-term debt. Monetary policy also reverted smartly to pre-war canons. 'The men of 1919 believed that the best monetary system was that of 1913; a world gold standard centred on London, with the Bank of England controlling the system by manipulation of the Bank Rate and acting as the watchdog of financial practice.' [38, p. 111] The government and the monetary authorities were overtly determined to restore the pre-war gold standard as soon as it was feasible to realign the exchange rate at the pre-war level of $4·86. This objective involved putting limits to the note issue, accumulating banknotes in the Currency Notes Redemption Account and getting prices down by manipulating the Bank Rate. The post-war boom carried the exchange rate down to $3·20 in February 1920 and in April the Bank rate was raised to 7 per cent: moreover, it was held at this traditionally high rate in the teeth of falling prices after the boom hit its peak. According to Hawtrey [17, p. 414]: 'Conditions in the Spring of 1920 were obviously unsound and the Government and the Bank of England were so evidently determined to stop the inflation that 7 per cent turned out to be enough.' With this view prevailing in the City, with wage rates still rising, prices beginning to falter and official policy aimed at checking the inflation, the climate of business expectations shifted from optimistic to pessimistic and boom turned into slump. The slump lasted until early 1923, but recovery was stifled by the official determination to return to gold at the pre-war parity and the slump turned into the phase which Pigou designated as the Doldrums and which lasted until the Wall Street crash in 1929.

Taken as a whole, then, the period of the First World War and the post-war boom involved an average annual rate of price increase over the six years 1914–20 of 18 per cent per annum. By 1920 the index of consumer prices was standing at roughly the same level (compared with 1914) as average weekly wage rates; but average earnings were somewhat higher, and if account is taken of the high and rising level of unemployment through the 1920s, the subsequent deflation can be seen to have had a depressing effect on working-class standards of living. There had been a welfare gain for labour in the wartime period of full employment but it was largely eroded in the Slump and the Doldrums. However, one significant legacy of this inflation episode was a marked increase in the share of incomes from employment in net national product. During the quinquennium 1909–13 incomes from employment accounted for just under 53 per cent of net national product: in the quinquennium 1919–23 the proportion was over 66 per cent (using Feinstein's estimates [10]. Most of this gain survived nearly two decades of high unemployment and in the quinquennium 1935–9 the proportion was still as high as 63 per cent.

The Second World War and its aftermath

The rise in UK prices associated with the Second World War was modest compared with the experience of the First World War, and also – as it was to turn out – less violent than the peacetime inflation which developed in the 1970s. Over the six war years from 1939 to 1945 the average rate of increase in the general price level (market prices of total final expenditure) was no more than 7½ per cent per annum compound. This was in spite of the fact that the Second World War was a much more expensive war in terms of the annual burden per head of population.[13] The crucial difference between the two episodes was that the men of 1939 had learned the lesson of the earlier experience. They had no delusions about an early end to the war and they were determined to minimise inflation. For it had been shown that the policy of diverting resources to government use by inflation was at best feasible in the short run: when applied over a long period it was evidently liable to degenerate either into a self-defeating wage–price spiral (as British experience had shown) or at worst into a hyper-inflation of the kind experienced in Germany and other European countries in the 1920s.

As before, the outbreak of world war initiated a sharp increase in UK import costs owing to a speculative rise in world prices and the high cost of war freight and insurance. The increase was aggravated by the 14 per cent devaluation of sterling and in 1940 import prices rose by 38 per cent. The dangers of a price–wage–price spiral were pointed up by the coal-miners whose early demand for a rise in wages to compensate for a rising cost of living brought a corresponding rise in the price of coal. In the light of this warning and under the influence of Keynes[14] the government explicitly rejected inflation as a way of financing the war effort and turned instead towards centralised planning of resource allocation. Sir Kingsley Wood's budget speech of 1941 outlined a new kind of macro-economic approach to national budgeting by calculating the total money demand of the war economy, measuring it against gross money incomes and thus identifying the size of the inflationary gap that had to be stopped by taxation or other fiscal means in order to prevent prices from rising, or intolerable shortages from developing. According to the historian of this aspect of the Second World War: 'The budget had in fact ceased to serve its peacetime purpose of providing finance for all Government activities and had become solely an engine for preserving, in the face of colossal defence expenditure at home, reasonable stability in the value of money and adequate incentives consistently with a distribution of the burden that people would accept as broadly just.' [40, p. 49]

In the event the stabilisation policy was remarkably successful in controlling both prices and wages as Table 1.7 illustrates. After the early upsurge in 1940 and 1941 the general price level (prices of total final expenditures) rose by 14 and 11 per cent, respectively, the annual rate of

13. Measured in terms of the total cost of public expenditure on current goods and services at 1913 prices, the four years of total war 1915–18 inclusive, involved an average annual outlay of £997 million (amounting to about £24 per head of the population of Great Britain). This compares with an average annual outlay (also at 1913 prices) of £169 million for the six years 1940–45 inclusive (i.e. about £35 per head of the population of Great Britain). See C. H. Feinstein [10], Tables 8–9, and 22, for estimates of public authorities' expenditure and corresponding price indices based on 1913.

14. R. S. Sayers [40] quotes Keynes to the effect that 'The traditional way out which we adopted in 1917 . . . is to let prices rise.. . . Today we have cut ourselves off from this expedient because many groups of wages are linked to the cost of living so that they go up automatically when prices go up.'

increase dropped back to 6 per cent in 1942, 5 per cent in 1943 and 1944 and then to between 2 and 3 per cent in 1945 and 1946. Consumer prices – reflecting government's pledge to restrain the cost of living – grew a little more slowly from 1942 onwards:[15] and even import prices grew by less than 24 per cent in total over the four years between 1941 and 1945. Weekly wage-rate rises generally lagged slightly behind the growth in consumer prices though – given the increase in employment and man-hours worked – there was scope for a non-negligible improvement in average real incomes for the labour force, as is indicated by the last column of Table 1.7.

Table 1.7   Price and wage indices, 1939–48 (1938 = 100)

Year	Total final expenditure	Consumers' goods	Imports goods and services	Average weekly wage rates	Real income per employee at 1938 prices
1939	102·6	102·8	100·9	101·1	100
1940	117·3	120·0	139·6	118·9	99
1941	129·9	133·0	159·8	122·2	101
1942	138·2	142·5	164·6	130·8	102
1943	145·7	147·3	185·2	137·3	106
1944	153·5	151·3	188·9	144·3	110
1945	157·3	155·6	197·7	151·4	111
1946	161·6	160·4	212·2	163·2	111
1947	180·4	171·7	257·6	169·2	112
1948	194·4	182·4	288·0	177·8	115

Source: Based on estimates in C. H. Feinstein [10]. Final column represents average incomes from employment per employee deflated by consumers' goods price index.

The suppression of the wartime inflation was achieved by an elaborate system of controls on production, distribution and prices. House rents were statutorily controlled at an early stage. Food prices were from the first a special area of concern. Domestic agricultural prices were fixed annually and the gap between rising producer or import prices and the tightly constrained retail price of food was plugged by subsidies. For some other manufactured products which bulked largely in the cost of living index (e.g. clothing and furniture) prices were held down by quality-control schemes associated with central distribution of raw materials.

In addition to imposing specific controls on a wide range of prices – a task which was facilitated by the battery of physical controls on labour and raw materials, including a sophisticated rationing system for consumers' goods and a centralised acquisition and distribution of industrial raw materials – the authorities used all the financial and fiscal

15. The Ministry of Labour retail price index grew more slowly still, but in view of the deliberate attempts to manipulate that index by offsetting controllable prices against non-controllable prices, it became less and less representative of consumer price movements generally.

policies they could devise to damp down the inflationary pressures inherent in a fully employed wartime economy. The inflationary impact of the government's short-term borrowing programme, for example, was reduced by introducing a new short-term borrowing instrument – Treasury Deposit Receipts – which amounted to a little more in total value than Treasury Bills and, in principle, were less liquid. The deliberately low interest rates designed to keep the cost of government borrowing to a minimum were associated with a tight control over private *capital* issues and bank advances to the private sector. The National Savings Movement was designed to tap the small savers' surplus. And a stiff rate of taxation was further jacked up by a system of forced savings through post-war credits. Tax liabilities which had accounted for 22 per cent of private income in 1938 had risen to 33 per cent in the years 1941–4: and the income tax collection system was rationalised by the Pay As You Earn scheme which enabled the Inland Revenue to require employers to deduct tax from wage and salary earners at source.

Inevitably, of course, repressed inflation on the scale achieved in the Second World War – effective though it was in controlling the price symptoms of excess demand – was piling up problems for the post-war period. Both consumers and businesses had been forced to accumulate idle balances or government securities (many of which were payable on demand or at short notice) to an extent that they would not have chosen had their choices not been constrained by controls and shortages. At the same time financial institutions enjoyed a degree of liquidity which must lend wings to credit expansion as soon the economy began to change direction from war to peace. Even more than in the aftermath of the First World War the late 1940s seemed tailor-made for a boom. Then the devaluation of 1949 and the Korean War boom of 1950–51 (which drove up import prices by nearly 50% in two years) gave successive boosts to inflationary pressures which had begun to tail off.

What prevented the post-Second World War boom from developing at the pace which had characterised the aftermath of the First World War was the fact that the authorities had learned the lesson of 1919–20 and were not disposed to scrap the wartime system of direct controls with all possible speed. On the contrary, the Labour government approached the task of reconstructing a peacetime economy in the same planning spirit as the wartime governments had dealt with the problem of organising for victory. In 1947, for example, it published the first of a series of *Economic Surveys* designed to precede the annual budget with an economic forecast, together with a statement of intent on policy, set in a national budgeting framework of ideas. After announcing that the present government had already begun 'to build up administrative machinery for economic planning' and specifying full employment as one of the self-evident aims of the planning exercise, the 1947 *Economic Survey* made absolutely clear that there was still no intention of dismantling the existing 'large number of direct controls, the purpose of which is to allocate scarce resources of all kinds between the various applicants for their use – rationing, raw material controls, building licensing, production controls, import licensing, capital issues control, etc.' [7, p. 8]

It was thus not until the 1950s (when the Conservative government, with its less interventionist bias, took over) that the armoury of physical controls were appreciably relaxed. Even then the process of freeing the market economy took several years. Clothes rationing had been ended in 1949 and petrol rationing in 1950, but food rationing lasted until 1954. Import controls were steadily lifted from 1952 onwards, while building licensing and the controls on private investment were also being relaxed until they were finally disbanded in 1954. By 1956 government was no longer bulk-buying raw materials in overseas markets and the last major allocation scheme (for coal) was abandoned in 1958. Having given up its powers of direct intervention at strategic points in the flow of resources government was henceforth thrown back on fiscal or monetary policies if it wished to restrain the rate of inflation.

Table 1.8 Movements in prices and wage rates, 1948–65. Percentage increases over index for preceding year

Year	General price level (%)	Consumers' prices (%)	Import prices (%)	Average basic weekly wage rates (%)
1949	2·3	2·3	2·7	3·0
1950	3·3	2·7	13·1	1·3
1951	7·9	9·4	31·6	8·1
1952	10·4	5·9	−1·9	8·7
1953	0·5	2·0	−9·6	4·7
1954	1·3	1·9	−0·4	5·2
1955	3·9	3·6	2·8	7·0
1956	5·4	4·5	1·0	8·0
1957	3·5	3·4	2·4	5·0
1958	2·3	2·8	−5·0	2·4
1959	0·9	0·6	–	3·0
1960	1·2	0·9	1·5	2·7
1961	2·7	3·0	–	4·3
1962	3·2	3·7	0·3	3·4
1963	1·7	1·4	2·3	3·7
1964	2·6	2·9	3·4	4·9
1965	4·2	4·5	1·0	4·0

Sources: First three columns based on data in Feinstein [10], Tables 11 and 17. The implicit price index for the general price level was based on estimates of total final expenditure at current and 1958 prices, respectively. The last column based on monthly indices of basic weekly rates of wages of all manual workers in June each year given in Department of Employment and Productivity, *British Labour Statistics Historical Abstract, 1886–1968.*

By this time, however, the climate of business expectations was conditioned by two related features of the post-war situation which were fundamentally different from all past peacetime experience. The first was the commitment of governments generally (not merely the UK government) to maintaining full employment. The second – also an international phenomenon – was a persistent inflation of prices. Taken together, these new characteristics of the economic situation in the UK justified the expectation of a high and rising level of demand, thus stimulating a rising level of investment. In 1948 gross domestic fixed capital formation stood at over 13 per cent of GNP at factor cost – already a historically high level for the United Kingdom: by 1953 it had risen to 15 per cent, by 1958 to over 17 per cent and by the mid-1960s to between 20 and 21 per cent (see Table 1.9, p. 33).

The post-war price inflation though not rapid (it averaged under 3½ per cent per annum over the seventeen years 1948–65) created increasing concern through the 1950s. There were two main reasons for concern. The first was the fragility of the balance of payments position as a result of the rapid expansion of imports associated with a steady loss of competitiveness for UK manufacturers in both home and export markets; the second was the persistent tendency for money wage rates to grow faster than prices. One reflection of government concern was the appointment in August 1957 of a Council on Prices, Productivity and Incomes with the following terms of reference: 'Having regard to the desirability of full employment and increasing standards of life based on expanding production and reasonable stability of prices, to keep under review changes in prices, productivity and the level of incomes (including wages, salaries and profits) and to report thereon from time to time.'[16] The first report of the Council [8, p. 46] came up with the conclusion that 'the factor principally responsible for too rapidly rising profits – as for too rapidly rising wages – has been the level of total demand, and that the main route towards preventing the excessive growth of money incomes of both kinds must lie through mastering the level of demand'. The fourth and last report [9, p. 3] concluded that while inflation 'has sometimes been due to the pull of excess demand . . . experience has shown that removing excess demand is not of itself enough. We have been brought to the conclusion that inflation has another cause, an upward push as rates of pay are raised and profit margins are maintained by raising prices.'

In effect, then, it was clear to informed observers that, apart from the factors mentioned above which were tending to maintain a buoyant level of demand in the domestic economy of the 1950s, there were certain other essentially new but more permanent features of the post-war economic situation in the UK that had implications for the current and expected rate of inflation. Basically the most significant was the abandonment of the gold standard. In a sense this dates from 1931,

16. The original members of the Council were Lord Cohen (Chairman), Sir Harold Howitt and Sir Dennis Robertson and the Council issued four reports – two in 1958 and two in 1961, after a reconstitution of membership in 1960 with the same terms of reference throughout.

though its significance in this context did not become apparent until after the Second World War. The abandonment of the gold standard was crucial because it removed the automatic constraint on the supply of money to the economy. Though exchange rates were fixed from 1949 to 1967 the vulnerability of the British balance of payments was such that the long-run trend in the purchasing power of the £ sterling was certain to be downward, and hence a long-run fall in the value of money could be regarded as virtually inevitable.

There was, however, another factor in the post-war situation which – when combined with the abandonment of the monetary discipline of the gold standard – was to transform the shape of the policy problems involved in maintaining a reasonable stability of prices. That was the strength and attitudes of organised labour. As Hicks pointed out in 1955 [18, p. 391]:

> Since 1931 . . . the *general* level of wages has become a monetary question. So long as wages were being determined within a *given* monetary framework, there was some sense in saying that there was an 'equilibrium wage', a wage that was in line with the monetary conditions that were laid down from outside. But the world we now live in is one in which the monetary system has become relatively elastic, so that it can accommodate itself to changes in wages rather than the other way about.. . . It is hardly an exaggeration to say that instead of being on a Gold Standard, we are on a Labour Standard.

In these circumstances, given a government pledged to maintain full employment and private economic growth, the problem of controlling inflation became a problem of finding ways to restrain the growth of money wages. Moreover, for an open economy such as the United Kingdom this problem was compounded by the fact that the post-war inflation has been an international phenomenon and that rising import prices have had effects on the cost of living which led straight into the dreaded price–wage–price spiral.

Two things held the pace of inflation to relatively modest levels in the 1950s and most of the 1960s. One was the time lag between rises in the cost of living and the induced rise in wages. The other was the fact that a fixed exchange rate kept in force a balance of payments constraint – an automatic discipline which, though less rigorous than the rules of the gold standard, did oblige the government to put periodic fiscal and monetary brakes on the rate of expansion of demand. The time lag in the price–wage spiral was destined to contract as trade unionists and employers learned to anticipate inflation. In the early stages of the post-war inflation Peacock and Ryan [34] had calculated, on the basis of a study of certain manufacturing industries, that there was normally a time lag between an increase in consumer prices and a rise in wages of 'about 6 to 7 months plus the unknown lag between the rise in the Index and the presentation of claims'. The time lag was much longer, of course, for salary earners and pensioners.

However, as trade unionists and employers matured in their experience of the continually inflating, fully employed, economy of the 1950s and early 1960s, the annual wage round developed a momentum of its own. Nor was cost of living the only propellant. To begin with, wages rose fast in those industries which were experiencing the rapid increases in prices and productivity. Later social justice required that wages in other industries should be raised on grounds of 'comparability.' Wages began to rise almost as fast in non-expanding industries or in government service as in the growth sectors: they rose in recession as well as in boom. Table 1.9 illustrates the steady growth in the share of labour in the national product that resulted from this process and the progressive worsening of the balance of payments situation in the 1960s.

Table 1.9   The UK economy 1948–65: principal economic indicators

Year	(1) Gross domestic fixed capital formation at 1958 prices as % GNP	(2) Unemployment as % insured population	(3) Current balance of payments (£m.)	(4) Central government surplus (£m.)	(5) Incomes from employment as % NNP
1948	13·3	1·8	+ 26	507	70·5
1949	14·1	1·6	−1	590	70·2
1950	14·3	1·5	+306	663	70·6
1951	14·0	1·2	−365	577	71·8
1952	14·1	2·1	+163	341	71·4
1953	15·0	1·8	+145	201	71·1
1954	15·7	1·5	+117	233	71·1
1955	16·1	1·2	−155	503	72·4
1956	16·5	1·3	+208	416	73·6
1957	17·0	1·6	+233	527	73·9
1958	17·1	2·2	+344	622	73·6
1959	17·9	2·3	+143	492	72·9
1960	18·7	1·7	−265	202	72·1
1961	19·8	1·6	−4	367	73·7
1962	19·4	2·1	+112	670	74·2
1963	18·9	2·6	+114	241	73·2
1964	21·0	1·7	−395	495	73·1
1965	21·2	1·5	−77	890	73·4

Sources: Columns 1, 4 and 5 based on estimates in Feinstein [10]. Columns 2 and 3 from [25].

Epilogue

The phase of modest post-war inflation that characterised the extended aftermath to the Second World War came to an end with devaluation in 1967. During the next quinquennium – partly as a result of devaluation, partly as a consequence of an increasing world rate of inflation and partly perhaps because the character of the inflationary process was changing in the UK – the general price level (total final expenditures again) rose almost twice as fast as it had in the previous couple of decades, i.e. at the compound rate of 6½ per cent. One indication of the change in the nature of the inflationary process was that for the first time since 1939 the unemployment rate was showing a tendency to advance: it rose above 3 per cent in 1971 and 1972. During the next few years, 1972–6, under the impact of three things – (1) a downward floating exchange rate, (2) a spectacular boom in world commodity prices, and (3) the government's attempt in 1973–4 to stem the rising tide of unemployment by stimulating the level of economic activity, – the rate of inflation accelerated to an average of over 18 per cent per annum. In terms of the retail price index, and hence the social pressure to increase wages, the inflation was faster still.[17]

The social strains and stresses created by rapid inflation brought it to the top priority position in the UK government's policy agenda in the mid-1970s. It is evident that in the long run the only solution to the uncomfortable conflicts between policy objectives – in particular to the confrontation between inflation, the level of unemployment and the balance of payments – is a restructuring of the UK economy so as to raise the annual rate of growth of overall productivity per unit of input to levels that are comparable with the rates actually being achieved by its main competitors. In the short run the authorities have been trying to buy time by persuading unions and employers to operate an incomes policy strong enough to restrain the wage-price spiral, and by using the benefits of North Sea oil to check another major recent cost element in UK inflation, namely declining exchange rates. Thus, there may be some prospect of maintaining a more moderate scale of inflation in the late 1970s and early 1980s: but the underlying pressures which may be expected to ensure a continually rising price level in the United Kingdom remain strong and persistent.

17. Entry into the Common Market led, for a variety of reasons, to a faster rise in the price of consumers' necessities than would otherwise have been the case.

References

1. **Braudel, F.,** 'The Mediterranean economy in the sixteenth century', trans. from 'La Mediterranée et le Monde Mediterranean a l'Epoque de Philippe II', in P. Earle, ed. *Essays in European Economic History, 1500–1800.* Oxford Univ. Press, 1974.
2. **Cagan, P.,** 'The monetary dynamics of hyperinflation' in Friedman [14], 1966.
3. **Cannan, E.,** *The Paper Pound of 1797–1821* (containing a reprint of *Bullion Report* and an introduction by Cannan) 2nd ed. Frank Cass, 1969.
4. **Carus-Wilson, E. H.** (ed.), *Essays in Economic History,* Vols. I and II. E. Arnold, 1954.
5. **Cipolla, C. M.,** 'The so-called price revolution: reflections on the Italian situation', trans. and reprinted in P. Burke, ed. *Economy and Society in Early Modern Europe: Essays from Annales.* Routledge, Kegan Paul, 1972.
6. **Clapham, J. H.,** *The Bank of England,* Vol. I, Appendix C. Cambridge Univ. Press, 1944.
7. **Command 7046,** *Economic Survey for 1947.* HMSO, London.

8. **Council on Prices, Productivity and Incomes,** *First Report.* HMSO, London, 1958.
9. **Council on Prices, Productivity and Incomes,** *Fourth Report.* HMSO, London, 1961.
10. **Feinstein, C. H.,** *Statistical Tables of National Income, Expenditure and Output 1855–1965.* Cambridge Univ. Press, 1971.
11. **Felix, D.,** 'Profit inflation and industrial growth: the historic record', *Quarterly Journal of Economics,* Vol. XXV, 1956.
12. **Fisher, F. J.,** 'Influenza and inflation in Tudor England', *Economic History Review,* Vol. XVIII, Aug. 1965.
13. **Friedman, M.,** (Ed.) *Studies in the Quantity Theory of Money.* Lerner & Seldon, 1966.
14. **Gayer, A. D., Rostow, W. W. and Schwartz, A. J.,** *The Growth and Fluctuations of the British Economy 1790–1850,* Vol. I. Oxford Univ. Press, 1953.
15. **Gould, J. D.,** 'The price revolution reconsidered', *Economic History Review.* Vol. XVII, Dec. 1964.
16. **Hatcher, J.,** *Plague, Population and the English Economy 1348–1530.* Macmillan, 1977.
17. **Hawtrey, R. G.,** *Currency and Credit.* Longman, 1950.
18. **Hicks, J.,** 'Economic foundations of a wages policy', *Economic Journal,* Vol. LXV, 1955.
19. **Hicks, J.,** *Critical Essays in Monetary Theory.* Oxford Univ. Press, 1967.
20. **Hoffman, W. G.,** *British Industry 1700–1950,* English ed. Blackwell, 1955.
21. **Horsefield, J. K.,** 'Origins of the Bank Charter Act, 1844', in T. S. Ashton and R. S. Sayers, eds, *Papers in English Monetary History.* Oxford Univ. Press, 1954.
22. **Kerridge, E.,** 'The movement of rent, 1540–1640', reprinted in Carus-Wilson, E. M. ed. [4], Vol. I.
23. **Keynes, J. M.,** *Treatise on Money,* Vol. II, *Collected writings of John Maynard Keynes.* Macmillan, 1971.
24. **Keynes, J. M.,** *Tract on monetary Reform,* Vol. IV, *Collected Writings of John Maynard Keynes.* Macmillan, 1971.
25. **London and Cambridge Economic Series,** *The British Economy Key Statistics 1900–1970.* Department of Applied Economics, Cambridge.
26. **Lipsey, R. G.,** 'Does money always depreciate?', *Lloyds Bank Review,* Oct. 1960.
27. **Lowe, J.,** *The Present State of England,* 1822.
28. **Mitchell, B. R.,** *Abstract of Historical Statistics.* Cambridge Univ. Press, 1971.
29. **Morgan, E. W.,** *Studies in British Financial Policy, 1914–25.* Macmillan, 1952.
30. **Nadal, J.,** 'La revolucion des los precios espanoles en el siglo XVI: Estado actuel de la cuestion', *Hispania,* 1959.
31. **Nef, J. N.,** 'Prices and industrial capitalism in France and England, 1540–1640', *Economic History Review,* **VII,** 1937.
32. **Nef, J. N.,** 'The progress of technology and the growth of large-scale industry in Britain, 1540–1640', reprinted in Carus-Wilson [4], Vol. I.
33. **Outhwaite, R. B.,** *Inflation in Tudor and Early Stuart England.* Macmillan, 1969.
34. **Peacock, A. J. and Ryan, W. J. L.,** 'Wage claims and the pace of inflation, 1948–51', *Economic Journal,* **XXII,** June 1953.
35. **Phelps-Brown, E. H. and Hopkins, S. V.,** 'Seven centuries of the prices of consumables', *Economica,* **XXIII,** 1955.
36. **Phelps-Brown, E. H. and Hopkins, S. V.,** 'Seven centuries of the prices of consumables compared with builders' wage rates', *Economica,* **XXIII,** 1955.
37. **Phelps-Brown, E. H. and Hopkins, S. V.,** 'Wage rates and prices: Evidence for population pressure in the sixteenth century', *Economica,* **XXIV,** 1957.
38. **Pigou, A. C.,** *Aspects of British Economic History, 1918–1925.* Frank Cass, 1971.
39. **Sayers, R. S.,** *The Bank of England, 1891–1944,* vol. I, Cambridge Univ. Press, 1976.
40. **Sayers, R. S.,** *Financial Policy, 1939–45.* HMSO, London, 1956.
41. **Schumpeter, E. B.,** 'English prices and public finance, 1660–1822', *Review of Economic Statistics,* **XX,** 1938.
42. **Smith, A.,** *Wealth of Nations,* Cannan edn. Methuen, 1950.
43. **Thornton, H.,** *An Enquiry into the Nature and Effect of the Paper Credit of Great Britain.* Ed. F. A. V. Hayek, 1939.

44. **Tooke, H.,** *History of Prices*, vol. 1. Longman, London, 1838.
45. **Vilar, P.,** *A History of Gold and Money 1450–1920*. Foundations of History Library, NLB, London, 1956.

Chapter 2

Monetarist views on inflation

Victoria Chick*

Introduction

Stating a unified, generally agreed monetarist theory of inflation is an impossible task. Monetarists believe that money is important, but beyond that there may be as many varieties of monetarism as there are monetarist economists. And money is not static, but responds to controversy and to changing events. Earlier monetarist models concentrated on the importance of money to the determination of nominal income rather than inflation. Only as inflation has emerged as a major problem, and particularly as it has 'gone international', have monetarist economists emphasised the connection between money and prices except in the very long run, or during hyperinflations.

Paradoxically, as monetarist economists began to consider shorter-run price fluctuations, their models took on Keynesian attributes, so that the monetarist contribution has become, with the exception of the work on international aspects of inflation, less distinctive. Added to these problems of pinning down a monetarist theory of inflation is the varied nature of the empirical evidence pertaining to it, and the regrettable fact that no monetarist model has, to our knowledge and that of Henry, Sawyer and Smith [48], been tested for the UK.

Nevertheless, monetarists have provided a valuable corrective to the oversimplifications of early postwar Keynesian theory. We shall proceed to review particular monetarist theories and evidence, and to state their policy conclusions, as the work was developed from the late 1950s, after a summary of the main theoretical issues. The survey does not claim to be comprehensive; rather, the studies reviewed are chosen as prominent landmarks in an approach which is continuously developing.

Monetarist theory

Varieties of monetarism

If monetarists can be brought together under one banner, it is probably

*I should like to thank Morris Perlman for his comments and suggestions, without implicating him.

Friedman's assertion that '. . . inflation is always and everywhere a monetary phenomenon'. ([36, p. 24] original in italics). At its vaguest and least operational, this statement could be interpreted to mean that prices cannot continue to rise without *either* an expansion of the money supply *or* a rise in the velocity of the existing supply. It is unusual, however, for monetarists to be as non-committal as Friedman is in the following passage [31, p. 174], taken from an earlier article: 'The relationship between changes in the stock of money and changes in prices, while close, is not of course precise or mechanically rigid. Two major factors produce discrepancies: changes in output, and changes in the amount of money that the public desires to hold relative to its income.' This statement may be translated: $MV_y = PQ$, the familiar truism that the value of aggregate income equals the amount of money times its income velocity. It does not even postulate a causal role for money, only that monetary factors are in some way involved.

Indeed, early in the development of monetarism, it was difficult enough to make the point that monetary change is a necessary adjunct to price changes, while not attributing to it the role of prime cause. In 1959, Selden challenged the 'non-monetary' character of the Keynesian cost-push and demand-pull theories of inflation by pointing out that ever-higher wage bills or levels of demand could not be sustained without a greater monetary circulation. In more recent times the idea has been accepted that wage claims in excess of productivity are 'validated' by expansive monetary policy in order to avoid the unemployment which would most likely follow in the absence of such a policy. And Laidler [55] has put Selden's point somewhat differently, arguing that excess demand, whether cost-push or demand-pull, can change *relative* prices, but that the 'absolute' level of prices, i.e. an index of money prices, cannot exhibit an upward trend in the absence of changes in the money supply.

While not attributing a causal role to money, Laidler and Selden are not merely reminding Keynesians of a truism. They stress the importance of changes in the money supply and assert that the variation in velocity is small, certainly inadequate to fuel inflation. Their view, held with great consistency by monetarists (see Chick [15], for documentation of this point) is in sharp contrast to the strong Keynesian view of the Radcliffe Committee, who argued that even in the short run there was no limit to velocity. A more moderate Keynesian view would assert a more limited, but still substantial, variability of velocity.[1]

---

1. Thus a wage–price spiral, for example, could be sustained if firms borrowed to the extent of the increased wage bill for sufficient time to bring output on to the market at higher prices, those prices being sustained by the higher level of demand supported by workers' increased money incomes. Of course, as time progresses, interest rate rises will eventually put a stop to the spiral, but monetarists would regard this mechanism as unlikely, even for relatively short periods.

Theoretical framework

The foundation of the monetarist approach is the quantity theory of money. This theory attributes a central role to money in the determination of income and prices. At its simplest, the theory runs as follows.

The private sector has a demand for money which is predominantly determined by the need to use money in transactions; thus it is a stable function chiefly of the level of income, which determines the volume of transactions. A specific hypothesis states that there is no 'money illusion': 'real balances' are demanded in sufficient volume to support a given level of real transactions. The supply of money is determined exogenously to the private sector – formerly, it was determined by gold discoveries and foreign trade, now by control of the banking system through reserve requirements and the supply of base money (reserve money). When the money supply increases (decreases), the public react by increasing (decreasing) the money value of their expenditures, thus raising (reducing) aggregate nominal income until demand again equals supply. The extent to which this change is reflected in prices depends partly on the time horizon considered, and partly on the rate of monetary change. We shall return to this point later.

The key relationship is the direct link from money to expenditure on goods and services. Keynesians, in contrast, postulate a demand for money which derives from the need to place accumulated wealth in financial assets, including money balances. Keynes accepted the transactions demand as a component of liquidity preference; his followers have given it diminished importance. They postulate that an excess supply of money finds its way chiefly into financial markets, affecting interest rates rather than goods prices. Interest-rate changes affect investment, thus 'transmitting monetary impulses' to the market for current output indirectly. The 'new quantity theory' [30] opposed this view, not by restoring transactions demand directly but rather by emphasising that goods, as well as financial assets, have rates of return and are alternatives to holding money. The original quantity-theoretic conclusion that excess money mainly affects expenditure is restored through a rather curious argument: while stressing the variety of alternatives to money-holding, and thus the large number of channels through which monetary policy could in principle make itself felt, Friedman argued that, since financial assets were so manifold, interest rates on each of them would be little affected. A similar argument was not made with respect to goods; thus it was implied that an excess of money would have its chief effect on the goods market.

Brunner and Meltzer (see references in Brunner [11]) have also emphasised the range of alternatives to money, but an excess supply of money feeds through to output by a different route. Monetary change affects security prices and the value of 'real assets' (equities or capital equipment) and thus changes the incentive to invest, raising prices of current output in so far as the capital goods industries do not adjust output. Although Brunner sees the transmission mechanism through a range of assets as a distinctive feature of monetarism, his mechanism and Friedman's are virtually identical to Tobin's [74] and very similar to Keynes's too, though concentrating on the incentive to possess assets rather than on the cost of borrowing to purchase them.[2]

Maintained hypotheses

The monetarist theoretical framework, which, although exhibiting variations, centres on the demand for money function, is based on some deeper assumptions or beliefs which are more fundamental than the customary level of debate. These can be called 'maintained hypotheses'.

(i) Stability of the private sector.   A belief in the underlying stability of the private sector of the economy is a fundamental tenet of monetarism (Brunner [10] has been most explicit). It is assumed (rather than demonstrated) that, if left to its own devices, the private sector would tend toward a full-employment level of output or, if the system is dynamic, a full-employment growth rate.[3] Disturbances are created by variations in government policy. This belief contrasts with Keynes's emphasis (not always fully reflected in the writings of the Keynesians) on fluctuations in investment caused by changes in expectations concerning the profitability of productive enterprise.

In monetarist models, this belief in stability takes the form of postulating a long-run level or rate of growth of output which is exogenously determined. In particular, this level or rate of growth, to which there corresponds 'full employment' or a 'natural rate of unemployment', is independent of monetary factors. In the long run, therefore, it follows without elaborate theorising that money can only affect prices (Friedman [37], Anderson and Carlson [2] are models of this kind). In Keynes's framework, in contrast, the ability of policy to alter the incentives to invest can change the rate of capital accumulation from what the private sector would do if unaided, and this changes the long-run level of capacity output.

Another way of putting this point is related to the first of Brunner's criteria for establishing that a model is monetarist [10]: namely, that the long run is determined by stock variables, especially the stocks of money and capital, which determine prices and output, respectively. The long run is thus assumed to be independent of short-run events in monetarism, where in Keynes's theory the long run is determined by the interaction of stocks and flows in the short run.

2. Indeed, Tobin (Stein [71, p. 8]) does not believe that Friedman's transmission mechanism supports monetarist conclusions.
3. At a still deeper level lies the classical view that the rate of capital accumulation (and hence the growth of output) is determined by productivity, thrift, and population growth, assumptions retained by modern neoclassical growth theory.

(ii) Perfect markets. Independence of the long run from short-run decisions can be assumed if capital is perfectly malleable or, alternatively, if investment takes place in conditions of perfect foresight. The same effect can be obtained, in logic if not in reality, by the assumption of perfect capital markets. This assumption is rarely explicit; more often it takes the form of treating equities and real capital as interchangeable, as they would be if equities perfectly reflected real rates of return on investment. (See, e.g. Brunner's and Meltzer's work, Brunner [11]). Some non-monetarists also do this; see, e.g. Tobin [75] 1963.) Friedman [37] is, however, explicit in his assumption that the interest rate is always equal to the marginal efficiency of investment. In other monetarist writings, the assumption is embodied in the hypothesis that the nominal rate of interest reflects an exogenously given real rate and anticipated inflation. Any failure of the capital market to achieve the 'correct' rate of capital accumulation is thus due to faulty inflation expectations rather than to a mis-estimate, due to over-optimism, of the real rate of return on capital.

Similarly, wages and prices are presumed to be flexible; the marginal productivity of labour determines the wage.

(iii) Allocative detail. Finally, monetarists (especially Brunner, Meltzer and Friedman) place little emphasis on 'allocative detail', that is, on the disaggregation of output into consumer and capital goods. The distribution of expenditure is not supposed to affect the level of output or the rate of inflation. Discrepancies between supply and demand are taken care of by price flexibility which changes relative but not absolute prices. Thus, money is related to aggregate income, not to its components.

The long run and the short

Monetarists are known for their greater interest in the long run than in the short. This is particularly marked when discussing inflation; in the short run they have tended to take nominal income as the variable to be explained, leaving aside the question of the division between changes in prices and output. Friedman [39, p. 21] has acknowledged this weakness: '. . . we know much more about the nexus between money and money income, or nominal income, than we do about the forces that cause the division between prices and output'.

There are good reasons for this difference, though the reasons for it are to be found not in the monetarist literature but in Keynes. Keynes demonstrated [51, pp. 304–6] that the division between prices and output depend on the extent of excess capacity, the rate at which returns diminish, the speed of response of wages and the expected price elasticity of product demand – a list of influences which cannot be expected to be stable over the cycle or insensitive to the many influences governing expectations.

However, monetarism is not devoid of work in this area. Friedman [34, 37] has postulated that the short-run effects of monetary change fall chiefly on real output, and there are models which attempt to apportion the impact of monetary change between output and prices on a theoretical basis (Andersen and Carlson [2], Laidler [52, 53]). Interestingly, however, a key component of these explanations is excess capacity – the cornerstone of the Keynesian theory of prices.

Monetarism is at its strongest in explaining price changes over the long run or in periods of very rapid monetary change and hyper-inflation. In the latter case, the money supply is growing so rapidly that output initially cannot adjust fast enough and then, when the true nature of the situation becomes widely understood, output expansion ceases to be a profitable strategy. And the assertion that the impact of monetary growth falls chiefly on prices in the very long term derives directly from the maintained hypothesis of an exogenously given real rate of long-term growth.

Policy conclusions

Most Keynesians would now agree that there exists a rate of growth of money sufficiently rapid to cause inflation. A strong monetarist position is that monetary growth is both necessary and sufficient to explain inflation. Friedman is prepared to state that 'inflation . . . can be produced *only* by a more rapid increase in the quantity of money than in output' [36, p. 28] (my italics). But this begs the question of what determines output. Again, Friedman accepts, without qualification, that 'money is *all* that matters for nominal income' [37, p. 27] (my italics), but he does not commit himself concerning inflation. In the long run, given the assumed exogenous rate of growth of real output, money must be all that matters for prices. In the short run, monetarists assert that monetary change is necessary to cause inflation (see Selden and Laidler, cited earlier), but few would go further and assert that it was also sufficient.

It is clear that, if monetary growth were both necessary and sufficient to generate inflation, and the money supply was fully under the control of the authorities, then these authorities are responsible for starting and ending any inflation. One could argue about the costs, in terms of other policy objectives, but that is all. That these propositions are not generally accepted is obvious from the continuing debate between monetarists and those who support fiscal policy. At the beginning of this debate, there was a tendency for monetarists to dismiss fiscal policy altogether. More recently (Friedman [38]), the monetary implications of budgetary imbalance were recognised and the efficacy of fiscal policy attributed by monetarists to attendant monetary changes. Fiscal policy financed by debt is still said to have little effect (this issue is debated in Stein [72]).

Monetarists are also known to favour a money supply target, and preferably the institution of a rule governing the rate of increase of the money supply, removing discretionary control from central banks. This prescription does not follow ineluctably from their theory(ies): the Federal Reserve Bank of St Louis work indicates that monetary policy is a powerful tool, presumably there to be used for good or ill (see for example [2], [3], [4], [5], [6], [7]). And all monetarists stress the stability of the demand for money, which should make successful monetary policy possible. Yet, rather than suggesting improved discretionary policy, most favour removing these powers. The chief reason is a lack of confidence that these powers will be used wisely. (See, in particular, Friedman and Schwartz [41], for evidence of poor policy in the past.)

Monetarism as a reaction to Vulgar Keynesianism

From the complexities of the *General Theory* (Keynes [51]), economists who had accepted its basic message (or so, at any rate, they thought) extracted the idea that monetary policy was ineffective while fiscal policy was a powerful tool, not just in the Depression for which Keynes made this assessment, but generally. These Keynesians argued that the quantity of money was of no consequence, and ignored it: explanations of inflation were variants on the theme of excess demand, with the analysis couched in real terms. Fiscal policy was defined as variations in government expenditure and taxation, without reference to any monetary consequences that an unbalanced budget might have, and monetary policy, seen mainly as the management of a roughly stable overall government debt, was relegated in the UK to the status of serving the needs of the Treasury at least cost, subject to other considerations for which the interest rate played an important role (mainly balance of payments considerations).

The willingness to ignore the influence of money on the domestic economy was reinforced by another simplification of Keynes, namely that monetary policy acted chiefly, if not solely, through the interest rate, and, as a result of a number of empirical studies, it was believed that the influence of the interest rate on investment was weak.[4]

Monetarism can usefully be interpreted as a reaction to these views and the assumptions concerning the role of government which they embody. In asserting the importance of a direct effect of money on expenditure – consumption as well as investment – they circumvented the weak link in the Keynesian chain. In formulating their theories in terms of aggregate expenditure rather than its components,[5] they also directed attention away from the component of aggregate demand which Keynes emphasised was highly volatile – investment. Thus, the aggregate approach lends support to the hypothesis that the private sector is highly stable.

4. See the articles by Henderson, Meade and Andrews, Andrews, and Sayers in Wilson and Andrews [79], and see Ebersole [25].
5. Brunner [10] believes this approach to be a fundamental feature of monetarism.

The monetarist reaction to Keynesian policy conclusions similarly operates on (at least) two levels. The Vulgar Keynesians overstated the case for government intervention. Keynesians of all stripes believe in government intervention when the private sector fails to pull itself out of a morass of self-fulfilling adverse expectations. (The monetarists appear to be prepared to wait.) But the Vulgar Keynesians translated the case for intervention in a crisis to continuous countercyclical policy, while slowly moving from the goal of stabilisation to the goal of continuous growth in national income. This latter shift imparted an expenditure bias in addition to that inherent in the unpopularity of taxation and the irreversibility of social welfare programmes with its attendant bureaucratic growth. All this leads to a secular growth of money and government debt, and tends toward a growing share of government in national income. In warning against the dangers of monetary growth, monetarists could hope to slow the growth of Big Government which, as noted above, they deplore as an interference in a stable and efficient private sector. Indeed, because of their distaste for government intervention, monetarists have concentrated on establishing the ineffectiveness of fiscal policy rather than the efficacy of monetary policy, although it should follow that, if money is important, so is monetary policy.

Models, evidence, policy conclusions

Early monetarist investigations of the relationship between money and income and prices concentrated on episodes of rapid monetary growth; Cagan's celebrated study of hyperinflation [12] is perhaps the best known. Friedman's study of US war finance [29] focuses on another classic example to which the applicability of the quantity theory would be widely expected. These studies did, however, call attention to the role of money in a climate of opinion in which denial of its influence tended to be rather extreme.[6]

The work of Friedman and Schwartz, on the other hand, was concerned with less dramatic circumstances; although their *Monetary History of the United States* [41] encompasses wartime episodes, the argument does not rely on them. The association of money and income is held to exist even in normal circumstances. However, unlike the studies involving rapid monetary growth, where inflationary consequences are the subject matter, the work of Friedman with Schwartz

---

6. It does not follow that, if a good correlation between money and income *is* found, there will also be a strong correlation between money and prices; however, if it is not found, money and prices are not likely to bear a close relationship. It is not impossible to obtain a relationship, for income and prices *could* move in an off-setting fashion. However, such a pattern is not expected; consider the surprise with which the recent phenomenon of 'stagflation' was greeted. (This period of data is not included in the tests, even those of recent critics.)

and Meiselman, and the initial study by Andersen and Jordan of the Federal Reserve Bank of St Louis [41][42], were prepared only to assert – and investigate – a relationship between money and income. Nevertheless, the results bear reporting, for they raise important issues and, furthermore, if doubt were cast on there being a relation between money and income, a direct connection between money and prices is unlikely to be found.

Friedman and Schwartz

The role of money in determining income is investigated in the work of Friedman and Schwartz, through careful examination of time series data, but with little use of formal econometric techniques. Their *Monetary History* [41] and their later papers on money in business cycles ([42], Friedman [33]), relied on pinpointing trends and turning points in the money supply and measures of economic activity. The *History* takes the perspective of long sweeps of monetary experience. While it demonstrates the association of the two variables, most economists would probably agree that the causal role of money was not established. Their papers address the shorter-run question of the cycle and present evidence bearing on the question of causation. National Bureau reference cycles of activity are used as a benchmark against which the growth rate of money is compared. (The growth rate is used because the series is dominated by trend, and cyclical fluctuations are difficult to distinguish.) They found that the fastest rate of monetary increase occurs very early in the cycle – so early as to raise the possibility that monetary growth lags income slightly, rather than preceding its fluctuations with a long lead. For the twenty-one cycles from 1870 to 1961, the monetary growth peak comes, on average, seventeen months before the reference peak, the trough thirteen months before the reference trough (half-cycles average thirty-two months in length). The amplitudes of fluctuations in the two series display similar patterns. On the grounds that the lead pattern is more regular (Friedman [33]), the lead interpretation is adopted.[7] The standard deviation of the gap between the peaks and troughs of the two series, even for the lead interpretation, is substantial; the authors emphasise that the lag is quite variable. From this work stems the policy conclusion which Friedman has stated over and over: that, because appropriate monetary policy in the short run may have unforeseen consequences over a longer run, discretionary policy is at best clumsy and at worst dangerous, and should be supplanted by a monetary rule.

Friedman and Meiselman

Evidence using regression analysis was offered by Friedman and

7. Sims [69] notes that establishing money's lead is not sufficient to establish causation, though the presumption is strong.

Meiselman (hereafter FM) in [40]. Their study was a direct challenge to Vulgar Keynesianism. They contested the Keynesian view that autonomous expenditure, whether investment or government spending, was the chief determinant of income, proposing instead the quantity of money. The two views were each represented by a single equation,

$$Y = \alpha + K'A \tag{1}$$
and
$$Y = a + V'M, \tag{2}$$

where Y is income, A is autonomous expenditure, and M is the money supply, broadly defined.[8] They ran a series of regressions designed to assess the relative ability of M and A to explain variations in Y or, for statistical reasons, the endogenous components of Y, denoted C. The equations were run over a long span of years (1897–1958) and various subperiods.[9,10]

On the basis of the significance of the coefficients of M and A and the size of the correlation coefficients, FM assert the consistently superior performance of the monetary variable, and the existence of a close relation, throughout, between M and C or Y, both in terms of levels of the variables and first differences. It is difficult to understand, however, how this latter claim is substantiated in full. While the association between C or Y and M is strong over long periods, the regressions in first differences, involving quarterly data from 1945 to 1958, are extremely badly determined. Since the equations in the levels of the variables are dominated by time trends, one is inclined to be agnostic about their significance and look to the first difference equations for confirmation. It is not there.

Another test of the reliability of an association is its performance in predicting the dependent variable outside the period for which it was

---

8. Private holdings of currency and demand and time deposits.
9. The actual estimating equations were:
$$C = \alpha + KA, \tag{1a}$$
obtained by subtracting A from both sides of equation (1) to avoid spurious correlation, and
$$C = a + VM \tag{2a}$$
adopted for direct comparison with equation (1a) but not directly derived from equation (2). The multivariate equation,
$$C = a + KA + VM,$$
was also estimated, and equation (2) was estimated directly, with and without lagged values of M.
10. The following data are indicative: note that $r_{CA.M}$, the partial correlation of C and A given M, has the wrong sign.

	1897–1958	1929–58
r_{CA}	0·756	0·705
$r_{CA.M}$	−0·222	−0·424
r_{CM}	0·985	0·974
$r_{CM.A}$	0·967	0·957

estimated. Applying estimates taken from 1929–58 to the period 1959–70, Poole and Kornblith [64] find quite substantial errors of prediction for both FM equations. Money performs much better than FM's definition of autonomous expenditure, but considerably less well than some of the measures of A suggested by FM's many critics.[11] Poole and Kornblith [64] surmise that a monetarist might argue thus: since the theory was long-run in nature, a run of residuals of the same sign is not surprising – it merely reflects the adjustment process working its way through. It could be objected, however, that underadjustment would not be expected to go on for as long a period as that found in the predictive tests – roughly a decade. Evidence on lags among the variables would perhaps be useful here, but FM's investigations, using ordinary least-squares regressions of Y with different lagged values of M, are distinctly unhelpful. There is too much autocorrelation in the M series.

Some other issues raised by the FM study apply also to the Andersen and Jordan work, to which we now turn.

Andersen and Jordan

Andersen and Jordan (AJ) [5] attracted attention with their startling results of a large and rapid money multiplier and an inconsequential effect of fiscal policy. Their basic equation,

$$\triangle \text{GNP} = \beta_0 + \sum_{i=0}^{3} \beta_{1i} \triangle M_{t-i} + \sum_{i=0}^{3} \beta_{2i} \triangle E_{t-i} + \sum_{i=0}^{3} \beta_{3i} \triangle R_{t-i}, \qquad (3)$$

regresses changes in GNP on current and lagged changes in the money supply, narrowly defined,[12] high-employment government expenditures,[13] and high-employment government receipts,[14] by means of the Almon lag technique.[15] They found, for 1952–68, that the cumulative fiscal expenditure multiplier was never greater than one, and indeed in the fourth quarter it was significantly negative, resulting in an inconsequential overall influence. Receipts had no effect, and AJ favour omitting the variable altogether, both on empirical grounds and the theoretical argument that financing expenditure whether by taxes or by borrowing has the same effect.[16]

11. Ando and Modigliani [8], De Prano and Mayer [23] and Hester [49] are the main references. The definitions proposed by Hester performed particularly well in Poole and Kornblith's study. The suggestion that the choice of the broad definition of money was important to the success of the monetary equation is also confirmed by their study.
12. Private holdings of demand deposits and currency.
13. Expenditures on goods and services and transfers adjusted to remove cyclical unemployment benefits.
14. Tax receipts adjusted to high-employment income. These adjustments are made in order to reflect policy intentions rather than the *ex post* result.
15. A technique designed (Almon [1]) to estimate the weights of a distributed lag by specifying a polynomial.
16. A debatable point. See the literature on 'crowding out' and Stein [72].

Current and lagged changes in M, on the other hand, explained about 50 per cent of the variance in GNP changes, and had an overall (four-quarter) multiplier effect of the order of 6, more than half of which takes place in the first two quarters.[14,18] These results upset Keynesian theoretical expectations and contradicted evidence generated by the large Federal Reserve Board–MIT model, which gave a money multiplier of no more than 2·2 after *twelve* quarters.

The St Louis results not only disturbed Keynesians. They are in some conflict with other monetarist empirical work, chiefly that of Friedman and Schwartz. Friedman and Schwartz interpret business cycle experience to show that money affects income with a long and variable lag; the St Louis study alleges that the connection is rapid and, judging from the significance of the estimates, reliable. The policy prescription associated with the monetarist school, namely that government intervention is undesirable and should be minimised, fits well with Friedman's results but not particularly well with those of this St Louis investigation. The latter supports the use of monetary policy as a powerful and flexible instrument – conclusions which are not surprising, considering a central bank is their source, but which run counter to the policy conclusions of most of the monetarist camp. Nor is fiscal policy ruled out. While it is true that AJ's lag structure suggests that fiscal policy will have no *lasting* effect, there is still the possibility of short-run gains.

The policy implications of the St Louis equation were investigated by Cooper and Fischer [17], [18]. In the later study, which is based more directly on the St Louis equation, they reached a number of conclusions pertaining to this policy conflict within the monetarist camp. They chose a point from an estimated Phillips curve of a rate of unemployment of approximately 5 per cent and a rate of inflation of approximately 3 per cent as the goal, and investigated 'active' (discretionary) and constant growth rate (CGR) fiscal and monetary policies' effect on the standard deviation of the targets in simulation studies. The 'optimal' monetary and fiscal policies were found by search, using an estimate of the St Louis equation for 1955. i to 1971. iv, for the values of the policy parameters in the following equations which minimised the standard deviations of the values of the target variables.[19] The equations for monetary and fiscal policy are, respectively:

$$\dot{M}_{1t}=a_1+a_2(\dot{P}_{t-1}-a_3)+a_4(U_{t-1}-a_5)-a_6(\dot{P}_{t-1}-\dot{P}_{t-2})+a_7(U_{t-1}-U_{t-2}),\ (4)$$

$$\dot{E}_t=b_1+b_2(\dot{P}_{t-1}-b_3)+b_4(U_{t-1}-b_5),\ \ \ \ \ \ \ \ \ \ \ \ \ \ \ \ \ \ (5)$$

where $X_t=(X_t-X_{t-1})/X_t$, a_3 and b_3 are the target inflation rate, a_5 and b_5

---

17. That is, a \$1 billion change in the money supply would raise GNP by \$6 billion in one year.

18. Artis and Nobay [9] in a study designed along AJ lines were unable to find a close relationship between money and income for the UK.

19. The authors point out that the search procedure did not guarantee that the rule was a true optimum.

the target unemployment rate, and the other a's and b's are policy control parameters, to be set at zero for the CGR rule, and positively for the active rule to be found by search. A joint monetary–fiscal policy was also found. Simulations were then carried out, with the policies following active or CGR rules or their historical paths, in nine combinations. The results definitely favoured both active monetary and fiscal policy, though the role of fiscal policy is more marginal – there was little difference between an active monetary policy alone and the joint policy rule, and active monetary policy, whether alone or with fiscal policy, was superior to fiscal policy alone. Comparing the money-only and fiscal-only rules with the joint rule, monetary policy's reaction to the level of unemployment is not reduced by the joint rule, while fiscal policy's responsibility for that variable is much reduced; conversely monetary policy's optimal response to inflation is reduced when fiscal policy is also active, though the rule does not indicate a direct fiscal policy response $(b_2 = 0)!$[20]

However, AJ's work has been subjected to a barrage of criticism and, like FM's work, it does not appear to stand up well to re-estimations designed to demonstrate the importance of the various objections. As with FM, the model yields biased forecasts, in this case overpredictions (Poole and Kornblith, [64]). McNees [57], [58] also found the equation predicted badly. These results suggest that the confidence intervals of the sample estimates cannot be taken as an indicator of the reliability of a response to changes in money, even for income, much less for prices. Davis' [21] investigation of the stability of the AJ results when broken into subperiods reaches the same conclusion. Particularly interesting is his finding that the relation between money and income is not strong in 1952–60, when US prices were virtually stable, suggesting that the relation between money and output is weak also.

A possible source of bias is the choice of an inappropriate measure for the independent variables. Early criticism of FM stressed this point, and its importance has been demonstrated (Poole and Kornblith, [64]) with respect to measures of autonomous expenditure. De Leeuw and Kalchbrenner [22] and Corrigan [19] similarly criticise AJ's definition of net government expenditure for its inclusion of endogenous components. And Gramlich [46] has shown that the St Louis equation is as sensitive to the chosen measure of money as FM's results are sensitive to measures of 'A'.

The St Louis results have also been shown remarkably sensitive to the chosen lag specification. Schmidt and Waud [67] have shown that freeing the estimates from an arbitrary lag length of four quarters, and

20. The policy parameters are as follows:

	a_1	a_2	a_4	a_6	a_7	b_1	b_2	b_4
Monetary policy only	0·01	1	0·5	2	1	0	0	0
Fiscal policy only	0	0	0	0	0	0·0175	0	4
Joint policy	0·01	1	0·5	1	0·5	0·0175	0	2

removing end-point restrictions on the lags, yields an optimal[21] lag of seven quarters, the money multiplier is reduced to 4, and the relative superiority of monetary policy is not so marked. One looks forward to policy simulations taking this point into account, particularly as Cooper and Fischer noted the sensitivity of the policy rule parameters to lags (shorter lags raise the 'proportional' control parameters a_2 and a_4 and lower the 'derivative' control parameters a_6 and a_7), and the question of the correct policy in the face of lags is crucial.

Direction of causation and the validity of the single-equation approach

Problems of measurement, choice of time period, and specification bedevil all econometric investigations. While we do not dismiss the points made above by critics, there are two remaining points which are more fundamental, and which apply to all the evidence so far cited. One concerns the extent to which the single-equation approach used in these studies can be interpreted as a condensed equation (commonly but incorrectly called a reduced form) of a larger system not specified by the authors.[22] The second, not unrelated, difficulty is that the crucial question of causality is not resolved, and a proper specification of a reduced form in the technical sense, needed for estimation, hinges on its resolution.

The possibility that money is passively supplied in response to demand generated by economic activity, or indeed fulfils the demand for loans on which an upturn in activity depends, has been a Keynesian objection since the beginning (and the debate goes back a long way – one should not expect a resolution in the near future). This possibility, which conforms only to the weakest monetarist position, is acutely obvious in the Friedman and Schwartz work, as pointed out by Culbertson [20]. Even if money could be shown unambiguously to lead changes in activity, the case for its causal role is not watertight. Sims [69], making this point, proposed a stronger test, using further information contained in the lag structure. Applying it to UK data, Williams, Goodhart and Gowland [78] could not confirm Sims's results for the US, which favoured causality running from money to both nominal and real income (evidence for the latter was particularly marked).

The more usual attack on this problem (sometimes known as the 'reverse causation' problem) is to break down the relation between money and income into two parts. First, the supply of money is related to a variable directly under the authorities' control, such as the monetary base, B, or unborrowed reserves. Second, the total money stock is related to income. Evidence in favour of the first relation, because it appears to support the case of close control of M by the authorities, is often taken as evidence that M is exogenous. On the

---

21. That which minimises the standard error of estimate.
22. Friedman and Schwartz's studies investigate an implicit equation, $Y = f(M)$.

grounds that, even if M were not exogenous, B is – in the sense that it is a variable controlled by the authorities – AJ re-estimated their equation, substituting B for M in the income equation. The relationship continued to explain about half the variation of changes in GNP, with no significant help from fiscal variables. (The money multiplier was of course greatly increased, having a much smaller base to begin with.)[23]

However, de Leeuw and Kalchbrenner gave reasons to suppose that the monetary base variable was not truly independent of current variations in income. Substituting unborrowed reserves in the St Louis equation, and adjusting tax receipts for changes in their purchasing power, greatly reduced the money multiplier (despite the smaller multiplicand) – to 2·4 – and brought the signs on E and R around to their expected values (they had been perverse over the sum of the four quarters in the original study using the base) and made these variables significant. Davis [21] investigating the prior relationship between B and M, found that relationship rather weak, which does not lend much support to the proposed causal relation between the base and money. In any case, merely establishing *responsibility* for increasing the base does not ensure the *exogeneity* of the variable: currency and reserves, while controlled by the authorities, may be supplied on demand. When the variables chosen as independent are in fact not independent, one cannot claim to have a reduced form equation.

A more serious problem arises in the studies cited, owing to the fact that the *structure* from which the 'reduced form' equations purport to derive is not specified, and indeed it has been alleged that no known model of the economy generates the FM or St Louis equations. In particular, the St Louis equation embodies the monetarist maintained hypothesis of a stable private sector, for it implicitly assumes that no component of private expenditure is autonomous [60]; no such variable is included among the independent variables. Modigliani and Ando [60] show that the omission of an 'A' variable biases the results and, if the authorities respond to variations in A, the bias will be in favour of monetary policy if it is assumed that fiscal policy is used to offset fluctuations in A and *a fortiori* if the monetary authorities stabilise interest rates.[24] The possibility of such interdependence among variables would not have arisen had the models been fully specified in the first place.

The single-equation investigations, then, leave many doubts as to the role of money in determining income in the medium or short run. Still more tenuous are any inferences one might make concerning money and prices. Part of the difficulty is that inflation was low and showed little variability over the period covered by these investigations; all the work

23. Andersen has offered empirical evidence against reverse causation for the period 1953.i^{iv}1968iv, but the relevance of his test has been convincingly challenged by Schmidt and Waud [67].
24. The positive correlation between M and A will bias the coefficient of M upward; the negative correlation between E and A biases the fiscal coefficient downward.

reported above was done in the US, where prices were remarkably stable until the late 1960s. The second generation of monetarist models moved away from the single-equation approach and began to incorporate explicit theories of price determination.

Complex models I: The role of expectations

It is a feature of monetarist models that expectations of prices or of rates of inflation enter into the determination of the price level or the rate of inflation itself. The rationale of this is not given in terms of the theory of the firm, although a case can be made.

1. Friedman's presidential address, and the Phillips curve

In the theory advanced in Friedman's presidential address to the American Economic Association [34], expectations explain the lag, not only between money and income, but between money and prices, and relate to the monetarist criticism of the Phillips curve as a theory of inflation. Taking for granted that an increase in the money supply would stimulate spending, the division of the change between prices and output is determined by two lagged responses. First, firms react to increased demand by raising output; prices are stable because 'people have been expecting prices to be stable, and prices and wages have been set for some time in the future on that basis' [34, p. 103]. However, firms are quicker to adjust prices than factors of production to demand higher rewards (indeed, the demand for higher wages is a response to observing a fall in real wages). Eventually, money wages rise to restore the real wage. Output falls back to its former level, and prices are permanently higher. Plainly, repeated monetary increases can be expected not only to result in steadily rising prices, but the lags which are responsible for the delay of prices rises behind monetary increases are likely to become shorter as the expectation of price stability is eroded.

Equally plainly, factors of production need not wait for actual price changes to erode real wages, but may learn to place wage claims which anticipate them. The Phillips curve relation suggests that wages will rise the faster the tighter are labour markets, measured by unemployment. Then, if prices are dependent on wages, attempts to reduce unemployment are likely to be inflationary and, conversely, excess supply in labour markets can alleviate inflation. Monetarists argue, in effect, that the money wage consistent with any particular state of the labour market is not unique; it is also contingent on price anticipations – on the part of employees, whose supply of labour depends on the anticipated real wage, and on the part of firms, who grant wage increases in the anticipation of being able to cover increased costs with higher prices. Thus the rate of inflation is also not uniquely related to the state of excess demand in either the labour market or the product market on which the demand for labour depends.

2. *Friedman's NBER model*

Expectations delay an immediate price response to changes in money demand in Friedman's *Framework for Monetary Analysis* [37] by a more circuitous route. The model specifies expenditure dependent on real income and the real rate of interest, ρ, the latter being the nominal rate, r, adjusted for the erosion of this rate of return by inflation, $\dot{P}$, according to the theory of Irving Fisher [28]:

$$\rho = r - \dot{P}. \tag{6}$$

The underlying real rate of growth is taken as exogenous. Hence, it is not surprising that the real and monetary sectors are dichotomised, and that it predicts that in the long run the rate of growth of the money supply determines the rate of inflation. It is the short-run properties of the model that are of interest here.

This model concentrates on monetary factors, and expectations affect the economy initially through the real rate of interest rather than through wages and prices as in the earlier model. A key assumption is that the expected real interest rate diverges from the (confidently) expected long-term growth rate, $\dot{y}^e$, by K_0, a factor which is virtually constant:

$$\rho^e - \dot{y}^e = K_0. \tag{7}$$

Thus, variations in the expected nominal rate are dominated by the rate of inflation,

$$r^e = \rho^e + \dot{P}^e. \tag{8}$$

Friedman assumes that $r = r^e$ continuously through arbitrate, so that

$$r = r^e = \rho + \dot{P} = \rho^e + \dot{P}^e = K_0 + \dot{Y}^e \tag{9}$$

A rise in the money supply creates money market disequilibrium, which must be eliminated by a change in one of the determinants of the demand for money, which is of the form

$$M^D = Y \cdot L(r) = Y \cdot L(K_0 + \dot{Y}^e). \tag{10}$$

Assuming expectations change in response to actual changes, the adjustment must begin with a change in Y, which could be either a change in P or in real income, y. However, a change in $\dot{P}$ will alter r, and since $r = K_0 + \dot{Y}^e$ this implies that expectations rise as quickly as actual income. Since this contravenes the assumption about expectations-formation, it must be assumed that initially it is real income or output which has changed. Later, as nominal income (and price) expectations begin to change, prices are free to move without upsetting any of the assumptions made. Money from the initial increased supply flows into the bond market as interest rates rise but, once the nominal rate reflects the new price expectations, subsequent increases in the money supply can fall directly on prices, confirming the new expected rate.

3. Expectations and equilibrium

Friedman's 1971 model bears a superficial resemblance to neoclassical quantity theory, with an important difference. Instead of the price level being determined by the quantity of money, the rate of inflation is determined by the rate of growth of money, although the model contains a perfectly orthodox demand for money equation in terms of levels. This fact indicates that Friedman has done more than simply 'slip one derivative'.[25] The essence of the matter lies in the expectations hypothesis, which assumes a concern with the rate of change of prices rather than the price level. Thus, a change in the rate of inflation, brought about by a change in the monetary growth rate, will at first be unanticipated. During the time between the change in the actual rate and its full anticipation, the gap between the actual price level and the level implicit in anticipations widens (unless the anticipations were based on a falsely high perception of the level, in which case the gap could actually be decreasing). The eventual learning of the new rate of inflation will not eliminate this gap between levels, which is permanent (unless the rate of money growth is negative at some future time) and is the larger the longer it takes for the new actual rate and expectations of the rate to become equal.

In contrast, if expectations of levels were formed, equilibrium would not exist until the actual level of prices was correctly anticipated. Equilibirum would, of course, require stable prices. Perhaps, therefore, Friedman's model is a concession to realism in an inflationary world. It is also firmly in the classical tradition that the equilibrium position is independent of one's starting point for, although a price level is implicit in a rate of change if one knows where the process of change began, no such presumption is made in Friedman's theory.

4. Laidler's Manchester School model

The role of a lag of price expectations behind actual price changes in producing 'real' consequences of monetary expansion in the short run is perhaps easier to see in Laidler's model [53], for it is much simpler than those above. He also provides some estimates, using US data from 1953 to 1972. The model is but three equations. All variables are expressed in logarithms. The notation is obvious apart from $y*$, full employment real income. There is a demand for money equation:

$$\triangle M = b \ \triangle y + \triangle P = b \ \triangle(y - y*) + b \ \triangle y* + \triangle P, \qquad b > 0, \tag{11}$$

a price inflation equation

$$\triangle P^e = g \ \triangle(y - y*)_{-1} + \triangle P^e_{-1}, \qquad g > 0, \tag{12}$$

and an adaptive expectations-formation equation

---

25. I believe this characterisation is due to Tobin.

$$\triangle P^e = d \triangle P + (1-d)\triangle P^e_{-1}, \qquad 0<d<1. \tag{13}$$

The model predicts that in equilibrium, when $y-y^*=0$, and $P=P^e=P^e_{-1}$,

$$\triangle P = \triangle M - b \triangle y^*: \tag{14}$$

full employment is independent of the rate of money growth but the rate of inflation is not, and in disequilibrium, from equations (12) and (13)

we get, $\triangle^2 P = g(y-y^*)_{-1} + dg(y-y^*)_{-2}.$ (15)

It can be seen that the inflation rate would lag behind cyclical variations in activity, purely because it takes time to change expectations and to change prices set on the basis of them.

The Laidler model is quite a departure for monetarism; where the long-run quantity-theoretic result used to derive from the homogeneity of the demand for money function, now the long run depends on the process by which expectations converge on actual inflation.[26] The results are made possible by the assumption that entrepreneurs forecast only prices, not levels of activity. (The latter is the source of the erratic behaviour of investment in Keynes's system and is rejected by monetarists.) Thus, prices can be dominated by past experience rather than current demand conditions, leaving output to vary as a residual, despite the implications for profits. (See Chick [15, pp. 113–14]. For theories of price-setting derived from hypotheses of firms' behaviour, see Heathfield, this volume.)

5. Some evidence

There are three areas in which empirical evidence bears on the models just cited: the extent to which price-setting behaviour is influenced by price expectations, the degree to which the nominal rate of interest incorporates inflationary expectations, and the extent to which the Phillips relation breaks down as expectations of stable prices give way to anticipated inflation.

It is, of course, notoriously difficult to test expectations hypotheses, for the expectations are subjective; the usual assumption that expectations are based on past observations of the same variable ignores the outside information, such as policy changes, which may be important determinants. Some investigations have used survey data; see, e.g. Turnovsky and Wachter [77], Parkin [62] and the ingenious study by Carlson and Parkin [14].

It does seem clear that it is important to incorporate expectations into the Phillips curve. There have been too many studies to mention; but for the UK, Parkin, Sumner and Ward [63] and Saunders and Nobay [66] confirm the importance of expectations when prices and incomes policies are not in operation.

Evidence on the incorporation of expectations into money rates of interest are rather more mixed. Sargent's extensive study [65] found

26. Laidler notes that this convergence does not hold in his *Economica* model [53].

Fisher's hypothesis an inadequate explanation of the data from 1870 to 1940, while investigators of the postwar period, e.g. Yohe and Karnosky [80], Feldstein and Eckstein [27], were more successful. The lag before $\dot{P}^e$ was fully reflected in r was thirty years for Sargent's period, one to two years in the postwar studies. Fama [26] has made a strong claim that the nominal rate of interest incorporates all relevant inflationary expectations. His investigation adopts the usual monetarist presumption of a stable expected real rate.[27] Carlson [13], using survey data, shows a cyclical pattern in the real rate; it falls during recessions. And the information content of nominal interest rates is not complete; predictions of inflation are improved by adding a measure of excess labour.

Laidler's [53] estimates of his price equation, using US data, are quite satisfactory, he feels. They are reasonably well determined for equations in first and second differences, and they imply reasonably rapid adjustment of expectations: the estimates suggest an adjustment period of about three years. The low Durbin–Watson statistics, suggesting autocorrelation in both the first and second difference estimates, do not appear to worry him, though they suggest serious misspecification, probably omitted variables. The UK estimates, however, are quite worrying: Henry, Sawyer and Smith [48] found an implied lag of *forty-four years* in adjusting to new rates of inflation.

6. Policy conclusions

No doubt it would be wise to await better evidence before basing policy on monetarist theories which rely heavily on expectations for their conclusions. For the moment, however, let us take the posited relations as given and explore their implications. Each of the models explains, in its own way, the short-run response of output and the long-run exclusive response of prices that has become conventional monetarist wisdom. To Friedman [34] they imply that the use of monetary policy to alleviate unemployment is ultimately futile, whether it attempts to influence the economy through interest rates or through temporary reductions in firms' real costs; there may be short-term gains for the economy, 'paid for' in the longer run. It is in a way curious, therefore, that he has argued for a monetary rule, for in his models, if any good at all is to come of monetary policy, it comes before expectations catch up. If it were thought that the temporary good outweighed the later costs, surely a constantly changing monetary policy would be appropriate. Gramlich [46] has determined that a short-run perspective is inappropriate for monetary policy on the grounds that it causes initial overshooting. This, of course, is damaging to the main case for using monetary policy – its flexibility.[28]

27. Laidler [52], cited below, is an exception among monetarist theoretical models in permitting the real rate to vary cyclically.
28. Models featuring overshooting in financial markets are Tucker [76], Tanner [73], Laidler [54]. See also the conclusions of this paper.

Perhaps most discouraging of all are the results of Laidler's business cycle model [52], for it gives the result that there is no unique relationship between inflation and excess demand. 'Either rising prices or falling prices could well persist throughout a complete cycle [in activity], depending upon the expectations about inflation held by economic agents at its beginning. . . .' [52, p. 128] The result arises from the assumption that the desired stock of capital, rather than the rate of investment, depends on (*inter alia*) the real rate of interest. It follows that investment, and hence expenditure, is a function of *changes* in the real rate and hence changes in the expected inflation rate. With full employment output given, excess demand (or supply) is related to accelerating (or decelerating) inflation, even though price increases depend on the expected *rate* of inflation as before, for they also depend on the extent of excess demand. It is debatable whether Laidler's postulate about investment is plausible, but if accepted it implies that, at best, policy can slow the rate of increase of inflation but not stop or reverse it.

These policy conclusions would be substantially altered, of course, if the intentions of the authorities were permitted to affect expectations directly. Much policy is conducted on the assumption that there is a substantial 'announcement effect'. They would also be altered if the assumption of a given full employment output or rate of growth were relinquished to allow for the capacity-increasing effects of investment expenditure. But that would give too much to the Keynesian approach.

Complex models II: Monetarist models with Keynesian overtones

Laidler's models incorporate a Keynesian feature: price changes (or in [52] their rate of change) are affected directly by excess supply of money. This is also the case in the model which has supplanted the single equation at the Federal Reserve Bank of St Louis (Andersen and Carlson [2]). Current and lagged changes in government spending and the money stock determine changes in expenditure as in the AJ equation. But now prices and output are treated explicity. The model comprises eight equations:

$$\triangle Y_t = f_1(\triangle M_t, \ldots, \triangle M_{t-n}; \triangle E_t, \ldots, \triangle E_{t-n}), \tag{16}$$

$$\triangle P_t = f_2(D_t, \ldots, D_{t-n}; \triangle P_t^e), \tag{17}$$

$$D_t = \triangle Y_t - (X_t^F - X_{t-n}), \tag{18}$$

$$\triangle Y_t = \triangle P_t + \triangle X_t, \tag{19}$$

$$R_t = f_3(\triangle M_t, \triangle X_t, \ldots, \triangle X_{t-n}; \triangle P_t, \triangle P_t^e), \tag{20}$$

$$\triangle P_t^e = f_4(\triangle P_{t-1}, \ldots, \triangle P_{t-n}), \tag{21}$$

$$U_t = f_5(G_t, G_{t-1}), \tag{22}$$

$$G_{t-1} = \frac{X_t^F - X_t,}{X_t^F} \tag{23}$$

where D is excess[29] demand, X is output, X^F is full employment output, U is unemployment, R is the rate of interest, and G is the 'GNP gap'. The rest of the notation is not new.

The rate of inflation in this model is proximately determined by expected inflation and excess demand, as in Laidler's models. In the model, expected inflation is determined solely by the history of price changes; excess demand is determined by monetary and fiscal policy and full employment output. But when Andersen and Carlson estimate the equations, they use, in the main text,

$$\Delta P_t^e = f_6(Y_{t-2}; \Delta P_t/U_t, \ldots, \Delta P_{t-n}/U_{t-n}), \tag{24}$$

modifying past price experience by an index of unemployment.[30] In an appendix they provide estimates of alternative price equations also

$$\Delta P_t = f_7(D_t, \ldots, D_{t-n}; R_{t-1}^L X_{t-1}), \tag{25}$$

where R^L is the long-term rate of interest, supposed to embody price anticipations and thus used as a proxy measure of them,[31] and

$$\Delta P_t = f_8(D_t, \ldots, \Delta D_{t-n}; \Delta M_{t-1}, \ldots, \Delta M_{t-n}). \tag{26}$$

This last equation is a rare direct test of the influence of money on prices. Both D and M are significant, and together they explain 86 per cent of the variation in the rate of inflation, using quarterly US data from 1955 to the end of 1969. Over a lag length of nine quarters, the cumulative effect of a 1 per cent change in the monetary growth rate raises the rate of inflation by 2·6 per cent on average. It is a pity that a direct comparison with the money multiplier in the spending equation cannot be made; there are four lags and a contemporaneous term in that equation, giving an overall multiplier of 5·6 – without $\Delta M_t, 4·3$.

However, the direct test does not perform significantly better than the alternative price equations: there is little to choose between them on any of the statistical criteria offered. Andersen and Carlson note that the price anticipations version (equation (24)) yielded the most classical conclusions in a thirty-year simulation; all versions gave equilibrium growth rates of output which were invariant with respect to the money growth rate chosen, but the interest rate and money stock versions stabilised at different unemployment rates, depending on the money growth rate. Perhaps this explains their preference for equation (24).

---

29. The model shares with Friedman's [37] the property that the interest rate does not affect expenditure. This helps to preserve the independence of long-term growth from changes in the rate of investment.
30. (The role of Y_{t-2} is not clear to me.)
31. See, above the empirical evidence on this.

When the model[32] as a whole is evaluated by looking at its predictive performance, it shows systematic overprediction of output and underprediction of prices (Andersen and Carlson, [2], [4]). Most disturbing is the evidence from the latter paper that predictive performance for *P*, *Y* and *X* *improve* as one predicts further into the future: the best results are predictions fifteen to seventeen quarters ahead. This casts a great deal of doubt on the early St Louis conclusions that monetary policy was quick and relatively certain in its effects on income, and confirms Friedman's scepticism on our knowledge concerning the division between price and output changes. It would seem that the evidence generated by this model should be regarded as highly provisional.

Complex models III: Portfolio considerations

Recently the orientation of the debate on the role of money has taken a new and fruitful turn. The interconnection between fiscal deficits and money creation, deriving from the government's financing requirements was turned to monetarist advantage.[33] Friedman [38] proposed that while fiscal deficits financed by taxation had little effect on the economy, deficits financed by money creation did have. This proposition was rather readily agreed, and work proceeded on the area in which, until recently, surprisingly little work had been done: the effects of fiscal policy involving changes in the amount of outstanding debt.[34] The papers of Stein [70] and Brunner [10] assess the effects on activity and prices of changes in the volume of government debt and money in the economy. While it is difficult at this early stage to evaluate these models and the evidence Stein adduces for his, their outlines should be sketched, for they bear on the increasingly frequent discussions of the role not only of fiscal deficits but the increasing size of government budgets, whether balanced or not, in generating inflation.

In both these models, the principal routes through which the creation of money and debt affect expenditure are the wealth effect on consumption and the interest rate effect on investment. It is assumed that increases in government debt have a positive effect on consumption, thus putting pressure on output and prices in the same manner as

---

32. A twenty-year simulation of the whole model, reported later (Andersen and Carlson, [3]), yielded results which are a monetarist's dream. Rates of monetary growth are chosen by the investigators. All variables are rates of change.

M	*Y*	*X*	*P*	*U*	R^L
0	1·0	4·1	−3·1	4·4	0·9
3	3·2	4·1	−0·8	4·4	2·7
6	6·0	3·9	2·1	4·0	5·0

33. Or the government's 'budget restraint'. This phrase was used by Christ [16], and Ott and Ott [61], in their celebrated articles, but it is rather misleading for a body which has powers to tax and print money.

34. The principal non-monetarist work is Tobin [75].

an excess supply of money (though not necessarily with the same strength). The negative effect on investment of the rising interest rates accompanying new debt issues acts to offset this. The interest rate changes stem from portfolio readjustments as the proportions of debt and money change.

1. Brunner's 1976 model

Brunner includes a further set of conflicting factors not treated by Stein, and they lead to paradoxical long-run conclusions. In Brunner, the government's financial balance equation is given by

$$pg + wg_1 + R - T = \triangle B + \triangle S, \tag{27}$$

where pg is the value of expenditure on goods, wg_1 is expenditure on labour services, R is interest payments on existing debt. These outlays are financed by taxes, T, an addition to the monetary base, $\triangle B$, or new government debt, $\triangle S$. In the short run, the demand–pressure consequences of financing by new money will be greater than if debt is issued, for there is no offsetting effect on expenditure through higher interest rates.[35] But in the long run, when $\triangle B = \triangle S = 0$, a history of money finance may lead the economy to settle at a lower price level and higher output than financing by borrowing! This result arises from two sources: (a) higher interest rates will retard private capital accumulation, thus resulting in a smaller final capital stock, (b) cumulatively, government outlays will be larger, as the debt must be financed. In the short run, the *speed of adjustment* to a deficit is faster the larger is the ratio of new money to new debt. In other words, in Brunner's model there is a tradeoff between a higher rate of inflation in the short run and a larger volume of output, at lower prices, in the long run.

This conclusion is a novel one, but one wonders how trustworthy it is. For there is one startling feature of Brunner's model which casts doubt on all his conclusions: the government's activities are entirely unproductive. All output is produced by the private sector and all capital (including, presumably, social overhead capital) accumulated by it. Thus, not only is it assured that new money will chase too few goods, but any interest rate rise is detrimental to capacity growth. If it were not for reservations arising from the dubiousness of this assumption, we could look forward to a lively debate between Brunner and Friedman on the long-run implications of monetary growth for output.

2. Stein

Stein, although he permits technical change (exogenously given), restricts his attention to a kind of short run, in the sense that although variables are deflated by the size of the capital stock and hence are

---

35. If government deficits were continuously maintained, the outstanding stock of money or bonds would be rising continuously. In long-run equilibrium, government expenditure must be self-financing.

compatible with growth, the growth of the capital stock is not explained. No conflicts arise, therefore, between short- and long-run results. It is the first of the two conflicts stated above on which he pins the debate between Keynesians and monetarists.

For our purposes, the price change equation is central. His hypothesis is

$$\pi = w + \lambda \; _pD, \tag{28}$$

where w is the rate of change of real wages in excess of productivity change (given by the rate of Harrod neutral technical change) and D is excess demand. Price expectations and unemployment determine w and excess demand is given by

$$D = C_k(U,m,z) + I_k(U,\pi^*,r) + G_k - y_k(U), \tag{29}$$

ignoring depreciation and the growth of the effective labour supply. Here, U, unemployment, is a measure of excess capacity, comparable to Laidler's $y - y^*$, but measured, as are the expenditure variables, in units of capital. It substitutes for income in the consumption relation. Consumption is also positively related to increases in financial wealth, either real balance per unit of capital, m, or real government debt per unit of capital z.[36] Investment depends on excess capacity, expected inflation, π^*, and the interest rate, which in turn is determined by

$$r = g(U, \pi^*, m, z); \quad g_1 < 0, \quad 0 < g_2 < 1, \quad g_3 < 0, \quad g_4 > 0: \tag{30}$$

monetary increases lower rates, debt flotations raise them, and price expectations are not fully reflected in nominal rates. The rate of change of prices is thus determined by five variables:

$$\pi = P(U, \pi^*, m, G, z); \quad P_1 < 0, \quad P_2 > 0, \quad P_3 > 0, \quad P_4 > 0, \quad P_5 \lessgtr 0. \tag{31}$$

As before, an excess of government expenditure over taxes must be financed by bonds or new money. The effect of the latter policy is twofold: pressure on resources comes not only from the government's demand but also from the response of consumption to increased money. The results of bond financing are, on the other hand, ambiguous, for the reason already stated. The effect of either policy on the rate of inflation will depend, as in earlier models with Keynesian overtones, on excess capacity and expected inflation. Taking these factors as given, Keynesians would argue that bond-financed deficits were permanently expansionary (perhaps inflationary), monetarists that they are either neutral or deflationary. Both would argue that the initial government spending is expansionary; conflict arises over the consequences of the permanent increase in assets that a period of deficit spending still leaves behind, even when the deficit has ceased. The effect hinges on the sign of P_5. If it is positive, demand will be higher than the pre-intervention level even after government expenditure ceases. The pure monetarist position

---

36. Stein uses θ, the proportion of debt to money. This gives rise to needless difficulties; the substitution made here is of no consequence.

that 'only money matters', is consistent with $P_5 = 0$. If P_5 is negative, investment demand will fall by more than consumption rises. Once the stimulus of the government expenditure is over and the effects are due to the larger stock of debt alone, prices will fall to clear markets. The growth of money income declines to *less* than its initial level, and unemployment *rises* – a kind of super-monetarist result.

There would seem to be evidence that, if money is not *all* that matters for inflation, it matters more than most other things. Stein's estimates of the price change equation for US data, quarterly from 1960. iv to 1970. iv, show the rate of growth of money to be significant while the growth of the debt has a t value of -1·9; the coefficient's negative sign supports the monetarist view. Government expenditure changes are not significant. Lagged values of π and U are also significant.[37] The effect of a change in monetary growth over an average lag of one and a half quarters is quite small (contrary to the St Louis results): a 10 per cent increase in monetary growth raises the inflation rate by only 1·7 per cent. In the steady state, however, Stein calculates that a 4·8 per cent rate of money growth implies an 'equilibrium' inflation rate of 4·18 per cent if government debt does not increase – and that it falls to 2·74 per cent if government debt increases at the same rate as money. The first result, of course, neatly confirms the long-run prediction of the quantity theory.

Stein runs similar equations for output. Only one aspect of this evidence is relevant to the present discussion. Stein compares the short-run effects of monetary change as a proportion of steady-state values for both employment and inflation. Finding that a much greater proportion of the total effect on employment takes place in early periods (as given by the regression equations cited above) than it does on inflation supports Friedman's contention [34], [36] that the impact effect is on output and feeds through into prices later. (The ratios are 0·91 for the employment equation when debt does not change, 0·65 when employment changes at the rate of monetary growth, 0·15 for the inflation equation with stable debt, 0·08 with growing debt.)

International factors

No survey of monetarist thinking on inflation should ignore the work on inflation as an international phenomenon, in which monetarists have predominated in recent years. However, only a brief sketch is provided here for international aspects of inflation, including the monetarist view, are discussed by McKenzie in this volume, and for an overview written by a monetarist see Parkin [62].

37. Money is defined as currency and demand deposits, in contrast to the theoretically relevant money base, presumably to capture later repercussions of changes in the base. Here, U and π are lagged three quarters, while the policy variables are measured as moving averages over the preceding three quarters to give a measure of a non-random change in policy stance. The data are transformed to correct for autocorrelation, but the Durbin–Watson statistics are still quite low. Estimates are also made for 1960.iv to 1973.iv, but they are less satisfactory. They include a period of price controls.

In the late 1960s it became obvious that inflation was not an affliction confined to particular unfortunate countries. Unaffected countries began to stand out as exceptions. At the same time, international reserves were growing rapidly, especially after the escalation of the Vietnam War drove the US balance of payments into heavy deficits. The major trading countries, linked by fixed exchange rates, not only used a (virtually) common currency for trade but their domestic money supplies could not be insulated from the major changes in international reserves that the world was by this time experiencing. Monetarists saw the explanation of world inflation as a problem to which the quantity theory was every bit as applicable at the international level as for a closed economy. 'World' (usually the ten OECD countries) price indexes, the weights determined by each country's contribution to 'world' GNP or trade, were related to the level of international reserves, the 'world' money supply, or similar monetary measure by many investigators (e.g. Genberg and Swoboda [43]; Meiselman [59]; Duck et al. [24]; Heller [47]; Keran and Riordan [50]) with fairly convincing results.

The breakdown of fixed exchange rates has, of course, rather changed the picture that this work was beginning to build up. Even without the theoretical challenge they present, international money is now difficult to measure. It has also become more difficult to ignore the divergences in inflation rates among countries. It would be foolish, however, to deny the importance of international influences on inflation or to under-estimate the possible influence of international liquidity, even if its measurement is now problematic.

Conclusion

In the light of monetarist theory and evidence, it is safe to say that money has some bearing on inflation. The questions that remain are how much and how quickly do monetary changes feed through to prices, and *who is responsible*. Evidence on the magnitude and speed of the link between money and prices is quite ambiguous, and in any case is liable to change both cyclically, as capacity utilisation changes, and after any significant change in experience with inflation or other factors likely to change expectations. It would seem unlikely, from an *a priori* standpoint, that a well-defined, stable, short-run relationship will be found.[38] In any event, it would not clearly establish that the monetary authorities were responsible for inflation in the sense that the money supply was determined by their initiative. The possibility of 'reverse causation' – monetary expansion initiated by the private sector – is always present in a monetary system comprising private-sector banks

38. If one were found, doubtless the authorities would discover that it was subject, like demand for money and Phillips relations before it, to Goodhart's Law: stable functions become unstable as soon as their stability is relied on for policy purposes.

and public authorities, unless the authorities' control of the banking system or their countervailing open-market operations are well-nigh perfect. In day-to-day management, the authorities would find it difficult to distinguish seasonal demand for bank reserves from demands due to overexpansion, and this could be enough to fuel a steady, though probably quite moderate, inflation. Asymmetrical interest rate policy, more concerned to keep rates down, would have a similar effect. It is the rather more spectacular episodes of inflation which are easier to attribute to the authorities, though even these may be due to monetary mismanagement which stems from the pursuit of other objectives. It is important that monetarist thinking has now recognised the role of fiscal policy in this matter. Any time that tax revenues are less than expected or interest rates higher than expected, the temptation to expand the money supply is present.

A major divergence of opinion on policy matters is, indeed, over the question of when monetary changes are justified. Keynesians would be more inclined to accept the risk of inflation emerging later in return for short-run benefits than would monetarists, for several reasons. The first has to do with the structure of their respective theories. Monetarists tend to take the long-run level or rate of growth of output as given by exogenous factors over which money has no influence. This means that the eventual emergence of inflation after monetary increases which exceed the rate of change of productivity is inevitable. To a Keynesian, inflation is not a certainty: a stimulus to investment today may speed the embodiment of technical progress, producing a greater output for the new money to chase, perhaps sufficiently greater to prevent inflation. The second reason stems from the monetarist rejection of demand anticipations as an important factor in investment decisions and the greater speed with which they, as opposed to Keynesians, expect money wages to adjust to inflationary erosion. On both these counts, an investment boom will be expected to be of shorter duration by the monetarists than by the Keynesians, so their estimate of the benefits of expansionary policy is less while their estimate of the risk of increasing costs is greater.

There is yet a third reason, which has to do with a much-debated but never resolved (and now rather *passé*) issue: the role of idle cash balances. In much of the pre-1972 debate between monetarists and Keynesians, the role of the interest rate in the transmission of monetary policy was a central issue. Keynesians took the view that excess money balances chiefly affected interest rates on financial assets, and subsequent effects on demand were channelled through interest-elastic investment. Monetarists countered with what amounted to a direct effect of money on expenditure.[39] Their differences over the transmission mechanism were never explicitly related to different time

---

39. The nature of the argument was sometimes rather tortuously expressed in terms of a spectrum of yields on assets including goods, but it comes to an expenditure effect in the end.

horizons, and the latter may explain their divergent assessments of inflation risk. Keynesians might have argued thus: money flows into financial markets; investment induced by lower interest rates raises output and transactions needs, and some of the money will come out of idle balances or security holdings to meet these needs. But this active circulation, being matched by increased output, is not inflationary. Even if security prices are so high as completely to discourage demand, it is unlikely that a monetary increase will find its way immediately into goods markets. *Some* may, producing price increases, but some, perhaps most initially, will be held idle. But no one will hold on to idle money indefinitely. In the absence of a rise in interest rates, securities remain unattractive and in the absence of a fall in interest rates investment does not increase. So when individuals tire of holding idle balances at zero yield, money comes on to a goods market which is now not expanding, and this is inflationary. This is not too different from the monetarists' long run, except that fewer idle balances would be held (because in their theories expected rises in interest rates stem from observed inflation, and that does not occur, initially) and – paradoxically – the ultimate inflationary pressure would be mitigated in the monetarist case by the progress of the underlying real rate of growth: the inflation would occur sooner, but be milder. In this perspective, Keynes's exposition of the causes of a long-run association between money and prices [51, pp. 306–7] should be a statement to which both sides could agree, leaving the question of the exogeneity of growth as the crucial question for a long-term theory of inflation and the determination of a wide range of expectations (not just those concerning interest rates) and speeds of adjustment as the causes of differences of opinion concerning the role of money in inflation in the short run.

There is another disagreement on policy matters which would arise even if both sides could agree to some intertemporal tradeoff between the costs and benefits of expansionary policy. That is the question of whether governments and central banks can be relied upon to adhere to a tradeoff established by private-sector preferences. The recent American – and world – experience with the use of inflationary methods of financing an unpopular war lies behind and gives strength to the monetarist proposal to supplement discretionary policy with a monetary rule – a given monetary growth rate of x per cent per year. Keynesians, on the other hand, would see a well-defined demand for a money equation or a successful forecasting equation relating monetary changes to inflation as improved knowledge on which to base discretionary policy. This issue has little to do with monetary theory or evidence over short periods; political theory and the broad sweep of monetary history are the appropriate intellectual base from which to argue.

References and bibliography

1. **Almon, S.,** 'The distributed lag between capital appropriations and expenditures', *Econometrica*, **33,** Jan., 178–96, 1965.
2. **Andersen, L. and Carlson, K. M.,** 'A monetarist model for economic stabilization', Federal Reserve Bank of St. Louis *Review*, **52,** Apr., 7–25, 1970.
3. **Andersen, L. and Carlson, K. M.,** 'An econometric analysis of the relation of monetary variables to the behaviour of prices and unemployment', in O. Eckstein, ed., *The Econometrics of Price Determination*. Federal Reserve Board and SSRC, Washington DC, 1972.
4. **Andersen, L. and Carlson, K. M.,** 'The St. Louis model revisited', *International Economic Review*, **15,** June, 305–27, 1974.
5. **Andersen, L. and Jordan, J.,** 'Monetary and fiscal actions: a test of their relative importance in economic stabilization', Federal Reserve Bank of St. Louis *Review*, **50,** Nov., 11–24, 1968.
6. **Andersen, L. and Jordan, J.,** 'Reply' to de Leeuw and Kalchbrenner, Federal Reserve Bank of St. Louis *Review*, **51,** Apr., 12–16, 1969.
7. **Andersen, L. and Karnosky, D. S.,** 'The appropriate time frame for controlling monetary aggregates: the St. Louis evidence', in *Controlling Monetary Aggregates II: The Implementation*. Federal Reserve Bank of Boston, Boston, Mass., 1973.
8. **Ando, A. and Modigliani, F.,** 'Velocity and the investment multiplier', *American Economic Review*, **55,** Sept., 693–728, 1965.
9. **Artis, M. J. and Nobay, A. R.,** 'Two aspects of the monetary debate', National Institute of Economics and Social Research, *Economic Review*, Aug., 33–51, 1969.
10. **Brunner, K.,** 'An aggregative theory for a closed economy', in Stein [72], 1976.
11. **Brunner, K.,** 'Inflation, money and the role of fiscal arrangements: an analytic framework for the inflation problem', in M. Monti, ed., *The New Inflation and Monetary Policy*, Macmillan, London, 1976.
12. **Cagan, P.,** 'The monetary dynamics of hyper-inflation', in M. Friedman, ed., *Studies in the Quantity Theory of Money*. Univ. of Chicago Press, Chicago, 1956.
13. **Carlson, J. A.,** 'Comment' on Fama, *American Economic Review*, **67,** June, 469–75, 1977.
14. **Carlson, J. A. and Parkin, J. M.,** 'Inflation expectations', *Economica*, **42,** May, 123–38, 1975.
15. **Chick, V.,** *The Theory of Monetary Policy*, rev. edn. Basil Blackwell, Oxford, 1977.
16. **Christ, C.,** 'A simple macroeconomic model with a government budget restraint', *Journal of Political Economy*, **76,** 53–67, 1968.
17. **Cooper, J. P. and Fischer, S.,** 'Stochastic simulation of monetary rules in two macroeconomic models', *Journal of the American Statistical Association*, **67,** Dec., 730–60, 1972.
18. **Cooper, J. P. and Fischer, S.,** 'Monetary and fiscal policy in the fully stochastic St Louis econometric model', *Journal of Money, Credit and Banking*, **6,** Feb., 1–22, 1974.
19. **Corrigan, E. G.,** 'The measurement and importance of fiscal policy changes', Federal Reserve Bank of New York *Monthly Review*, June, 133–45, 1970.
20. **Culbertson, J.,** 'Friedman on the lag in effect of monetary policy', *Journal of Political Economy*, **67,** Dec., 617–21, 1960.
21. **Davis, R. G.,** 'How much does money matter? A look at some recent evidence', Federal Reserve Bank of New York *Monthly Review*, June, 19–31, 1969.
22. **de Leeuw, F. and Kalchbrenner, J.,** 'Comment' on Andersen and Jordan, Federal Reserve Bank of St Louis *Review*, **51,** Apr., 6–11, 1969.
23. **De Prano, M. and Mayer, T.,** 'Tests of the relative importance of autonomous expenditures and money', *American Economic Review*, **55,** Sept., 720–2, 1965.
24. **Duck, N. et al.,** 'The determination of wages and prices in the fixed exchange rate world economy, 1956–1970', in J. M. Parkin and G. Zis, eds., *Inflation in the World Economy*. Univ. of Manchester Press, 1976.

25. **Ebersole, J. F.,** 'The influence of interest rates upon entrepreneurial decisions in business – a case study', *Harvard Business Review,* **17,** Autumn, 35–40, 1939.

26. **Fama, E. F.,** 'Short-term interest rates as predictors of inflation', *American Economic Review,* **65,** June, 269–82, 1975.

27. **Feldstein, M. and Eckstein, O.,** 'The fundamental determinants of the interest rate', *Review of Economics and Statistics,* **52,** Nov., 363–75, 1970.

28. **Fisher, I.,** *The Theory of Interest.* Macmillan, New York, 1930.

29. **Friedman, M.,** 'Price, income and monetary changes in three wartime periods', *American Economic Review,* **42,** May, 612–25, 1952.

30. **Friedman, M.,** 'The quantity theory of money: a restatement', in M. Friedman, ed., *Studies in the Quantity Theory of Money.* Univ. of Chicago Press, Chicago, 1956.

31. **Friedman, M.,** 'The supply of money and changes in prices and output', in Friedman [35], 1958.

32. **Friedman, M.,** 'The lag in effect of monetary policy', *Journal of Political Economy,* **69,** Oct., 447–66, 1961.

33. **Friedman, M.,** 'The monetary studies of the national bureau', from the *44th Annual Report* of the National Bureau of Economic Research, and reprinted in Friedman [35], 1969.

34. **Friedman, M.,** 'The role of monetary policy', *American Economic Review,* **58,** Mar., 1–17, 1968.

35. **Friedman, M.,** *The Optimum Quantity of Money.* Macmillan, London, 1969.

36. **Friedman, M.,** *The Counter-revolution in Monetary Theory.* Institute of Economic Affairs Occasional Paper No. 33, London, 1970.

37. **Friedman, M.,** *A Theoretical Framework for Monetary Analysis.* National Bureau of National Research, New York, 1971.

38. **Friedman, M.,** 'Comments on the critics', *Journal of Political Economy,* **80,** Sept./Oct., 906–50, 1972.

39. **Friedman, M.,** Discussion, in 'A monetarist controversy', Federal Reserve Bank of San Francisco *Economic Review,* Supplement, Spring, 12–22, 1977.

40. **Friedman, M. and Meiselman, D.,** 'The relative stability of monetary velocity and the investment multiplier in the United States', in Commission on Money and Credit, *Stabilisation Policies.* Prentice-Hall, Englewood Cliffs, NJ, 1963.

41. **Friedman, M. and Schwartz, A. J.,** *A Monetary History of the United States, 1867–1960.* Princeton Univ. Press for the National Bureau of Economic Research, Princeton, NJ, 1963.

42. **Friedman, M. and Schwartz, A. J.,** 'Money and business cycles', *Review of Economics and Statistics,* **45,** Feb., Supplement, and in [35], 189–235, 1963.

43. **Genberg, H. and Swoboda, A. K.,** 'Causes and origins of the current worldwide inflation', in E. Lundberg, ed., *Inflation Theory and Anti-inflation Policy.* Proceedings of the International Economic Association Conference at Saltsjöbaden, Macmillan, London, 1977.

44. **Gibson, W. E.,** 'Price expectations effects on interest rates', *Journal of Finance,* **25,** Mar., 1970.

45. **Gibson, W. E.,** 'Interest rates and inflation expectations: new evidence', *American Economic Review,* **62,** 854–65, 1972.

46. **Gramlich, E.,** 'The usefulness of monetary and fiscal policy as discretionary stabilisation tools', *Journal of Money, Credit and Banking,* **3,** May, 506–32, 1971.

47. **Heller, H. R.,** 'International reserves and worldwide inflation', International Monetary Fund *Staff Papers,* Mar., 61–87, 1976.

48. **Henry, S. G. B., Sawyer, M. C. and Smith, P.,** 'Models of inflation in the United Kingdom: an evaluation', National Institute of Economic and Social Research *Economic Review,* **60,** 60–71, 1976.

49. **Hester, D. D.,** 'Keynes and the quantity theory: a comment on the Friedman–Meiselman paper', *Review of Economics and Statistics,* **46,** Nov., 364–8, 1964.

50. **Keran, M. W. and Riordan, M.,** 'Stabilisation policy in [the] world context', Federal Reserve Bank of San Francisco *Economic Review,* Fall, 5–19, 1976.

51. **Keynes, J. M.,** *The General Theory of Employment, Interest and Money.* Macmillan, London, 1936.

52. **Laidler, D.,** 'Simultaneous fluctuations in prices and output: a business cycle approach', *Economica*, N. S. **40**, Feb., and in [56], 120–33, 1973.
53. **Laidler, D.,** 'The influence of money on real income and inflation: a simple model with some empirical tests for the United States, 1953–72', *Manchester School*, **41**, Dec., and in [56],134–65, 1973.
54. **Laidler, D.,** 'Expectations, adjustment and the dynamic response of income to policy changes', *Journal of Money, Credit and Banking*, **5**, Part I, 157–72, 1973.
55. **Laidler, D.,** House of Commons Expenditure Committee (*Ninth Report*, HC 328, 1974), paras. 155, 165, 1974.
56. **Laidler, D.,** *Essays on Money and Inflation*. Manchester Univ. Press, Manchester, 1975.
57. **McNees, S. K.,** 'An evaluation of economic forecasts', Federal Reserve Bank of Boston, *New England Economic Review*, Nov/Dec., 1–39, 1975.
58. **McNees, S. K.,** 'An evaluation of economic forecasts: an extension and update', Federal Reserve Bank of Boston, *New England Economic Review*, Sept/Oct, 1976.
59. **Meiselman, D. I.,** 'Worldwide inflation: a monetarist view', in D. I. Meiselman and A. B. Laffer, eds., *The Phenomenon of Worldwide Inflation*. American Enterprise Institute, Washington, DC, 1975.
60. **Modigliani, F. and Ando, A.,** 'Impacts of fiscal actions on aggregate income and the monetarist controversy: theory and evidence', in [72], 1976.
61. **Ott, D. J. and Ott, A. F.,** 'Budget balance and equilibrium income, *Journal of Finance*, **20**, 71–7, 1965.
62. **Parkin, J. M.,** *Inflation in the World Economy*, Surrey Papers in Economics No. vii, Nov., The Univ. of Surrey, Guildford, 1976.
63. **Parkin, J. M., Sumner, M. and Ward, R.,** 'The effects of excess demand, generalized expectations and wage–price controls on wage inflation in the UK: 1956–71', in K. Brunner and A. H. Meltzer, eds., *The Economics of Price and Wage Controls*. North-Holland, Amsterdam, 1976.
64. **Poole, W. and Kornblith, E. B. F.,** 'The Friedman–Meiselman CMC paper: new evidence on an old controversy', *American Economic Review*, **63**, Dec., 908–17, 1973.
65. **Sargent, T. J.,** 'Interest rates and prices in the long run', *Journal of Money, Credit and Banking*, **5**, 385–449, 1973.
66. **Saunders, P. G. and Nobay, A. R.,** 'Price expectations, the Phillips curve and incomes policy', in M. Parkin and M. T. Sumner, eds, *Incomes Policy and Inflation*. Manchester Univ. Press, Manchester, 1972.
67. **Schmidt, P. and Waud, R. N.,** 'The Almon lag technique and the monetary versus fiscal policy debate', *Journal of the American Statistical Association*, **68**, March, 11–19, 1973.
68. **Selden, R. T.,** 'Cost-push versus demand-pull inflation, 1955–1957', *Journal of Political Economy*, **67**, Jan., 1–20, 1959.
69. **Sims, C. A.,** 'Money, income and causality', *American Economic Review*, **62**, Sept., 540–52, 1972.
70. **Stein, J. L.,** 'Inside the monetarist black box', in [72], 1976.
71. **Stein, J. L.,** 'Introduction', in [72], 1976.
72. **Stein, J. L.,** ed. *Monetarism*, North-Holland, Amsterdam, 1976.
73. **Tanner, J. E.,** 'Lags in the effects of monetary policy: a statistical investigation', *American Economic Review*, **59**, Dec., 794–805, 1969.
74. **Tobin, J.,** 'Money, capital and other stores of value', *American Economic Review*, **51**, May, 26–37, 1961.
75. **Tobin, J.,** 'An essay on the principles of debt management', in Commission on Money and Credit, *Fiscal and Debt Management Policies*. Prentice-Hall, Englewood Cliffs, NJ, 1963.
76. **Tucker, D.,** 'Dynamic income adjustment to money supply changes', *American Economic Review*, **59**, June, 433–49, 1969.
77. **Turnovsky, S. J. and Wachter, M. L.,** 'A test of the "expectations hypothesis" using directly observed wage and price expectations', *Review of Economics and Statistics*, Feb., 47–54, 1972.

78. **Williams, D., Goodhart, C. A. E. and Gowland, D. H.,** 'Money, income and causality: the UK experience', *American Economic Review*, **66,** June, 417–23, 1976.

79. **Wilson, T. and Andrews, P. W. S.,** *Oxford Studies in the Price Mechanism.* The Clarendon Press, Oxford, 1951.

80. **Yohe, W. P. and Karnosky, D. S.,** 'Interest rates and price level changes, 1952–1969', Federal Reserve Bank of St Louis *Review*, **51,** 18–38, Dec., 1969.

Chapter 3

Inflation and the labour market

J. D. Byers

Questions concerning the interrelationship of the operation of the labour market, in particular the rate of unemployment thereby generated, and the rate of change of the average price level, have beset post-war generations of economists. Probably more ink has been spent on this than any other issue. It was not always so. Little can be found in the writings of earlier generations. Without claiming that justice is being fully done we can summarise their position as one in which inflation was seen to result from an excess demand for commodities in general and that, since labour is required to produce these goods, the economic system, which tended to generate full employment anyway, would certainly do so when aggregate demand was greater than potential supply.

Why the change of emphasis? It is pretty much of a cliché to begin a survey of any strand of modern macroeconomics by tracing its roots back to the *General Theory* [18]. It is also very nearly unavoidable. Keynes induced a permanent change in the way that economists view the world. His famed 'long struggle to escape' from pre-existing modes of thought is mirrored in the difficulties faced by post-Keynesian generations of economists in shedding the ruling Keynesian preconceptions. Of particular relevance for the present study is the way in which he, and his interpreters, perceived the role of the labour market in the economic system. It was understood to be essentially passive; the demand for labour by firms was determined by the level of aggregate demand for commodities, and money (or wage) illusion on the part of workers meant that the supply of labour adjusted to demand. More importantly, Keynes concentrated attention on the possibility of what he called 'involuntary' unemployment, and even though he admitted the existence of – and specifically excluded from central consideration (see [18, Ch. 2] esp. pp. 15, 16) – 'frictional' and 'voluntary' unemployment his followers tended to identify all observed unemployment of labour as being involuntary in nature, i.e. only amenable to reduction by an expansion of the level of aggregate demand. Indeed it became, and in some quarters still is, almost an article of faith to deny the existence of voluntary unemployment.

At its most fundamental, the *General Theory* constituted an attack on the traditional belief that the economic system was a self-correcting mechanism, that, although the economy was subject to shocks caused by parametric shifts, e.g. in tastes, any disequilibrium thereby generated would eventually be removed by forces integral to the system itself. The 'natural' position of the system was one of market-clearing equilibrium. In particular, the economy always tended towards full employment as a normal state of affairs. This Keynes denied. There did not, he claimed, exist forces to guarantee full employment; equilibrium, of a sort, would be achieved but would quite possibly be characterised by involuntary unemployment. It is but a short step from this to the belief that less than full employment is the 'natural' condition unless positive offsetting action is taken by the only body capable of such, the government.

Now if unemployment is observed to exist and if it is, or we choose to regard it as, involuntary, we must also conclude that aggregate demand is inadequate. Suppose that, in addition, we observe the level of prices to be rising. Obviously we cannot believe that the inflation is a result of the pressure of aggregate demand in excess of potential supply. The demand-orientated approach is not open to us. Inevitably, appeal must be made to a supply-side theory of inflation predicated on the operation of the labour market or on other factors entering into costs. By and large this is the post-Keynesian story. Paradoxically, the apportionment of a passive role to the labour market in so far as the determination of output and employment are concerned requires the allocation of an active role when we turn to price-level determination.

The crucial influence on the development of the labour market theory of inflation was the assumption of money illusion on the part of suppliers of labour, i.e. the contention that behaviour is affected by changes in the nominal wage rate, even if the price level changes in proportion to keep real wages constant. In particular, it was assumed that workers would supply all the labour required at the going money wage rate, but would refuse to accept a reduction. We shall look at this matter in greater detail below. For the moment the important point is that the typical Keynesian model takes the money wage rate as a datum: it is what it is because it is not as some other value. Clearly, things could not be left to lie there and so appeal was made to various institutional or sociological factors as determinants of the money wage rate. The role of the trade unions in fixing the level of money wages was, and is, often stressed and has the added polemical attraction that the existence and influence of these bodies are not well integrated into non-Keynesian theory.

Given that the money wage rate is an exogenous variable, the Keynesian system is capable of fixing the price level and, naturally, the price level moves every time the level of money wages does, although the exact relationship, e.g. of proportionality or not, remains to be determined. This approach leads naturally to a cost-push theory of inflation and this was the line taken by the earlier post-war work on the problem. Of course, factors other than wages enter into prime costs – account should also be taken of the rate of return on capital and, in open economies, the cost of imported factors of production.

Dow [7] provides an example of the sort of calculations made. The general approach may be illustrated by means of a very much oversimplified example. By definition the value of national output is divided between wages and profits, i.e.

$$WN + R = Py, \tag{1}$$

where: W = money wage rate,

N = employment,

R = total profits,

P = price level,

y = real output

Letting π represent the rate of return on labour cost, we can write this as

$$WN + \pi WN = Py \tag{2}$$

or

$$P = \frac{kW}{A}, \tag{3}$$

where: $k = (1 + \pi)$, and

A = average productivity (y/N).

This looks like the basis of a cost-push theory of inflation, but is in fact an identity. It only starts to become a theory when we can say something about the determination of the mark-up, k, and average productivity, A. Given consistent calculation of each of the individual elements, equation (3) will, of course, give a good statistical 'explanation' of price movements over time, as will its equally simple competitors derived from the 'equation of exchange', but a satisfactory explanation of inflationary processes requires a more carefully specified model in which the different elements are simultaneously determined. Nevertheless, despite the many criticisms laid against it ([3] and references), the cost mark-up approach has retained its popularity in some quarters (e.g. [37]) and indeed, the macroeconomic forecasting model used by the UK Treasury uses essentially this method [17].

In the wider context, however, progress was being made. The demand-orientated approach to inflation was always available as an alternative to the cost-push arguments. It was, of course, Keynes' own explanation for a state of 'true' inflation [18, Ch. 21]. Hence, controversy arose over whether the forces of demand-pull or cost-push provided the better explanation of the rate of inflation. Such controversies arise because many prefer sequential theories to simultaneous theories and regard one equation as better than two. In fact, the differences between the two sides were more apparent than real. Demand-pull theorists saw prices as rising in response to excess aggregate demand for commodities, while proponents of the cost-push approach saw prices rising in response to increases in money wages in a situation where trade union bargaining power was enhanced by the existence of excess aggregate demand [31]. The turning point was reached with the publication of Phillips' renowned article in 1958 [28].

Judged by the response in terms of the number of further publications on the theme, few articles can have had anything like the influence of this one, for Phillips provided a peg on which almost the whole of the subsequent debate over the causes of inflation was hung. What made the article a smash hit and all-time bestseller? Partly it was the simplicity of the idea of a stable long-run relationship between the rate of change of money wages and the rate of unemployment (see Fig. 3.1) such that wages rose faster when unemployment was low and slower (or even fell) when unemployment was high, and partly it was the fact that Phillips was concerned with the statistical regularity of the relationship and attempted no more than a smattering of theoretical foundation. Thus, both demand-pull and cost-push theorists could use the tool he provided as being amenable to their point of view. Other influences no doubt played their part. If the UK had a 'Phillips curve' so much many other countries, and anyone who knew enough econometrics to do ordinary least squares – and by this time many people did – and could find the relevant data, could estimate the relationship and publish the results. Since academic prowess is often measured, even if only in an ordinal manner, by the length of the publication list, the temptations must have been strong. However, no doubt this is but a tiny part of the truth. Again, the task of theoretical underpinnings provided opportunities for theorists of all shades and hues to show their paces and provided a background for the armies of the old and new orthodoxies. The bounty was not at all diminished when the turn of governments came. Politicians could ascribe their failure to achieve their promised price stability and full employment to the fact that the two aims were mutually incompatible, though that usually did not stop the promise being made again. Economic policy became, or seemed to become, the reasonably simple matter of choosing the most preferred point on the trade-off between inflation and unemployment and instigating policies to get there.

Despite the manifold attractions of the Phillips curve approach, criticism has been directed from many sides. It would not be going too far to say that the idea was very nearly stillborn; several early replies to Phillips' attitude attempted to cast quantities of cold water on his results. A preliminary point to note is that, in an apparent attempt to identify equilibrium configurations of rates of wage change and unemployment, Phillips collapsed his date for the period 1861–1957 into just six observations. The plot of the observations (see [28, figs. 1, 9, 10, 12]) had suggested that the postulated relationship was in the form of a hyperbola, and he used four of these six to estimate its shape and the remaining two to determine its position by trial and error. Routh [32] criticised Phillips' data and the estimation procedure followed, claiming that it exaggerated the closeness of the relation. Knowles and Winston [20] found the stability and simplicity of the relationship surprising in view of the many institutional changes that had taken place over the period, and noted that a wide range of rates of wage inflation had been compatible with low rates of unemployment while wage stability had been associated with many different unemployment rates. Griffin [13], in a comment on Lipsey's consequent research, and using US data for the period 1946–61, found that, although it was possible to interpolate a hyperbolic curve, the observations in fact divided into two quite distinct groups. The period 1948–57 was one of low unemployment rates and a wide range of rates of wage inflation, suggesting a vertical relationship, while for the period 1923–39, with higher levels of unemployment, a downward-sloping relationship seemed to exist. He concluded that it would be more reasonable to fit straight lines to each group of data rather than a hyperbolic curve across the groups and that the Phillips curve shifted as the rate of unemployment was reduced, conjecturing that as governments became committed to policies of maintaining full employment, wages and prices would become less sensitive to what would be regarded as temporary fluctuations in the rate of unemployment.

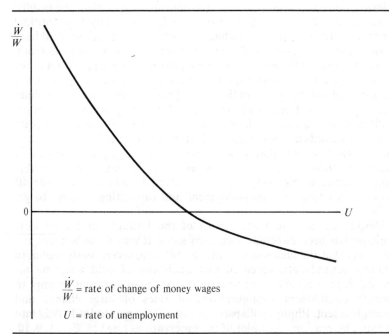

$\dfrac{\dot{W}}{W}$ = rate of change of money wages

U = rate of unemployment

Fig. 3.1

Nevertheless, the future of the Phillips curve was made secure by Lipsey [23] and Samuelson and Solow [33]. Lipsey's contribution was to suggest a theoretical foundation for the observed relationship derived from the behaviour of the labour market and to estimate the curve by standard econometric techniques. The theory of the Phillips curve was derived from the orthodox theory of price change in markets, i.e. that in situations of excess demand the price of a commodity will rise, while in conditions of excess supply the price will fall. Since the required relationship refers to the proportional rate of change of a price (the wage rate), a further assumption is needed to relate the speed of price change to market conditions. It is usual to suppose that the percentage rate of change of prices is greater the further the market is from equilibrium. Figure 3.2 graphically depicts the linear reaction function usually

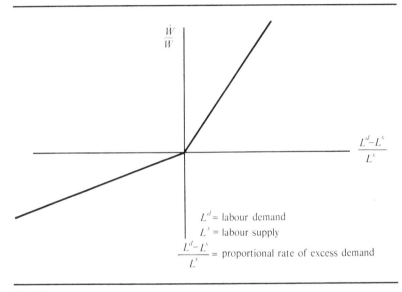

Fig. 3.2

assumed in discussion. The higher is the percentage excess demand the greater is the rate of increase of wages. In negative excess demand (i.e. excess supply) situations, the rate of growth of wages is negative (wages fall), but wages fall more slowly in an excess supply situation than they rise in an equivalent excess demand situation. Hence the kink in the relationship. This analysis implies that in equilibrium situations where excess demand equals zero, the rate of change of wages is also zero and thus conflicts with the Phillips curve result that zero wage change is consistent with a positive rate of unemployment. The apparent discrepancy is removed by noting that observed unemployment is at best a crude measure of the excess demand situation, as even in equilibrium some frictional unemployment will normally exist. Any maintained rise in excess demand will reduce even this 'equilibrium' frictional unemployment, while decreases will have the opposite effect. Thus, we could expect a relationship between the theoretically valid excess

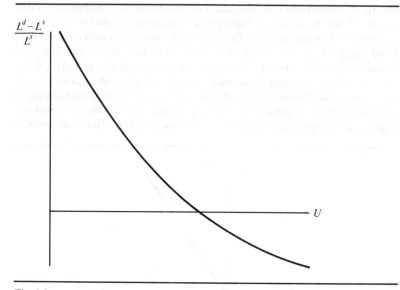

Fig. 3.3

demand variable and that which we actually observe (Fig. 3.3), and conclude that zero wage change is consistent with a positive amount of measured unemployment. By choosing various levels of excess demand and plotting the related rates of wage change and unemployment, the required relationship between the latter two variables may be derived.

The two papers [23] and [33] contain many of the strands around which the theory and practice of the Phillips curve developed. Lipsey pointed out that the rate of wage change was likely to be affected not only by the level of unemployment but also by the distribution of unemployment among the various labour markets in the economy since, even with identical but asymmetric reaction functions, for a given aggregate level of unemployment wages will rise faster in the markets with excess demand than they fall in those with excess supply. Thus, the macroeconomic Phillips curve was based on microeconomic foundations and the way was opened to mitigate the painful effects of the trade-off via policies designed to affect the workings of individual labour markets. Samuelson and Solow derived a Phillips curve for the US. They noted that the curve seemed to have shifted over time and speculated that this might be the result of increasing trade union power or a change in behaviour caused by the expectation of continuing full employment. They referred to the idea that policies to increase the mobility of labour or to improve the flow of information in the labour market would have anti-inflationary effects. Samuelson and Solow seem to have been the first to consider the Phillips curve as a relationship between the level of unemployment and the rate of price inflation rather than wage inflation. They concluded that it would be wrong to think of the trade-off as remaining constant in the longer run; shifts may be generated by the influence of expectations engendered by the pressure of aggregate demand or by such things as structural and institutional changes.

The concept of the Phillips curve as a relationship between the rates of unemployment and price inflation is indicative of a major change in emphasis. The Phillips curve, Mark I, with the rate of wage change on the vertical axis, could be considered a result of the operation of the labour market almost in isolation from the rest of the economic system. The Phillips curve, Mark II, with the rate of price inflation on the vertical axis, had to be derived from the operation of the economic system as a whole, and to explain the observed relationship we require a model of the general equilibrium of the economy. In such a system the rate of change of the price level and the rate of employment would be mutually determined along with, among other things, the real wage rate. This latter, the level of money wages deflated by the average price level, has an important role to play for, despite the fact that Lipsey and others (e.g. [6, 19]) had included current and lagged price inflation as explanatory variables in wage-change equations, the general approach had, by and large, been to regard labour market events as determining the level or rate of change of the money wage rate. In fact, orthodox theory specifies that it is the real wage rate that moves to equilibrate labour demand and labour supply. If this is indeed the case then a given level of unemployment can be associated with any rate of change of money wages as long as the rate of price inflation is sufficient to keep real wages constant. The matter is complicated by the institutional facts of life in the labour market, e.g. that wage contracts are only remade at finite intervals, implying that employees and employers must 'take a view' as to the future movements of the price level when settling wage bargains. In this context labour market equilibrium is one in which the expectations on which wage bargains have been based are fulfilled so that the actual real wage ruling at any time is that which was expected to rule when the wage bargain was made. A whole literature has evolved around this point [26, 27, 36] which, fundamentally, is just orthodox economic theory. The simple point, to invert the previous statement, is that, in equilibrium, a given level of unemployment may be associated with any rate of price inflation as long as the rate of wage inflation is such as to keep real wages constant. In a full analysis account must be taken of the fact that other nominal variables must grow at the required rate and that, for example, technical progress may result in a steady rise in the real wage rate and therefore money wages must grow faster than prices.

The most recent approach to the theory of the Phillips curve views the existence of a trade-off between unemployment and inflation as essentially transitory – the common adjective is 'short-run' but, as usual in economics, there is no implication about the actual duration of the state of affairs – and as reflecting the fact that the economy and the decision-takers within it have not yet adjusted to a change in some parameter of the system. The usual story goes something like this: Consider a position of long-run equilibrium characterised by a constant level of unemployment, and suppose also that in this long-run equilibrium the rate of price inflation is zero and, given the absence of technical progress, so is the rate of wage inflation. In this situation the real wage rate has adjusted so that all existing unemployment is voluntary in nature, consisting of workers whose marginal valuation of leisure is higher than the equilibrium real wage rate. Depending on the social security system and the means by which the unemployment rate is calculated, a proportion of these voluntarily unemployed individuals will be (incorrectly) included in the labour force and counted as unemployed.

Now suppose that the government, in good Keynesian fashion, identifies the observed unemployment as involuntary and decides to increase the level of aggregate demand in order to attain what it defines as full employment. The precise sequence of events which follows depends upon the speed with which the various participants in the labour market react to the changed state of affairs, but obviously any expansion of employment requires simultaneous decisions by firms and households to increase the amount of labour demanded and supplied. Since, given the initial equilibrium, an increase in the amount of labour demanded requires a fall in the real wage rate, while a rise is necessary to call forth an increase in the amount of labour supplied, it would seem to be questionable whether the levels of output and employment would actually change. However, because decisions are taken not only with reference to current values of variables but also on expectations about their future values, it is possible to find a situation in which a fall in unemployment occurs in the short run.

When the initial situation is disturbed by the new aggregate demand policy, output expands and unemployment falls because employers bid up money wages in the expectation that eventually prices will rise by an amount sufficient to lower the real wage rate to the level required to support the new, higher, level of employment. At the same time, households are willing to supply more labour because they value the new money wages at the original price level and hence expect a higher level of real wages to be maintained. When prices actually do rise, employment remains at its increased level until households adjust to the higher level of prices. This results in a downward revaluation of the real wage rate and a consequent decline in the supply of labour. Eventually, output and employment return to their original levels with the initial real wage rate but with money wages and prices increased in proportion.

The story is unchanged in essentials if we adopt a dynamic scenario in which the initial situation is characterised by money wages and prices growing at the rates required to keep real wages constant and the level of output stable. Here, an increase in the rate of growth of aggregate demand brings about a divergence between the rate of growth of money wages and the expected rate of inflation sufficient to reduce unemployment, but only in the short run. Eventually the economy returns to the original level of output and employment, but with a perpetually higher rate of money wage and price inflation.

This approach implies that it is only possible to trade-off some unemployment at the cost of a higher inflation rate for the length of time that it takes individuals in the system to adjust to the new higher level of inflation, and that in the long run the Phillips curve is vertical at the 'natural' rate of unemployment. Figure 3.4 provides a diagrammatical representation of the sequence of events outlined above.

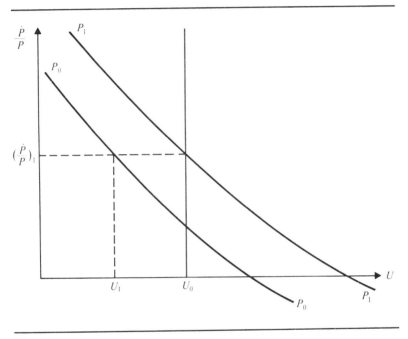

Fig. 3.4

The economy is initially at point U_0 with the natural rate of unemployment and a zero rate of inflation which is expected to continue. The government desires to reduce unemployment to U_1, and in order to do so increases the rate of growth of aggregate demand, for example by increasing the rate of growth of the stock of money. As a result the economy moves to a point on the short-run Phillips curve P_0P_0 with unemployment at U_1 and inflation at $(\dot{P}/P)_1$. But this trade-off only exists because the expected rate of inflation is zero and as the new, higher, rate of inflation is built into expectations the curve shifts upwards until a new equilibrium position is reached with employment again at U_0 and inflation now at $(\dot{P}/P)_1$, and expected to continue at that rate. Thus, the locus of long-run equilibria is the vertical line through U_0. If the government attempts to maintain unemployment at U_1 it must constantly increase the rate of growth of aggregate demand and hence engender a perpetually rising rate of inflation.

Given acceptance of its premises, the logic of this argument seems unassailable, particularly when viewed as a proposition about the comparative dynamics of the system. There is, of course, much room for discussion about the time paths of the variables in disequilibrium. What is open to dispute, however, is the usefulness of the approach as a guide to practical policy, and that question revolves around the behavioural characteristics of individuals and firms in the labour market. The crux of the matter, the recurring theme in discussions of the impact and importance of the labour market, is the old question of the nature of observed unemployment: is it voluntary or involuntary? transitory or permanent? Will it disappear of its own accord, given reasonable flexibility of wages and prices, or does its elimination require positive application of aggregate demand policies? To put it at its simplest: if the economy works in such a way as to generate one, and only one, level of employment per level of the real wage rate, in the long run the Phillips curve trade-off does not exist and hopes of reducing unemployment below its natural level are illusory.

The previous pages have surveyed the development of economists' views of the role of the labour market in the inflationary process. Yet although the various theories comprise an attractive plant which has flowered in many directions and colours, its roots are not clearly visible and to these we must now turn. In many ways the shift from static to dynamic analysis made necessary by the study of inflation has served to obscure the fact that apparently strange and novel theories are derived from orthodox economics. Moreover, the newer theories often do not allow easy differentiation of the roles of the labour market in the inflationary process. To this end, and because one of the main aims of this chapter is to examine the extent to which it is true that the rate of inflation depends upon the rate of increase in money wages, we now turn to the primary building blocks of the theory of inflation.

The popularity of Hicks' IS–LM, or income–expenditure approach, to macroeconomic analysis [15], in which the price level is taken as given, has meant that it has not always been recognised, even by the foremost practitioners of economics [e.g. 10, 11], that there is available a more complete model in which output and the price level are simultaneously determined. If we are to have a theory of the way in which the price level moves over time and the causes of that movement, then it seems reasonable to begin with a model of how the price level is determined in the first place. This model should be general enough to include the various demand-pull and cost-push factors which have been suggested as important in inflationary processes, and also to give some indication of their relative importance. At the same time, given the confines of this chapter, simplicity of exposition is not so much a virtue as a necessity. The approach, then, is not to derive a complete theory of inflation but to provide an analytical framework general enough to separate the causes of inflation from the effects and to contain, as special cases, the various particular explanations for inflation that have been suggested.

The main simplifying assumption is that the economy is closed to foreign trade and payments and so there is no room for the cost-push influences of increases in the prices of raw materials. The model could be extended in this direction, but only at the cost of increased complication and with little return to the categorising purposes in hand. Cost-push via wage increases is, of course, central to our concern and the model will be able to take account of that. Among other things, this means that, far from denying their role in inflation, institutional factors must be explicitly allowed for. We cannot ignore the existence of trade unions and the possibility that their actions help to generate and maintain inflation. Indeed, perhaps the most important question from the viewpoint of current practical policy concerns the extent to which trade unions can autonomously cause inflation. If it is found to be so, as many people claim, then wage-restraint must become the characteristic economic policy of modern economies. Even if it is not the complete truth, then we can still ask whether an incomes policy has a role to play in macroeconomic stabilisation. Unfortunately, we have no theory of institutional behaviour to integrate into the macroeconomic model, and accordingly must be satisfied with specifying particular aims of the unions, for example a certain level, or rate of increase, of (real or money) wages, thence to examine the economic consequences as they pertain to the level of unemployment or the rate of inflation.

A macroeconomic model

Any economy can be viewed as a collection of interacting markets. Macroeconomics, being concerned with aggregative variables such as the rates of output and employment and 'the' price level generally, collapses the very large number of markets of a modern economy into a very few – those for commodities in general, financial instruments and labour services. Macroeconomic equilibrium obtains when all these markets clear.

Final output is treated as a single homogeneous commodity, produced by employing a certain amount of labour and capital services, and demanded by households and firms for consumption and investment and by the government for various social and political purposes. For convenience we aggregate the demand for output by households and firms into total private sector expenditure. The level of real private expenditure is determined by the level of real income, the rate of interest and the real net wealth of the private sector; it rises when real income increases, falls when the rate of interest increases and rises when net private sector wealth increases. This latter consists of the stock of capital in private hands (assumed constant in real terms) and the quantity of government debt owed to the private sector (assumed to consist only of 'outside money'; see [25].) The real level of public expenditure is determined by the government. These assumptions are summarised in equation (4).

$$e = F(y, \ r, \ K_0 + \frac{M}{p}) + g,$$ (4)

where: e = real total private expenditure,
$\quad r$ = the rate of interest,
$\quad K_0$ = the constant real value of private capital,
$\quad M$ = the nominal quantity of money, and
$\quad g$ = the real level of government expenditure.

The financial side of the economy is represented by a single market – that for the government's monetary debt. The nominal supply of money is determined by the government and the demand for real money balances is a function of real income, the rate of interest and real private wealth, rising with real income and real private wealth and falling with increases in the rate of interest. Instead of proceeding in the normal fashion of equating demand and supply we can regard the money market as determining the rate of interest, given the levels of real income and wealth. This allows us to write,

$$r = L(y, \ K_0 + \frac{M}{p}).$$ (5)

We can now substitute equation (5) into equation (4) to obtain

$$e = F[y, \ L(y, \ K_0 + \frac{M}{p}), \ K_0 + \frac{M}{p}] + g$$

or

$$e = D(y, \ K_0 + \frac{M}{p}) + g.$$ (6)

Equation (6) summarises the demand side of the economy. It shows the level of total real expenditure given the levels of real output and real wealth. The government can influence this total either by changing its own expenditure (g) or by altering the supply of money. This latter makes its effect felt through two channels, firstly directly via an increase in private sector wealth, second indirectly via its effect on the rate of interest. The total effect of a change in the money supply is to change real expenditure in the same direction. Since equilibrium requires that real aggregate expenditure equals real aggregate income (or output) we can also regard equation (6) as a relationship between the demand for output and its price level, i.e. as the 'aggregate demand curve'. This curve is graphed as the curve DD in Fig. 3.5. It slopes downwards towards the right because at lower price levels the real value of a given nominal quantity of wealth is higher and, on the above assumptions, so is the demand

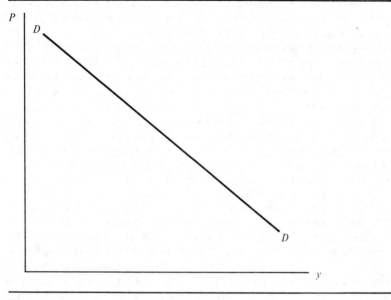

Fig. 3.5

for output. Higher levels of government expenditure, or increases in the stock of money, result in higher levels of real expenditure at any price level and therefore shift *DD* to the right and vice versa.

However, consideration of the demand side alone of any market is not sufficient to determine the equilibrium quantity transacted and its price, we also need to examine the conditions of supply. In our model economy the single, homogeneous, output is produced by the cooperation of labour and capital services and inputs are related to outputs by a production function. And that is about as far as we can go without encountering the controversies arising from different assumptions about the supply side of the economy which are at the core of the problem of the causes of inflation and what ought to be done about it. Indeed, as far as those economists who deny the existence of capital as a factor of production and the validity of production functions [14] are concerned, we ought not even go this far. We have, however, enough troubles of our own without looking for more, so it will be assumed that the necessary relationship between inputs and outputs exists.

Our aim is to construct an aggregate supply curve analogous to a market supply curve, that is to say a relationship between the price of output as a whole and the level of production. In order to do this we have to take account of two types of information. Firstly there is the technology of the economy and, in particular, the degree to which one factor may be substituted for another as relative factors prices change. Secondly there are the motivations of the decision-makers in the economy and, in particular, the degree to which their actions are influenced by money illusion. In the latter respect we shall assume that firms' decisions are not at all affected by money illusion; they always attempt to maximise profits by equating the marginal product of labour and the real wage rate. This provides us with four possible cases, depending on whether there are fixed or flexible coefficients of production and whether suppliers of labour do, or do not, suffer from money illusion.

Consider first the case of flexible factor ratios and absence of money illusion. Given the stock of capital each firm maximises profit by setting the marginal product of labour equal to the going real wage rate. Since the marginal product of labour depends on the amount of labour (and capital) employed we can invert the relationship to give the level of employment, or the demand for labour, as a function of the real wage rate and capital stock so that, with capital stock constant, a rise in the real wage rate is associated with a reduction in the demand for labour, i.e. the demand for labour curve slopes downwards and to the right. This relationship is depicted in Fig. 3.6. On the other side of the market are utility-maximising suppliers of labour who are equating the marginal rate of substitution between goods-in-general and leisure, to the real wage rate. On the usual assumptions a rise in the real wage rate will induce an increase in the amount of labour offered, and thus the supply curve of labour slopes upwards and to the right (Fig. 3.6).

The intersection of these two curves determines the market-clearing

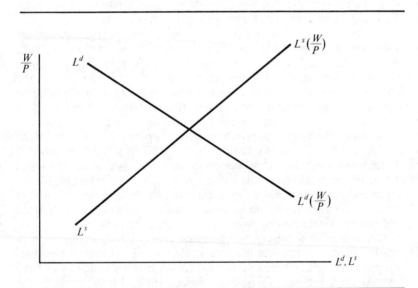

Fig. 3.6

real wage rate and the equilibrium level of employment. Since the equilibrium position is 'on the supply curve' the total amount of actual employment at this real wage rate is equal to the total amount of planned or desired employment and thus this position is one of 'full employment'. That is not to say that this is a position of maximum employment. The fact that the labour supply curve continues to slope upwards indicates that more labour would be forthcoming at a higher real wage rate, and equally the fact that the demand curve continues to slope downwards shows that firms are prepared to increase employment if the wage rate falls so the only sense in which this is a maximum is that it is the greatest possible employment *at the going real wage rate* and that all other real wage rates will be associated with a lower amount of employment since at other rates the 'short' end of the market will dominate: at higher rates firms will demand less labour than households seek to supply, and at lower rates households will offer less than firms desire to employ. In fact this equilibrium position is compatible with three sorts of observed unemployment. One stems from the fact that voluntarily unemployed people may find it worthwhile to register as unemployed and hence appear to be in the labour force in order to qualify for certain benefits, the level of which has, in turn, affected the decision about whether to actually be a member of the labour force or not. The second type results from the fact that our concept of labour market equilibrium is, in some senses, rather approximate. In any real-world economy there is always change of one sort or another, some firms are declining and laying-off men, others are expanding and increasing their staffs; some individuals are leaving the labour force and others are joining. The result is a regular and indeed very sizeable flow of persons into and out of employment and into and out of the labour force. Since, in the nature of things, one cannot always move instantaneously from job to job or from non-labour force status into employment there will always be a certain amount of 'frictional' unemployment compatible with overall equilibrium in the labour market. In addition, when the labour market as a whole is in equilibrium, there may be certain real factors in the economy which produce a higher rate of unemployment in some regions than in others. It is precisely these sorts of unemployment which governments sometimes seek to eliminate by aggregate demand measures when the correct policy is microeconomic in nature.

If we assume, as is likely, that these types of unemployment exert no pressure to change the equilibrium real wage rate then, given the stock of capital and the amount of employment generated by the operation of the labour market the level of production is given via the production function. The aggregate supply curve of output is a straight line extending vertically above the rate of output consistent with 'full employment' of labour. To see why this is so conduct a conceptual experiment in which the price level rises. If money wages stay constant real wages will fall and there will be an excess demand for labour as firms try to expand production. This will result in money wages being bid upwards until equilibrium is regained at the initial level of real wages, the only one consistent with equilibrium given our assumptions. Thus, even if there is a temporary expansion of output and employment, production will eventually return to its original level though with a higher price level, money wages having risen in proportion.

The vertical aggregate supply curve derived from the assumptions of flexible factor ratios in production and absence of money illusion in the labour market is graphed as ZZ in Fig. 3.7. Drawing in the aggregate

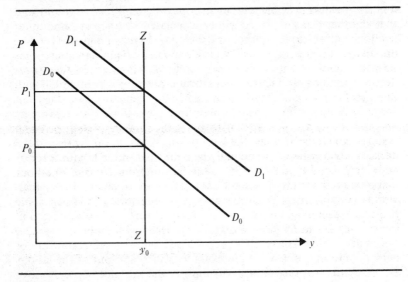

Fig. 3.7

demand curve enables us to demonstrate how the levels of output and prices all simultaneously determined in the economy. Suppose that initially government policies are such that the aggregate demand curve is D_0D_0, then the price level is P_0 and output is at the full employment level, y_0. Now let the government expand aggregate demand such that the curve shifts to D_1D_1. After sufficient time has passed to allow equilibrium to be regained the level of prices will have risen to P_1 and the rate of output will have returned to y_0. In this instance, then, because of the neoclassical assumptions employed, the level of output is determined solely by the production sector of the economy, represented by the aggregate supply curve. The levels of output and employment in the long run are independent of the level of aggregate demand which influences only the price level. The greater is aggregate demand the higher is the levels of prices. In the short run, as hinted above, employment may increase if the level of wages reacts sluggishly to the rise in prices consequent on an expansion of aggregate demand. The question which naturally arises is whether it is possible for an expansion of aggregate demand to produce a sustained rise in output and employment, even if at the expense of a somewhat higher price level. It turns out that there is such a case if we make the standard Keynesian assumption that there exists money illusion on the part of suppliers of labour.

Suppose that this is the case. We maintain the assumption of flexible factor ratios in production, but assume that the supply of labour depends on the money wage rate. It may also depend upon the level of prices as well, and hence partly upon the real wage rate, but for the moment we shall assume that the money wage rate alone is important. Afterwards we can work out the consequences of money illusion not being complete. It is worth pointing out that this assumption of money illusion on the part of households as suppliers of labour conflicts with the absence of such illusion when households make expenditure decisions implied by the usual consumption-function formulation and that the subsequent analysis requires that households as owners of capital will accept any return to that resource consistent with full employment of the capital stock (see [34, 35]). Consider an initial situation which happens to be on the aggregate supply curve, the labour market is clearing at a certain real wage rate and, given the price level, the level of money wages is determined. Now let the price level rise: with money wages constant real wages fall and firms attempt to hire more labour. What happens next depends on the condition of the labour market. If there exists involuntary unemployment, i.e. if there are suppliers of labour who are prepared to work at the going money wage rate but so far have been unable to find jobs, then the expansion of employment and output which firms desire will take place with no alteration in the level of money wages. Therefore we can draw an aggregate supply curve which slopes upwards and to the right such that the money wage rate is a constant along its length. Now suppose that the initial situation is one of full employment and again conduct a conceptual experiment in which prices rise. We can analyse the sequence of events in terms of Fig. 3.8.

The L^s curve reflects the fact that labour supply will rise with increases in the money wage rate irrespective of what is happening to the price level and hence to real wages. The demand for labour, however, depends upon both wages and prices in such a way that if both changed in the same proportion the amount of labour services required would be unchanged. In the Fig. 3.8 the increase of prices from P_0 to $2P_0$ shifts the demand for labour curve upwards so that at $2W_0$ the amount N_0 of labour services would be demanded. This, of course, simply reflects the absence of money illusion on the part of employers of labour. The initial situation is one with price level P_0, employment N_0 and hence, via the production function, output y_0. The level of money wages W_0, clears the labour market. Consequently (P_0, y_0) is a point on the aggregate supply curve. The figure illustrates the case of a doubling of the price level. The

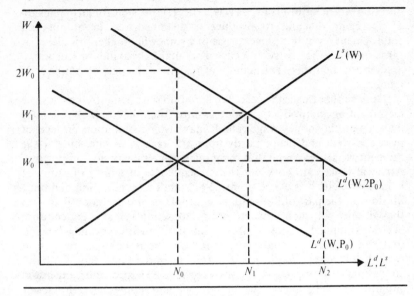

Fig. 3.8

labour demand curve shifts upwards to twice its former height, but the labour supply schedule, being independent of the price level, is unchanged. Given the halving of the real wage rate implied by the doubling of the price level firms would like to expand employment to N_2, but in fact the maximum amount of labour forthcoming at money wage rate W_0 is already employed. Consequently, the money wage rate must rise to the point of intersection of L^d *and* L^s where money wages have risen to W_1, employment to N_1, and output to y_1, Once again a higher price level is associated with a higher output level and we could draw an upward-sloping aggregate supply curve, but this time one along which the money wage rate is changing. Note that in terms of Fig. 3.8 the case of involuntary unemployment is precisely the case where the money wage rate does not rise so that employment expands to N_2 (and output to y_2) since the labour supply curve is, in effect, horizontal. Moreover, if labour supply depends partially on the price level the experiment in which prices were doubled would involve a leftward shift of L^s since less labour would be supplied at lower real wage rates. The result would be equilibrium money wage rates somewhere between W_0 and $2W_0$ with employment ending up between N_0 and N_1.

The foregoing arguments imply that the equation for the aggregate supply curve can be written as

$$y = Z\,(W,\,P,\,K_0) \tag{7}$$

and that the slope of the function (see Fig. 3.9) depends on the interaction of wage rates and price levels. We are now in a position to

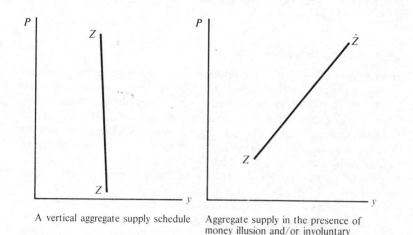

A vertical aggregate supply schedule   Aggregate supply in the presence of
money illusion and/or involuntary
unemployment

Fig. 3.9

draw some conclusions about this shape. Firstly, it is quite clear that
higher levels of output and employment are compatible with higher
price levels only because a lower real wage rate is induced. This
conclusion stems from the orthodox theory of production and the
assumption that firms behave rationally. Such a short-run relationship
between employment and real wages was, indeed, accepted by Keynes
[18]. It is precisely this fall in real wages that allows and encourages the
expansion of the economy. In other words aggregate demand policies
designed to alleviate unemployment are effective only if the real wage
rate is able to decline. Secondly, a decline in the real wage rate will occur
in only two circumstances (a) if workers suffer from money illusion,
and/or (b) if there initially exists a quantity of involuntary unemployment. Take the case of money illusion; if it is absent any rise in the price
level will inevitably lead to a proportional rise in wages and the return of
output to its original rate, implying a vertical aggregate supply schedule.
The greater the degree of money illusion the more real wages can fall,
given the change in prices, and accordingly the less steep the slope of the
aggregate supply schedule. The limiting case is reached when the labour
supply schedule under money illusion is horizontal, as it would be if
there existed involuntarily unemployed labour resources since these
workers are prepared to accept work at the going money wage rate if
only employment is offered to them. Thus, the nominal wage will not
rise until all the involuntarily unemployed are employed. Note that this
does not imply a horizontal aggregate supply schedule and hence a price
level determined solely by supply-side considerations. Even in this case a

rise in prices is necessary to reduce the real wage rate before output and employment can expand.

Changes in prices and output

Macroeconomic equilibrium requires that aggregate demand equals aggregate supply, i.e. that the volume of expenditure is equal to the level of output, the two things being measured in either real or in value terms. Geometrically, equilibrium occurs at the intersection of the schedules of aggregate demand (*DD*) and aggregate supply (*ZZ*) and involves the simultaneous determination of the rate of output and the level of prices. Thus, the apparatus that we now have is a first step in the construction of a theory of the rate at which the price level changes and the movement of the volume of employment over time.

Clearly, prices and output can change as a result only of shifts in the schedules of aggregate demand or supply and the extent of the changes will depend upon the size of any shifts which change place and the slopes of the schedules. To what degree can it be said that the level of prices, and hence their rate of change, depends only upon forces arising from one side or other of the economy? In particular, how far is it true that the price level is determined by the level of money wages and inflation by their rate of change? Obviously such extreme situations can only arise if either the aggregate demand curve or the aggregate supply curve is horizontal or vertical, for, if either is horizontal, the level of prices is determined solely by forces on that side of the market and, if either is vertical the level of prices is determined by the other side of the market. We shall examine four cases:

1. a horizontal aggregate supply curve, implying a supply-determined price level;
2. a horizontal aggregate demand curve, implying a demand-determined price level;
3. a vertical aggregate supply curve, implying a demand-determined price level;
4. a vertical aggregate demand curve, implying a supply-determined price level.

Note that in each case prices being determined by one side of the market implies that output and employment are fixed by the other side. For each of these possibilities we must consider the possibility of its occurrence and the possibility of its continuance over time. Since inflation is a sustained rise in prices this latter is of particular importance.

1. The horizontal aggregate supply curve
It might be thought, from the arguments of the previous section, that a horizontal aggregate supply curve is a limiting case of money illusion, for we saw there that the greater the degree of money illusion the smaller

the slope of *ZZ*. That this is not so may be seen from the fact that, even with the supply of labour a function only of the money wage rate, a rise in prices is required to bring about the fall in real wages necessary for an expansion of output and employment. Two conditions must be met for a horizontal aggregate supply curve to exist: a constant marginal product of labour and involuntary unemployment. Consider, for example, a fixed-coefficient technology situation where capital and labour are available in the required proportions but are less than fully employed. In such a case output can increase, employing more capital and labour in the 'correct' proportion, while the marginal product of labour remains constant [8]. Note that this 'marginal product' requires that sufficient capital be available for the newly employed labour to work with and that the marginal product of labour equals its average product equals the inverse of the labour input coefficient. Constancy of the marginal product of labour implies a horizontal labour demand curve and hence a fixed real wage rate, given a fixed real return on capital. The higher is the nominal wage rate, the higher must prices be. Accordingly, any level of employment is possible, and if the economy finds itself operating at some initial level any slight rise in prices will induce firms to attempt to expand output without limit, while any slight fall in prices will send output to zero. However, this is not sufficient to generate a horizontal aggregate supply curve, for suppose that the supply of labour is the usual upward-sloping function of the level of real wages, then the demand for labour determines the level of real wages and the supply determines the level of employment and output (see Fig. 3.10) which is, therefore, not free to vary between zero and infinity. Any rise in money wages which happens to take place, for example as a result

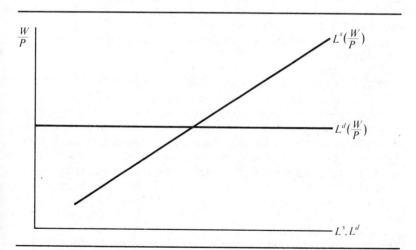

Fig. 3.10

of trade union pressure, will lead to a proportional rise in prices with output constant, i.e. a vertical aggregate supply schedule. Equally, if there is a degree of money illusion in the labour supply function, a rise in money wages accompanied by an equal proportional rise in prices will shift L^s to the right, producing an upward-sloping ZZ curve. Only if nominal wages stay constant will the price level be unchanged as output increases and, in turn, nominal wages will be constant only if there exists involuntary unemployment, for involuntarily unemployed factors will accept employment offered at the existing money wage rate and will therefore hold the rate steady until they are all employed.

The case of a horizontal aggregate supply curve seems more of a logical possibility than a practical phenomenon. Even if the real world was characterised by a fixed-coefficient technology, the fixity would be absolute only in the very short run and even then fixed coefficients in each process are compatible with varying coefficients overall as relative outputs change. More importantly for the purpose in hand, as output expands there will come a time when all factors are fully employed and thus there exists an upper limit to output. At and beyond that point expansion of aggregate demand will result only in higher prices – the aggregate supply curve becomes vertical.

2. The horizontal aggregate demand curve
To all intents and purposes this case can be disregarded. Differentiating equations (4) and (5) and solving for the slope of the aggregate demand curve will show that it is horizontal only when the marginal propensity to spend is unity and the money demand function does not have real income as an argument. In this situation any decline in the price level produces infinitely large multiplier repercussions on the demand for output. A marginal propensity to spend of less than one is a necessary condition for stability of the macroeconomic system. Consequently, we shall be safe in regarding a horizontal aggregate demand curve as impossible.

3. The vertical aggregate supply schedule
We have already examined in some detail the causes of this case, in which the level of prices is determined by the position of the aggregate demand curve. In essence it is the situation which orthodox economic theory would have us expect. We have also seen that the vertical aggregate supply schedule is the limiting situation of zero money illusion, and since we are interested here in the possibilities of the various 'extreme' cases existing we must look further into the matter.

The observation that behaviour in the labour market is affected by money illusion does not permit us to say which of several sorts of illusion is actually present. Firstly, there may be 'true' money illusion in which behaviour is determined partially by the nominal values of variables as well as by their relative values. If this actually exists in the real world, then the aggregate supply curve must have an upward, non-infinite slope and the vertical ZZ relationship is an impossibility. However, there is no evidence that money illusion is absolute in this sense.

Secondly, what looks like money illusion may exist in the short run if suppliers of labour (and, indeed, demanders) do not adjust sufficiently rapidly to change conditions. This line of argument has a long tradition in economics. It is the basis of the concepts of 'normality' – normal profits, normal price – which are part of the economist's stock-in-trade and of the analysis of the 'microfoundations of macroeconomics' which has been so popular in recent years [26, 27]. The essence of the approach lies in the recognition that it takes time for decision-makers to react to any change in economic conditions when they have become used to those initially existing. Thus, a firm will wait for a certain period before increasing prices in response to an increase in the demand for its output. The managers may originally believe that the expansion of demand will be very shortlived and may hold both output and price constant, allowing the market to physically ration the available quantity. As time passes and the higher level of demand persists, a decision will be taken to work the existing capital of the firm more intensively so as to expand output with somewhat higher prices, i.e. the firm moves up its short-run supply curve. If the higher level of demand persists for even longer periods, it will be recognised as a change in the economic climate in which the firm works and enter into the firm's long-run calculations. Eventually the firm will alter its investment plans in order to generate extra capacity and will move to a position on its long-run supply curve. Similar stories may be told concerning the behaviour of suppliers of labour. If the level of demand for labour changes it may take some time before the realisation that the level of wages can be changed and so, in response to an increase in aggregate demand, money wages may react more sluggishly than prices, allowing a fall in real wages and an expansion of employment. In time, however, competition among employers and workers will cause the initial level of output and employment to be regained. Thus, although the short-run aggregate supply curve may slope upwards, in the long run it would be vertical.

Thirdly, and perhaps of the greatest practical importance, in an economy dominated by large institutions, money illusion may be observed at the aggregate level, even though each individual is free of it. Take a situation in which trade unions bargain for economy-wide money wage rates. It may be that each of their members is absolutely free of money illusion, but because it takes time to rouse a large organisation into action real wages may be allowed to fall in the short run because the trade unions react slowly to an increase in prices. If such a situation exists, and it seems likely that it does, then the inconsistency between economists' assumption of money illusion in labour supply decisions and no money illusion in commodity demand decisions by households in the economy is removed. As in the previous case, the 'money illusion' will not persist into the long run and hence any expansion in employment would be temporary, eventually the initial level of real wages and output being restored.

In the above examples the long-run aggregate supply curve is vertical at some level of output and employment. This may be associated with substantial amounts of observed unemployment owing, say, to regional disparities which have not been adequately dealt with by economic policy. In order to allow for the fact that the long-run aggregate supply curve may be vertical at some level of employment, quite different from what may reasonably be called 'full', the term 'natural rate of unemployment' [9] is often used instead. Just as Keynesian 'involuntary' unemployment may be removed only by acting on the level of aggregate demand, 'natural' unemployment requires policies at the microeconomic level if it is to be reduced.

There is one more circumstance in which the aggregate supply curve is vertical. It occurs when trade unions bargain for a higher level of real wages than is consistent with equilibrium in the labour market. Inevitably employment is lower than it would be and those who have a job, often the members of the stronger unions, gain at the expense of those who have no job (see Fig. 3.11). Potentially, full employment could

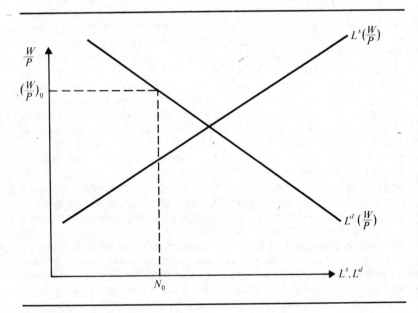

Fig. 3.11

be brought about if non-unionised labour worked for wages which were sufficiently low to bring the average real wage to the right level. However, the point to be established here is simply that such institutionally determined unemployment could exist. We may merge this possibility with that immediately preceding to say that in the long run trade unions may exercise monopolistic power to raise the real wage rate above the competitive level and hence produce long-term unemployment. Such unemployment is 'voluntary' at the aggregate level since it results from a voluntary coalition of workers using the power which coalition entails, but 'involuntary' at the individual level since no one, of course, wants to be unemployed. In the short run, however, if the unions react slowly to changes in economic conditions, real wages may fall and employment may rise. This will not persist. Eventually the unions will enforce the old real wage rate and the old level of unemployment will be restored. This 'equilibrium' level of unemployment is 'natural', since it results from the exploitation of microeconomic monopoly power and cannot be removed by macroeconomic means.

When we associate a vertical aggregate supply schedule with a downward-sloping aggregate demand curve we get the 'orthodox' neoclassical case (see Fig. 3.12). The level of output and employment is

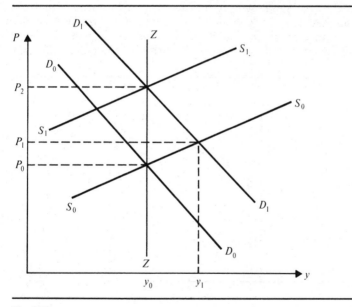

Fig. 3.12

set at the natural rate by forces on the supply side, given sufficient time for these forces to work through the system. The position of ZZ is determined by the level of real wages such that the higher the level of real wages the further to the left is ZZ. Movement of ZZ to the right is limited by the full employment position in which labour demand equals labour supply. The actual position of ZZ depends upon the degree to which monopoly power exists and is exploited and the importance of 'frictions' in the economy. As argued above, output may rise in the short run if wages lag behind prices. Consider an initial equilibrium giving a price level of P_0 and output of y_0, and suppose that an expansion of aggregate demand takes place so that D_0D_0 shifts to D_1D_1. The result is a rise in prices to P_1 and in output to y_1 as the economy moves up the short-run aggregate supply function S_0S_0. Sooner or later, however, money wages are bid up and the short-run aggregate supply function shifts upwards and to the left. Equilibrium is regained where the new aggregate demand schedule intersects the vertical long-run aggregate supply schedule at price level P_2 and output level y_0.

4. A vertical aggregate demand curve

When a vertical aggregate demand schedule is associated with an upward sloping aggregate supply curve we get the typical Keynesian case (see Fig. 3.13), which is used in opposition to the typical neoclassical case just discussed. How can a vertical DD arise? Obviously we must find some way of making the level of expenditure independent of the price level. The simplest way to do this is to assume that the consumption demand for commodities is a function of real income only and that the investment demand is the autonomous result of the 'animal spirits' of entrepreneurs. Consequently, there is only one level of real

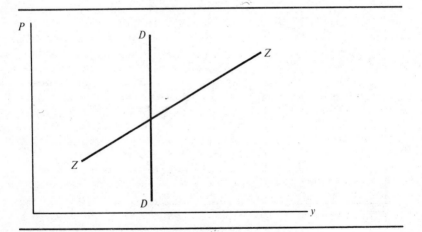

Fig. 3.13

income at which real savings equals real investment. Since no behaviour changes as a consequence of changes in the price level, neither does real expenditure, resulting in a vertical aggregate demand schedule. If we admit that investment may also depend upon the rate of interest, then the Keynesian must appeal to the existence of a liquidity trap in the money market for otherwise a fall in the price level increases the real supply of money and leads to a fall in interest rates. This, in turn, stimulates investment and hence results in an expansion of output and employment. The liquidity trap stops all this; the price level can be what it may since- whatever the real supply of money, interest rates are constant. In addition to the liquidity trap, a vertical aggregate demand curve requires that private sector expenditure (consumption plus investment) is not influenced by real private sector wealth. For if this were indeed the case a fall in prices would stimulate expenditure directly, there being no need for the interest rate to change.

In the Keynesian case the price level is determined by the aggregate supply side of the economy. Any trade union push on money wages is reflected in upward shifts of the aggregate supply curve and, accordingly, a constant push leading to a steady rate of increase of money wages will result in an inflation of the price level at the same rate. We may note an apparent similarity with the orthodox case previously discussed. There a steady expansion of aggregate demand would sooner or later lead to a price inflation at the same rate, but whichever rate of inflation was established the level of output and employment would be constant in the long run. In the Keynesian case the rate of price inflation depends on the trade union-determined rate of growth of money wages and is also independent of the levels of output and employment. However, this equivalence is illusory. The rate of output in the Keynesian model is determined by the level of aggregate demand which, in turn, is a variable under the control of the government; thus, output and employment will be increased if government expenditure is expanded. Under the conditions necessary to generate a vertical aggregate demand curve the schedule shifts bodily rightwards, resulting generally in a higher price level (which has no effect on demand behaviour) and an expansion of output equal to the change in real government expenditure times the multiplier. We are at the heart of the Keynesian model with fiscal policy fully effective, monetary policy absolutely ineffective, the ability to reduce unemployment by expenditure measures and the necessity to control the trade unions in order to control inflation.

How likely is a vertical aggregate demand curve? We have already seen the rather extreme conditions necessary for its existence. As soon as the liquidity trap is removed, and as soon as real private sector wealth is allowed to influence expenditure decisions, the aggregate demand curve ceases to be vertical. Even given a vertical schedule, macroeconomic policy cannot repeatedly shift it further to the right, cannot forever buy higher levels of output at the expense of higher price levels, because ultimately the aggregate supply curve will set a constraint. There will come a point at which full employment is reached, i.e. when further price rises will stimulate proportional money wage increases. At Keynesian full employment the aggregate supply curve becomes vertical and our previous analysis comes into play. It may be possible to bring about an increase in output by engineering a movement up the short-run aggregate supply curve, but the fall in real wages necessary for this will eventually be reversed and the economy will return to its initial level of output at a higher price level. Any longer-run attempts to reduce unemployment below the full-employment level will result in inflation.

An extreme case would be one in which the vertical aggregate demand curve moved to the right of the vertical aggregate supply curve, producing a perpetual state of excess demand and causing prices to rise without limit. This, however, seems unlikely. We have already seen the very special assumptions necessary for a vertical *DD* curve and that we may, in general, expect it to slope downwards from left to right since lower price levels increase the real value of private sector wealth and therefore stimulate expenditure. On the supply side of the economy, even if we start off in a position where there exists pure Keynesian involuntary employment, there will be some expansion of aggregate demand which will reduce it to zero. Beyond that point we are in a situation wherein unemployment is voluntary in one of the aggregate or individual senses discussed above. We are in the realm of the orthodox model.

Prices and output in the long run

At any moment in time the level of output and the price at which it is sold are determined by the ruling conditions of aggregate demand and supply. Any movements of output or prices which take place over time must therefore result from shifts in the schedules of aggregate demand and supply. The position taken here, supported by the arguments made above, is that the long-run aggregate supply curve is vertical. If no expansion of capacity is taking place the economy will eventually settle at some point on the curve with output and employment at the 'natural level'. Since our concern here is not with the growth of output over time, we shall ignore factors leading to rightward shifts of the aggregate supply schedule. Though it would not be difficult to incorporate economic growth into the analysis, we are here interested in the static long run rather than the dynamic, at least as far as output is concerned. We can summarize the basics as follows:

1. The long-run aggregate supply schedule, given zero growth in the capital stock, is a constant function of the long-run real wage rate. The higher is the latter, the further to the left is the aggregate supply schedule, while the rightward limit is associated with the real wage determined in a competitive labour market.
2. The aggregate demand schedule is a downward-sloping function of the level of real income (output). With the capital component of private wealth constant, the schedule is shifted by changes in the money supply and in government expenditure policies. In the long run these latter are linked by the fact that the government needs to finance its expenditure by taxation, by borrowing or by increases in the money supply so that in the simple case where there is no borrowing or taxation, absolute growth of the money supply in any year is equal to the level of government expenditure.

We are now in a position to investigate the generation and maintenance of inflation and the extent to which the labour market plays an active or a passive part in the process. Consider first the simplest inflationary process. Let real output be fixed at the full employment level by the operation of a competitive labour market so that real wages are at the equilibrium level and any reduction in them brought about by a rise in the price level will be removed by money wage increases resulting from competitive bidding by employers, each individually attempting to expand output and employment in his own concern. If we leave out of account the (constant) capital stock, the model can be written as

$$y = Z(\frac{W}{P}), \tag{8}$$

$$e = D(y, \frac{M}{P}) + g, \tag{9}$$

along with the equilibrium condition

$$y = e. \tag{10}$$

Analysis of this model is trivial: with y set by the operation of the labour market the only long-run equilibrium configuration is that in which all the nominal variables, i.e. W, M and P, are growing at the same rate. Since, by assumption money wages respond to price-level changes and prices are endogenous, the exogenous variable driving the system is the rate of growth of the money supply as set by the government. Given sufficient time for short-run influences to work themselves out, the rate of inflation will equal the rate of monetary expansion. A slight wrinkle arises in that if the inflation rate is not equal to zero then the real rate of interest and the money rate of interest diverge according to the equation:

$$i = r + \frac{\dot{P}}{P}, \tag{11}$$

where: i=the money rate of interest,
$\quad\quad r$=the real rate of interest, *and*
$\quad\quad \frac{\dot{P}}{P}$=the rate of inflation (strictly the expected rate of inflation).

This means that the aggregate demand curve is somewhat different from (8) since the real rate of interest is normally taken as being relevant for investment decisions, while the money rate of interest, reflecting the opportunity costs of holding money, is relevant for money market equilibrium. Thus, instead of equations (4) and (5) we should have:

$$e = F(y, r, \frac{M}{P}) + g \tag{12}$$

and

$$r + \frac{\dot{P}}{P} = i = L(y, \frac{M}{P}), \tag{13}$$

giving the aggregate demand equation,

$$e = D(y, \frac{M}{P}, \frac{\dot{P}}{P}) + g. \tag{14}$$

Clearly, a rise in the inflation rate brings about a fall in the real rate of interest [24].

An examination of the short-run aspects of the model gives some indication of the probable temporal course of events. In Fig. 3.14 the economy is initially in equilibrium at P_0, Y_0.

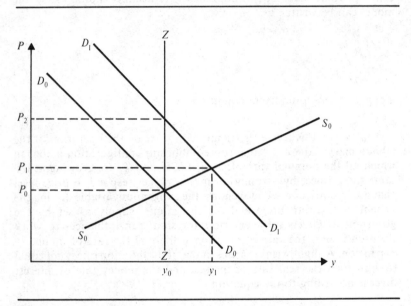

Fig. 3.14

Suppose the government is dissatisfied with the rate of unemployment associated with y_0 and prefers that corresponding to y_1. With y_1 as the target of macroeconomic policy some expansion of aggregate demand will bring the economy to y_1 at the expense of a higher price level P_1. As we have seen previously, such an increase is nearly always possible by inducing an expansion of the labour force. However, a higher level of employment can only be maintained at a lower real wage rate and, by assumption, there are forces at work to restore the real wage rate to its original level. Eventually the level of output returns to y_0 with prices rising to P_2. If the government again tries to expand output to y_1 by aggregate demand policies, the process is repeated, unemployment initially falls, then rises and prices increase. Though this is the basic step, any actual sequence of events will probably differ from the above since governments will usually try to stop the fall in output by a further expansion of aggregate demand before the economy returns to y_0.

The conclusion drawn from the simplest model is that the rate of inflation is determined by the rate of expansion of aggregate demand – prices rise as the aggregate demand curve shifts up along the long-run aggregate supply schedule. An inflation of this sort is set off by an increase in aggregate demand resulting from an increase in the rate of growth of government expenditure, say from zero to some positive number. This extra expenditure is financed by expansion of the money supply, and in equilibrium the rate of growth of real government expenditure returns to zero – money supply must grow at the rate of inflation just to keep real government expenditure constant. If the government tries to maintain a higher level of real expenditure, perhaps in order to reach a rate of unemployment lower than the natural rate, then the result will be a perpetually rising rate of inflation.

The generality of this model is demonstrated by the ease with which it can be converted from a demand-pull to a cost-push version of the inflation process, since technically equilibrium requires only that all nominal variables grow at the same rate in order to keep real values constant. It follows that we could just as easily choose the money wage rate as the exogenous variable and take the quantity of money as endogenous. This Keynesian variant requires a different story to be told, but is analytically much the same as the foregoing. Take the static version first. Suppose trade unions demand and receive a rise in the level of money wages in order to increase real wages. This shifts the aggregate supply curve to the left with the result (see Fig. 3.15) that output falls (y_0 to y_1), unemployment rises and prices increase (P_0 to P_1). If the government is committed to a policy of holding employment at the level generated by a rate of output of y_0 it will react by expanding aggregate demand to bring economic activity back to its initial level. In this way output increases again to y_0, but prices rise even further to P_2. Unfortunately, real wages are now back at their original level, leading the trade unions to demand a rise in money wages to reach their real wage target. As long as the government holds on to its employment targets it must always validate the wage increases brought about by trade union pressure. In equilibrium, prices and the money supply will rise at a rate equal to the rate of growth of money wages determined by the trade unions.

There are only two ways to remove the problem. Firstly, the government could refuse to expand aggregate demand in response to wage increases, allowing the trade unions to have higher real wages at the expense of lower output and employment. Secondly, the government could legislate away the monopoly power that allows trade unions to determine the rate of growth of money wages and hence the rate of inflation. Neither of these alternatives has proved particularly palatable to politicians. I believe an economist is very nearly bound to say that a removal of the monopoly power will be best for all in the long run, but

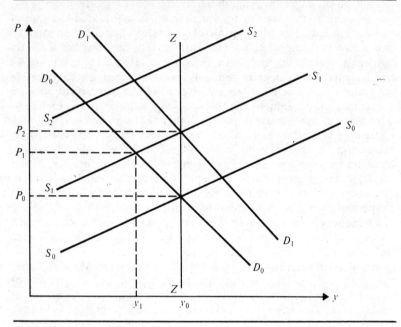

Fig. 3.15

that, if such proves to be politically impossible, the former policy will have to be put into action.

The foregoing leads to the conclusion that, in the long run, those who decide economic policy (and essentially this means those who control the money supply) can choose the rate of inflation, but that the level of output is not amenable to change by macroeconomic measures. This means that, whether inflation is brought about by 'demand-pull' or 'cost-push', the long-run Phillips curve is vertical at the natural rate of unemployment. In the short-run, divergences from the natural rate will take place in response to changes in the rate of growth of policy parameters, but these will work themselves out and return output to its previous level, though perhaps at a different rate of inflation. However, we have already seen that the long-run natural rate of unemployment is fixed by the level of the real wage rate. It is therefore possible that the economy will gravitate to a long-run, less-than-full level of unemployment, the divergence between the natural and the potential 'full' rate being determined by the difference between the actual level of real wages and the competitive equilibrium level. All this means, of course, is that the long-run aggregate supply schedule moves to the left, reducing the natural rate of unemployment. Otherwise the analysis goes through as before – it is decisions about the rate of growth of aggregate demand that determine the rate of growth of prices and it is decisions about the real wage rate that determine the level of unemployment. To give an example of the above, suppose that the trade unions bargain for a minimum real wage rate – by refusing to work for less – and for a given rate of growth of money wages. The analysis still holds; the real wage rate determines the equilibrium level of employment, and since, in the long run, all nominal variables must grow at the same rate, the rate of inflation will equal the rate of growth of money wages. If the trade unions choose a different rate of growth of money wages, the rate of inflation will be different but the rate of unemployment will be the same. The long run trade-off is vertical.

Conclusion

The price level is one of a set of nominal variables in an economic system. In equilibrium, and taking account of real growth over time, these nominal economic variables must share a common rate of growth. The simple model constructed above has the supply of money and the level of money wages as the other nominal variables to which the price level must adjust, and allows either of these two to be the fundamental determinant of inflation. Thus, if government macroeconomic policies require a steady rate of growth of the money supply, then eventually prices and money wages must adopt that same proportional rate of increase otherwise there will be a steady growth or decline of real wages over time, carrying in its train a steady rise or decline of the unemployment rate. Since this cannot continue for ever, prices and wages must grow at the same rate. If trade union power is such that they can enforce a steady rise in the level of money wages, then prices and now the money supply must adjust to this rate of growth. Whereas in the first case trade unions must be willing to allow money wages to rise – an assumption which will usually be satisfied – in the second the government must take positive action to expand the nominal supply of money – this they may not always be prepared to do. Directly or indirectly the government controls the rate of inflation. The major difference, then, between cost-push inflation and demand-pull inflation is that in the former there will be a tendency of unemployment to be higher than its equilibrium level during the process of inflation, while in the latter there will be a tendency of unemployment to be below that level.

Whatever the rate of inflation, the level of unemployment in the long run is determined by the level of real wages: the higher are the latter the higher is the 'equilibrium' unemployment rate, and vice versa. The fullest level of employment is, given various frictions, that set by a competitive labour market, though there is no guarantee that this level will be reached if monopolistic elements are present. At its crudest: 'governments cause inflation and trade unions cause unemployment', though adoption of such slogans tends to result in confusion rather than understanding. As we have seen in the foregoing, the role of the labour market in inflation depends to a great deal on the nature of the institutions existing in the economy and on the nature of the political processes in the society as a whole.

References and Bibliography

1. **Barro, R. and Grossman, H.**, *Money, Employment and Inflation.* Cambridge Univ. Press, 1976.
2. **Black, S. W. and Kalejian, H. H.**, 'A macro model of the U.S. labour market', *Econometrica*, **38**, 712–41, 1970.
3. **Bronfenbrenner, M, and Holzman, F. D.**, 'A survey of inflation theory', in R.E.S./A.E.A., Surveys of Economic Theory, Vol. I. Macmillan, London, 1968.
4. **Byers, J. D.**, 'The supply of labour', in D. F. Heathfield, ed., *Topics in Applied Macroeconomics.* Macmillan, London, 1976, and references therein.
5. **Daniel, W. W.**, 'A national survey of the unemployed', *P.E.P. Broadsheet No. 546*, 1974.
6. **Dicks-Mireaux, L. A.**, 'The interrelationship between cost and price changes, 1946–1959: a study of inflation in post-war Britain', *Oxford Economic Papers*, **13**, 267–92, 1961.
7. **Dow, J. C. R.**, 'Analysis of the generation of price inflation. A study of cost and price changes in the United Kingdom, 1946–54', *Oxford Economic Papers*, **8**, 252–301, 1956.
8. **Fergusson, C. E.**, *The Neoclassical Theory of Production and Distribution.* Cambridge Univ. Press, 1969.
9. **Friedman, M.** 'The role of monetary policy', *American Economic Review*, **58**, 1–17, 1968.
10. **Friedman, M.**, 'A theoretical framework for monetary analysis', *Journal of Political Economy*, **78**, 193–238, 1970.
11. **Friedman, M.**, 'A monetary theory of nominal income', *Journal of Political Economy*, **79**, 323–37, 1971.
12. **Goldstein, M.**, 'The trade-off between inflation and unemployment: A survey of the empirical evidence for selected countries', *I.M.F. Staff Papers*, **19**, 647–95, 1972.
13. **Griffin, K. B.**, 'A note on wages, prices and unemployment', *Bulletin of the Oxford university Institute of Statistics*, **24**, 379–85, 1962.
14. **Harcourt, G. C.**, *Some Cambridge Controversies in the Theory of Capital.* Cambridge Univ. Press, 1972.
15. **Hicks, J. R.**, 'Mr. Keynes and the "Classics"; A suggested interpretation', *Econometrica*, **5**, 147–59, 1937.
16. **Hines, A. G.**, 'Trade unions and wage inflation in the United Kingdom, 1893–1961' *Review of Economic Studies*, **31**, 221–52, 1964.
17. **H.M. Treasury**, 'Macroeconomic model', *Technical Manual, H.M. Treasury*, Section 10, 1976.
18. **Keynes, J. M.**, *The General Theory of Employment, Interest and Money.* Macmillan, London, 1936.
19. **Klein, L. R. and Ball, R. J.**, 'Some econometrics of the determination of absolute prices and wages', *Economic Journal*, **69**, 465–82, 1959.
20. **Knowles, K. G. J. C. and Winston, C. B.**, 'Can the level of unemployment explain changes in wages', *Bulletin of the Oxford University Institute of Statistics*, **21**, 113–20, 1959.
21. **Kuh, E.**, 'Unemployment, production functions and excess demand', *Journal of Political Economy*, **74**, 238–49, 1966.

22. **Laidler, D. and Purdy, D. L. (eds.),** *Inflation and Labour Markets.* Manchester Univ. Press, 1974.
23. **Lipsey, R. G.,** 'The relationship between unemployment and the rate of change of money wages in the United Kingdom, 1862–1957: A further analysis', *Economica,* **27,** 1–41, 1960.
24. **Mundell, R.,** *Monetary Theory,* Ch. 2. Goodyear, Pacific Palisades, California, 1971.
    Patinkin, D., *Money, Interest and Prices.* Harper and Row, New York, 2nd edn, 1965.
26. **Phelps, E. E. et al.,** *Microeconomic Foundations of Employment and Inflation Theory.* Norton, New York, 1970.
27. **Phelps, E. S.,** *Inflation Policy and Unemployment Theory.* Macmillan, 1972.
28. **Phillips, A. W.,** 'The relationship between unemployment and the rate of change of money wage rates in the United Kingdom, 1861–1957', *Economica,* **25,** 283–99, 1958.
29. **Rees, A.,** 'The Phillips curve as a menu for policy choice', *Economica,* **37,** 227–38, 1970.
30. **Rees, A. and Hamilton, M. T.,** 'The wage–price–productivity perplex', *Journal of Political Economy,* **75,** 63–70, 1967.
31. **Robertson, D.,** *Growth, Wages and Money.* Cambridge Univ. Press, 1961.
32. **Routh, G.,** 'The relation between unemployment and the rate of change of money wage rates: a comment', *Economica,* **26,** 299–315, 1959.
33. **Samuelson, P. A. and Solow, R. M.,** 'Analytical aspects of anti-inflation policy', *American Economic Review,* Papers and Proceedings, **50,** 177–94, 1960.
34. **Tobin, J.,** 'A note on the money wage problem', *Quarterly Journal of Economics,* **55,** 508–16, 1941.
35. **Tobin, J.,** 'Money wage rates and employment', in S. E. Harris, ed., *The New Economics.* Knopf, 1947.
36. **Tobin, J.,** 'Inflation and unemployment', *American Economic Review,* **62,** 1–18, 1972.
37. **Weintraub, S.,** *A General Theory of the Price Level, Output, Income Distribution and Economic Growth,* reprinted by Greenwood Press, 1973.

Chapter 4

Natural resources and inflation

S. P. Chakravarty

A note of caution

There are matters of fact and there are matters of opinion. But in only the most sterile works of economics is it possible to keep facts and opinions entirely separate. It may be argued that factual accounts, 'since they involve selections and emphasis, turn out on inspection to be interpretations' [22, p. 275]. Zinn [22, pp. 275–6] puts forth with considerable logical force the proposition that

> there can be no inherent 'meaning' of any interpretation – its meaning would consist of its effect on the actions of those who read it. And if so, we would have to go beyond the ostensible meaning of the words of that interpretation, because the effect on the reader is not created only by those words, but by the total setting of those words – who the author is, the context in which he writes, the emotive as well as rational emanations of the writing, the particular condition of the reader as he receives the message. The meaning of any writing then is the total interaction between the writer, the reader, and the setting in which the reading takes place.

The setting in which any discussion of inflation could take place would be so charged with towering passions that an author must tread very carefully. Talking about natural resources is an even more perilous occupation. I, therefore, venture to combine these two subjects with great trepidation.

Not very long ago the *New York Times* issued a strident call to the 'United States and its allies' to show 'that they mean business' in dealing with 'the double threat of world inflation and world depression', the 'major source' of which, according to the *New York Times*, was dependence on imported energy supplies whose price had risen [12]. Not quite three months later another article asserted in the *New York Times Magazine* that 'the fourfold oil price' rise contributed at the most 'between 1 and 2 per cent to the cost of living', which was rising at a rate well over 8 per cent [13].

If I were to argue in the following pages that scarcity of natural resources could lead to inflation, the effect of these words on some energetic reader might indeed be catastrophic in our emotionally charged world. Since every budding economist learns that export is good, import is bad and inflation is disastrous, our reader might feel impelled to the perpetration of arson, pillage, murder and such other acts of super patriotism which he would think necessary to gain complete control over natural resources by his country, tribe or whatever other body to which he owes allegiance. We can only hope that men of action will not read this chapter.

In any case, those who are looking for simplistic causes of inflation to convince themselves that their lack of well-being is entirely due to the machinations of enemies with creeping feet and shiny eyes would find this article not very useful. I do not argue even for a moment that constraints on natural resources have ever played any discernible role in creating or sustaining inflation. My purpose here is simply to investigate the movement of real wages under different assumptions concerning the relative difficulty with which resources might have to be extracted as the reserves dwindle. Other chapters in this book provide clues as to whether such movements in real wages are compatible with political reality. If not, we could have inflation. We might also have a revolution. I do not know and, for the purposes of this chapter, I do not much care.

Words and their meaning

The greater the frequency with which a word is used, the less likely is it going to be clearly defined. Inflation is such a word, inspiring almost superstitious awe. A senior British politician once compared inflation to Hitler. Tinpot dictators equate inflation to a condition which would prevail in the absence of their tyranny. Chancellors of the Exchequer increase the Civil List, freeze child allowances and raise taxes – all these we are told are attributable to inflation. None of them provide particularly illuminating clues for defining this alleged outrage, and the average citizen feels bewildered and haunted by some ill-defined Kafkaesque adversary.

To make matters simple, we shall stick to a narrow definition of inflation: ' . . . the process resulting from competition in attempting to maintain total real income, total real expenditure and/or total output at a level which has become physically impossible or in attempting to increase any of them to a level which is physically impossible' [21, pp. 534–5].

Consider, for example, the case where wage is defined as per-capita consumption of finished goods, obtained after subtracting per-capita investment from production per head. (This definition of wage includes distributed profits spent on consumption.) Let us suppose that constraints on extraction of primary commodities require wages to follow a trajectory which is not politically palatable. A situation could arise where the rate of increase in consumption of finished products might have to slow down, halt or even decline. Two options would be open to society: (a) to accept this situation as being inevitable until such time when technical change could provide amelioration, or (b) to obscure this limitation by making money wages rise faster than real wages. If in our model we allow for the fact that various groups in society have different access to material goods, there would be a third option, of redistributing income. If total consumption has to decline owing to the inexorable laws of physics, each person might think that the burden should be entirely borne by all other persons living in the community.

Option (a) would not result in inflation. Option (b) in so far as it attempts to create an illusion of consumption possibilities physically unobtainable, is inflationary according to our definition. The third case is very much more complex.

According to one version of economics, attempts at redistribution of income through altering relative prices are necessarily inflationary because they are based on logical contradictions. If we believe that wages are the marginal products of labour, and there is a unique solution to the system of equations governing prices and wages, starting from a given initial endowment, how could we hope to alter the relative share of different groups without making prices indeterminate? If a set of equations for wages and prices, given a set of initial conditions, has a unique solution, surely it is logically impossible to arbitrarily assign a 'solution' to it which is different.[1] To alter the initial endowment would require a consensus which there is no reason to suppose would necessarily exist. Thus, an effort to redistribute income through political action is tantamount to an attempt to maintain wages at a level which is inherently unstable.

Like so much else in the social sciences, mathematical models are essentially expressions of personal preferences [5], and there is no universal agreement that products of labour can be accurately, if at all, counted without introducing very many extraneous assumptions. The literature is full of recondite arguments [14, 19]. One need not, however, strain oneself very much to realise that outputs of ministers of religion and professors of economics are precisely what society determines they are. The great scientist and engineer Michael Faraday's official salary as an academic was a mere £200 per annum. Bishops of religion were paid over ten times that amount. But all that was in the last century when the clergy were more powerful than the technologists. Nowadays, even some of the most indolent professors of engineering could command salaries higher even than that of the Archbishop of Canterbury.

If it is indeed the case that the share of wages between different groups is determined by the relative strength of these groups in moulding social consciousness in their favour, a whole new Pandora's box opens up every time the question of income redistribution arises. There is no inherent reason to suppose that equations governing perceptions of just distributions of income have a solution, let alone a stable one, at all.

We note, therefore, that if natural resources constraints on the growth

---

1. This system of equations follows from general equilibrium theory, a version of which is presented in Baumal [2].

of total consumption were to open up debates on income distribution, the consequences might well be that no consensus would emerge. An attempt would be made to maintain income and expenditure at a level which is physically impossible.

Malthus, Ricardo et al.

Father Jonathan Swift suggested that children should be killed and eaten to provide a check on population growth. 'I have been assured by a very knowing American of my acquaintance in London, that a young healthy child well nursed is at a year old a most delicious, nourishing, and wholesome food, whether stewed, roasted, baked, or boiled. . . . [18, p. 101]. Those who find these sentiments unpleasant to contemplate might conclude that Father Swift was a disagreeable person. But the truth may be that Swift was a kind, genial man who occasionally displayed a macabre sense of humour. A solitary quotation from the writings of a prolific author can indeed create a wrong impression of his personality and cause dismay among those who know him better. We run this risk in our chapter by quoting from the writings of controversial men.

But if we remember the basic purpose of our chapter, this risk is not serious. We do not quote from Malthus or Ricardo to ascertain their actual beliefs. We use terms like Malthusian and Ricardian to denote certain specific world views, without necessarily implying at the same time that these opinions were central to the works of these men. The objective is to give some convenient names to these visions of the world and proceed from there to discuss matters which are not affected by the choice of a particular terminology. We are, therefore, not interested in settling disputes about hidden meanings behind quotations.

Through laborious exercise a diligent graduate student might indeed discover some day a number of moth-eaten, barely legible epistles on frail yellowish paper from Malthus to some hitherto unknown concubine, whose charm this puritanical parson could not resist. These letters might indicate that Malthus changed his views twenty-three times. Scholarly dialogue would ensue as to which among the twenty-three opinions should be called truly Malthusian. Dissertations would be written, conferences would be held, arguments would rage, passions would flow. However useful such weighty discourse on amorous letters to a mistress might be for enhancing scholarship, it is not relevant for our essay.

' . . . Man is necessarily confined in room. When acre has been added to acre till all the fertile land is occupied, the yearly increase in food must depend upon the melioration of the land already in possession. This is a fund, which, from the nature of all soils, instead of increasing, must be gradually diminishing.' [10, p. 4] This observation is not unique to Malthus as Adam Smith noted fifty years earlier that every 'species of animals naturally multiplies in proportion to the means of their subsistence, and no species can ever multiply beyond it' [20, p. 182].

But we still attribute the notion of man being confined in room to Malthus. In the following pages the term 'Malthusian' refers to that view of natural resources which emphasises a fixed limit to these commodities. In the case of minerals such as coal, once the total endowment is used up, there is no more and the law of diminishing return does not apply. But for land, the law of diminishing return sets in after the physical boundaries are reached. The gratuitous observation that population 'invariably increases where the means of subsistence increase [11, p. 261] is not central to what we call a Malthusian model here.

The distinction between the Malthusian and the Ricardian world lies in the fact that Ricardo allowed for the law of diminishing return more explicitly. He assumed three things to begin with: (a) the extent of available reserves is known, (b) resources are heterogeneous in quality and (c) better-quality resources are used up first. The last assumption is alleged to be dictated by economic rationality. Thus, the law of diminishing return sets in at the very outset. Also, Ricardo was more forthcoming than Malthus about discussing mineral resources, which are not singled out for attention by Malthus. We quote some passages from Ricardo [16, pp. 46–9] below:

> In the future pages of this work, then, whenever I speak of the rent of land, I wish to be understood as speaking of that compensation, which is paid to the owner of land for the use of its original and indestructible powers.
>
> . . . If all land had the same properties, if it were unlimited in quantity, and uniform in quality, no charge could be made for its use, unless where it possessed peculiar advantages of situation. It is only, then, because land is not unlimited in quantity and uniform in quality, and because in the progress of population, land of an inferior quality, or less advantageously situated, is called into cultivation, that rent is ever paid for the use of it.
>
> . . . The most fertile, and most favourably situated, land will be first cultivated, and the exchangeable value of its produce will be adjusted in the same manner as the exchangeable value of all other commodities. . . .

In the following pages we work out some numerical examples designed to illustrate the effect of Malthusian and Ricardian assumptions on the movement of real wages.

A simple model

Solely because a proposition may be simple, there is no guarantee that it will therefore always be more easily grasped than a complex thought. The reason why this paradox should be there we cannot tell. But of the fact that it does exist, we are certain. Hence the justification for repeating an idea, in words and through algebra. What follows is a numerical pursuit of a fraction of the thesis intimated earlier.

Consider again the law of diminishing return mentioned in the last section. One manifestation of that law in mining or agriculture would be the onset of declining output per unit of labour. In a Ricardian world this decline would be gradual, starting at time zero. A Malthusian model will exhibit a sudden fall in labour productivity once the boundary of available agricultural land or the limit of extractable minerals reserve is reached.

The economy described in this section is an island which has no contact with the outside world.[2] There are only two industries – *IND1* and *IND2*, denoting agriculture and food processing. As economists, we are not fettered by mundane aspects of reality and can assume that products of each industry are inputs to the other. The production relation may be written as follows:

A_1 tons of *IND1* + B_1 tons of *IND2* + L_1 number of workers
$$\rightarrow A \text{ tons of } INDI1,$$
A_2 tons of *IND1* + B_2 tons of *IND2* + L_2 number of workers
$$\rightarrow B \text{ tons of } IND2.$$

Here, A_1 tons of *IND1* and B_1 tons of *IND2* are combined to produce A tons of *IND1*. Likewise, A_2 tons of *IND1* and B_2 tons of *IND2* are used up in making B tons of *IND2*. The surplus generated in production is paid out in wages, or profits; we need not distinguish between them for the purposes of our exercise.

$$A_1 + A_2 \leqslant A \quad \text{and} \quad B_1 + B_2 \leqslant B.$$

The inequality holds if labour input is non-zero. Introducing prices p_a and p_b for commodities *IND1* and *IND2* we obtain:

$$A_1 p_a + B_1 p_b + L_1 W = A p_a \tag{1}$$

and

$$A_2 p_a + B_2 p_b + L_2 w = B p_b,$$

where w is the wage rate. Supposing that all workers are equally diligent and productive it follows that the total labour force, L, is employed and

$$L = L_1 + L_2.$$

Dividing the first equation by A and the second one by B,

$$a_1 p_a + b_1 p_b + \lambda_1 w = p_a$$

and $$\tag{2}$$

---

2. The purpose of our model is to focus on a very narrow and specific aspect of economics, the law of diminishing return. To achieve this objective, it is not necessary to represent reality through our assumptions and equations. It is sufficient to develop a construct, however artificial, which brings out the relevant arguments.

$$a_2p_a + {}^b{}_2p_b + \lambda_2 w = p_b,$$

where: $a_1 = A_1/A$, $b_1 = B_1/A$, $\lambda_1 = L_1/A$,
    $a_2 = A_2/B$, $b_2 = B_2/B$, $\lambda_2 = L_2/B$.

The coefficients λ_1 and λ_2 are measures of the productivity of labour. Here, λ_1 is the number of workers required to produce one unit of the output of agriculture, also called *IND1*; λ_2 is the number of workers needed to produce one unit of processed food, earlier referred to as *IND2*. If there is no technical change, the coefficients a_1 and b_2 would remain constant and the law of diminishing return in agriculture would manifest itself through an increasing λ_1.

If λ_1 increases gradually from the beginning, we would have a Ricardian case. If, on the other hand, λ_1 remains constant until the land boundary is reached and then starts increasing, the model would be Malthusian.

Let us assign some numbers and solve the set of equations (2) for prices, p_a and p_b, and wage, w. Since there are only two equations but three unknowns, one of the unknowns has to be designated the numeraire. The commodity chosen as a numeraire is arbitrary and for no particular reason we delegate that role to p_a and measure w and p_b relative to the price of agriculture and rewrite equation (2) as

$$p_b = -(\lambda_1/b_1)w + (1-a_1)/b_1,$$
$$w = (p_b - a_2)/\lambda_2 - (b_2/\lambda_2)p_b. \tag{3}$$

With some numbers given to the coefficients, we have:[3]

$$p_b = -(\lambda_1/0\cdot5)w + (1-0\cdot375)/(0\cdot5),$$
$$w = -(p_b - 0\cdot20)/\lambda_2 - (0\cdot30/\lambda_2)p_b. \tag{4}$$

As we indicated earlier, λ_2 is the number of workers needed to produce one unit of processed food and would remain constant if the level of technology remains the same. Set $\lambda_2 = 1$. But as population multiplies and better lands are used up, the productivity of labour in agriculture would decline in the Ricardian system. This effect is shown in the graph in Fig. 4.1[4], where two alternative manifestations of the diminishing return on labour are illustrated. For each alternative we solve equation (4) for w and p_b (see Figs. 4.2, 4.3).

As one would expect, if we postulate a sudden decline in productivity, movements in wages and prices are sudden. But a slow change in output per worker would have a more gradual effect. These are straightforward conclusions which may not remain so blantantly obvious if the model becomes complicated and very many additional interactions are

3. Numbers in this model are arbitrarily chosen to illustrate an argument although I do not doubt that, with some ingenuity, econometric techniques and other such chicanery these coefficients could be shown to follow as indubitable consequences of empirical observation.
4. In an appendix we produce tables of numbers used in plotting Fig. 4.1–4.12. To save space, these numbers are only shown at intervals of four periods.

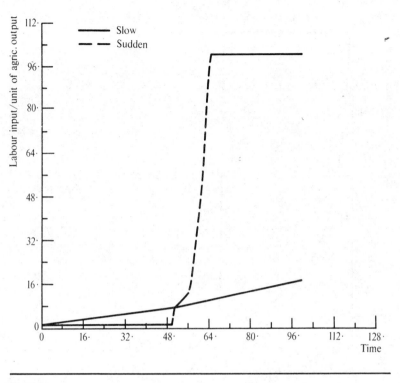

Fig. 4.1

introduced. We therefore stick to simple models which focus entirely on the difference between Malthusian and Ricardian scenarios.

Another formulation

We discussed a particular case in the last section and traced the movement of wages under different assumptions about how the law of diminishing return in agriculture sets in. Let us consider what might happen if we should choose an alternate system where the dynamic properties are more explicitly introduced. There are three variables, population, natural resources and capital, interacting with each other. The model as described below owes a great deal to Forrester [6].

5. Many of the variable names, *NRMM*, *ECIR* are the same as those appearing in [6], but they are used in a slightly different context. Initial conditions on natural resources, population and capital are taken from Forrester.

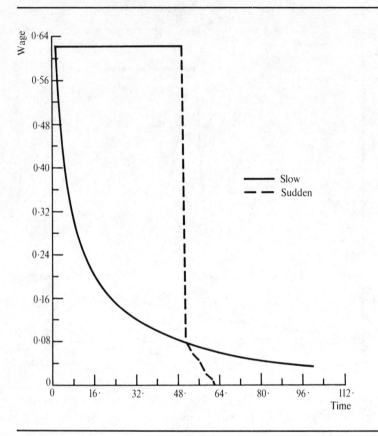

Fig. 4.2

$$\frac{\delta P}{\delta t} = BR - DR, \tag{5}$$

where: P = level of population,

BR = birth rate, and

DR = death rate.

$BR = P*BRN$ and $DR = P*DRN$.

We assume $BRN = 0 \cdot 04$ and $DRN = 0 \cdot 028$, constants derived using a population series from 1900 to 1970, the details of which are of no concern here.

$$\frac{\delta CI}{\delta T} = s * Y - \delta CI, \tag{6}$$

where: CI = capital stock,

s = savings ratio, assumed to be $0 \cdot 1$,

δ = depreciation rate, assumed to be $\frac{1}{40}$, and

Y = non-extractive output.

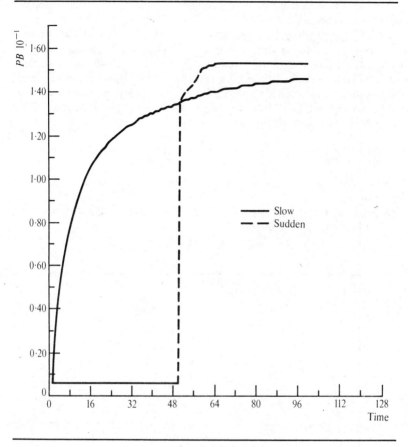

Fig. 4.3

$$\frac{\delta NR}{\delta t} = -NRUR, \tag{7}$$

where: NR=stock of natural resources remaining, and
$NRUR$=usage rate for these materials.

Natural resources and capital are used to produce non-extractive output, Y. Here, Y can be regarded as a proxy for material standard of living. This output follows a Cobb–Douglas-type production function so that

$$Y=(ECIR*P)^{\alpha}(NRUR)^{\beta}, \tag{8}$$

where: $\alpha = 0.6$, and $\beta = 1 - \alpha$.

The new variable $ECIR$ denotes the effective capital stock, out of the total amount CI, available to the non-extractive sector of the economy.

Part of the capital stock is tied up in getting natural resources out of the ground.

The amount which is so tied up depends on the nature of diminishing return postulated in the model. If it is argued that progressively it becomes more and more difficult to retrieve minerals because their quality deteriorates, we have a Ricardian world. If, on the other hand, the resources are regarded to be of uniform quality but finite quantity, the assumption is Malthusian. These ideas can be mathematically expressed in equation (9).

$$ECIR = \frac{CI}{P} *NREM, \tag{9}$$

where: $NREM$ = function of the fraction, $NRFR$, of natural resources remaining.

Depending on the shape of $NREM$, we have a Malthusian or a Ricardian case (see Fig. 4.4).

At any given point of time, we can obtain

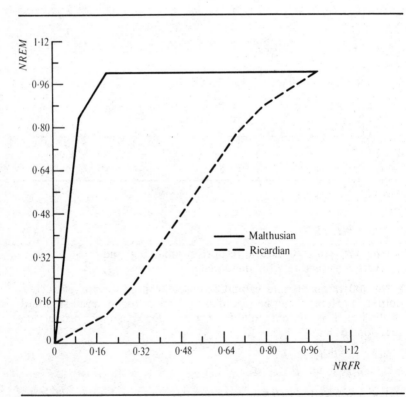

Fig. 4.4

$$NRFR = NR/NRI, \tag{10}$$

where: NRI = total stock of resources.

At the initial point in time, NR should, therefore, be equal to NRI.

The rate at which minerals are used up depends on the level of population and per-capita income, Y/P, and we can write,

$$NRUR = P * NRMM, \tag{11}$$

where: the multiplier $NRMM$=function of Y/P, a proxy for per-capita access to material goods manufactured using raw materials endowed by nature (see Fig. 4.5).

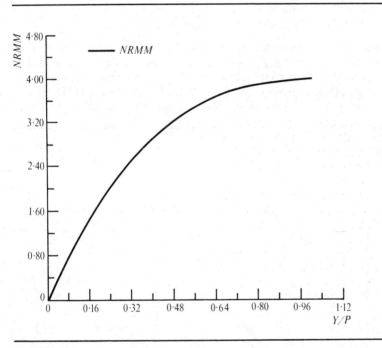

Fig. 4.5

In the above model we assumed constant return to scale and could therefore deduce prices by taking partial derivatives of Y.

$$PRNR=\text{price of natural resource}=\frac{\partial Y}{\partial NRUR}=\beta(\frac{ECIR*P}{NRUR})^{\alpha}$$

and

$$PRCAP=\text{price of capital}=\frac{\partial Y}{\partial (ECIR*P)}=\alpha(\frac{NRUR}{(ECIR*P)})^{\beta}.$$

Thus,

$$\frac{PRNR}{PRCAP} = \frac{\beta}{\alpha}(ECIR^*P/NRUR) \tag{12}$$

$$= \frac{\beta}{\alpha}\left(\frac{CI}{NRUR}^*NREM\right).$$

Wages can be obtained by noting that

$$WAGE = (1-s)Y/P. \tag{13}$$

Consider now a solution to the set of equations set out above with the following initial conditions:

$NRI = 900 \times 10^9 = $ total amount of natural resources available,
$CI = 0.4 \times 10^9 = $ initially endowed capital stock,
$P = 1.65 \times 10^9 = $ level of population at initial time.

These three values are required to solve the three differential equations in our model. Furthermore, we have to assign some number to the starting value for Y. Otherwise, $NRUR$ in equation (7) remains undefined. Here, $NRUR$ depends on $NRMM$ (see equation (11), which is a function of Y/P. We have already obtained the initial value of P and

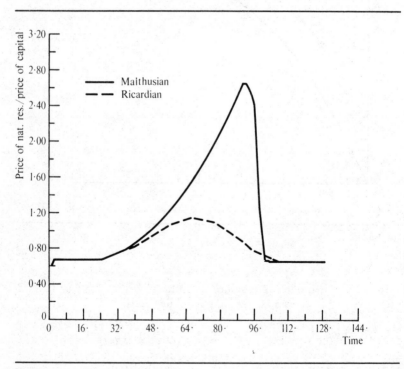

Fig. 4.6

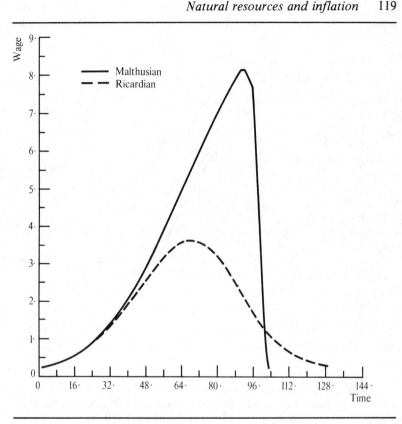

Fig. 4.7

we choose the starting point for Y at 0.394×10^9.

We are now almost ready to solve our model. There is only one more choice to be made. We have to define the shape of the function *NREM*. We solve the system for two possible *NREM*, shown in Fig. 4.4. Solutions pertaining to the (almost) Malthusian model are shown in heavy ink and those relating to the Ricardian version are depicted by broken lines (see Figs. 4.6, 4.7, 4.8).

In the Malthusian picture wages begin at 0.239 and rise to a maximum of 8.17 in ninety years, but then suddenly fall rapidly and reach a value of 0.536 in only ten more years. After another five years the collapse is complete. A similar abrupt effect is observed in *NRFR* which gradually declines for the first ninety-odd years, but then quickly plummets to almost zero. These dramatic results are inherent in the nature of the Malthusian assumption, that resources are all of the same quality but there is a rigidly defined finite amount available.

Ricardo allowed for different quality of resources, and he assumed

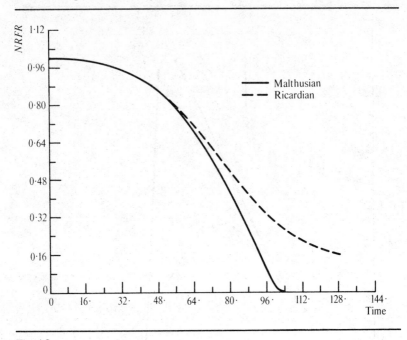

Fig. 4.8

that they would deteriorate with time, as the better and more easily accessible minerals and soils were progressively used up. Such a scenario leads to quite different results. Wages go up from 0.239 at $t = 1$ to 3.62 in sixty-seven years, but then falls gradually and slowly. Likewise, $NRFR$ does not show any abrupt change (see footnote 4 on p. 112).

Perhaps it would be worthwhile drawing attention to the interdependence between equations in this model. Consider Figs. 4.4 and 4.6, for example. Here, $PRCAP$ rises with time until the fraction of natural resources remaining, $NRFR$, constrains this ratio (equation (12) through the function $NREM$ in Fig. 4.4. Again, in Fig. 4.7 we see the effect of rising population on per-capita income. As population pressure grows, wages start going down and therefore the multiplier $NRMM$ declines (Fig. 4.5). This decline is even faster than the increase in P, causing $NRUR$ to plummet in accordance with equation (11). This effect is fed back into equation (12). The block diagram in Fig. 4.9 illustrates these interactions.

A question of numbers

The economics profession

has paid a good deal of attention to data ever since some unrecorded

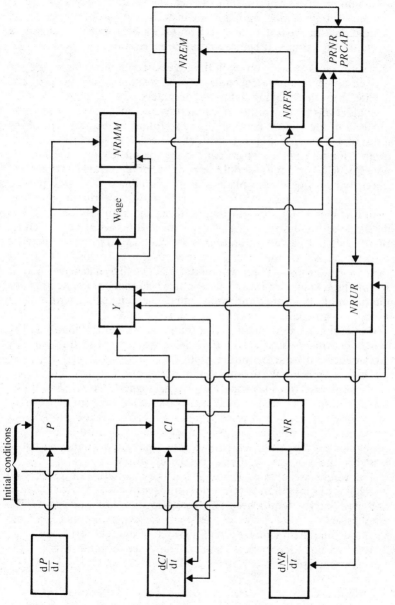

Fig. 4.9

genius had the original idea of finding out whether a live person weighs more, less, or the same as a dead person, not by speculating on the Vital Principles and the Intrinsic Substance of the Soul, as described in Aristotle and the Church Fathers, but by weighing a condemned criminal before and after execution [8, p. 393].

Our genius was hanged, but with the advent of computers his legacy was revived and economists began dispensing wisdom gained by gazing at gleams from the blinking lights of computers.

Suggestions that scarcity of natural resources may some day threaten our way of life and we may even have to follow in the footsteps of the dinosaurs do cause a great deal of concern. Given the record of destruction and pillage which constitutes the history of mankind, it is not clear why our demise should be a matter of regret, at least to the rest of the living beings on this planet. But such doubts we are not supposed to entertain. We would like to presume that our continuation on earth, even it is merely by proxy through future generations, to be almost as desirable as the destruction of our enemies. It is inevitable, therefore, that we should pay attention to oracles, clairvoyants and econometric forecasters. We are told that if 'the present growth trends . . . continue unchanged, the limits to growth on this planet will be reached sometime within the next hundred years' [9]. We also hear that 'the application of a modicum of intelligence and good management in dealing with current problems can enable economic growth to continue for a considerable period of time, to the benefit, rather than the detriment, of mankind' [7]. It may reasonably be asked if our model in the previous section can allay anxieties about what the future holds.

The answer is no. We do not attempt to forecast, and even if we did try to do so the balance of probability would suggest that we should fail. First point first. We wish to demonstrate the qualitative difference in the trajectories of wages and prices which follow from two scenarios, one postulated by Malthus and the other one by Ricardo. Ours is a pedagogic exercise designed to illustrate a particular point and not to establish the correctness of any specific hypothesis.

The results we obtain, although not the qualitative differences on which it is our intention to focus, are quite sensitive to coefficient values and it is instructive to keep this limitation in clear perspective. To emphasise this point, let us ponder the wage trajectory obtained from the model in the previous section for two different (almost) Malthusian *NREM* versus *NRFR* graphs shown below (see footnote 4 on p. 112). Let us designate the alternatives as *MLTHUS1* and *MLTHUS2* (see Figs. 4.10, 4.11).

Consider case *MLTHUS1*. Starting from 0·239, wage rises to a maximum of 8·17 in about ninety years and then plummets to almost zero in the next fifteen years. In the second case, starting from the same value, the maximum is 7·66, reached in eighty-five years. The decline is slow for the next ten years, although scaling factors obscure this phenomenon in Fig. 4.11 and then suddenly wage plunges to zero. Let us

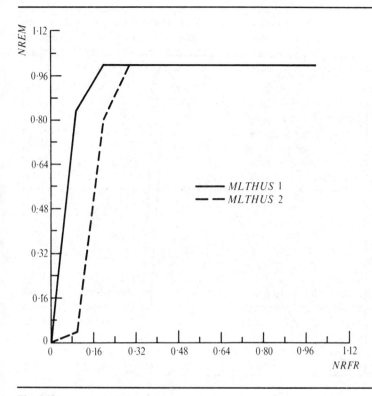

Fig. 4.10

suppose that the real world was more accurately described by *MLTHUS1*, but we assumed in our model that *MLTHUS2* was the appropriate description of resources constraint. We made this mistake because the available data did not contain sufficient information for us to be able to choose between *MLTHUS1* and *MLTHUS2*. In a situation of this sort, our model could indeed be very misleading. We would assume a breathing period of ten years after the peak is reached only to discover too late that no such respite could be hoped for.

Now let us come to the second point. Could we impart some empirical basis to our model? The simple answer is that it would be a difficult task well beyond the scope of a short chapter in an anthology. Even if we did undertake a major project on collecting data, there would remain grave doubts whether such an attempt could succeed. Controlled experiments being impossible in economics, we have to rely on interpreting existing data according to our own ideological and methodological bias.

Estimates of the energy content of uranium reserves vary from 190×10^{15} Kcal to $410\,000 \times 10^{15}$ Kcal, depending on one's judgement concerning the state of current and near-current technology [17]. Not

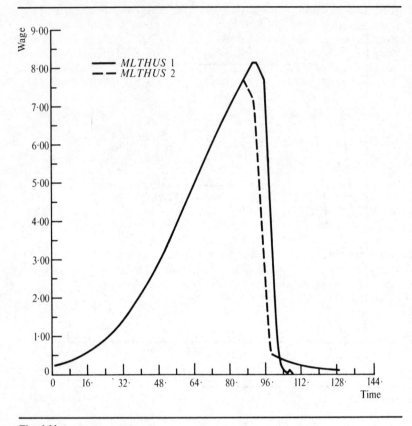

Fig. 4.11

everybody would concur in the statement that the 'earth and technology can provide food for a population of 40 to 50 billion' [15, p. 161]. We already noted how sensitive our conclusions are to the choice of function *NREM* versus *NRFR*. If the data available to us are subject to widely different kinds of interpretation, empirical work on the model is unlikely to be useful. H. J. Barnett and C. Morse [1] studied US data to obtain the effect of *NRFR* on non-extractive output. Their conclusions are not sufficiently positive to allow for the estimation of the exact relationship in Fig. 4.4. There are broadly three sets of problems: (a) choice of a proxy, (b) choice of period and (c) statistical techniques. Let us suppose that we take data from the coal industry. Could we use this data as a proxy for all extractive output? If not, what indicator do we use? The time period over which the data are collected could also colour our perception. If it is a period of rapid technological growth which may not be sustained for ever, we may draw wrong conclusions looking into the future by extrapolating the past. The last difficulty lies in the choice of statistical techniques, and we consider the problem below.

Let us look at Fig. 4.5. Here, *NRMM* is depicted as an increasing function of per-capita output. But what should be the exact shape of this function? Suppose we use UK data (1948–75) for industrial production per-capita and total primary fuel consumption per person as proxies for *Y/P* and *NRUR/P*, respectively (data from [3] and [4]). It then follows from equation (11) that a graph of primary fuel consumption per-capita (*FUELINPUT*) versus industrial production per-capita (*INDPROD*) should correspond to *NRMM* in Fig. 4.5. We produce this relationship below after scaling *FUELINPUT* and *INDPROD* to be 100 in 1970. The scaling factor is purely for convenience in representation and no significance should be attached to it (see Fig. 4.12).

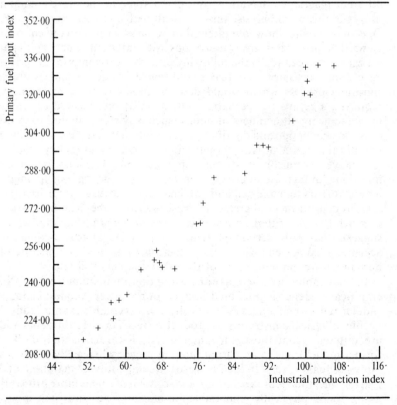

Fig. 4.12

We now have to ask ourselves a number of questions. What line do we draw through points in the above picture? How do we extrapolate the graph for values of *INDPROD* outside the range shown? We leave the reader to contemplate problems of measurement which we have raised but cannot solve.

Conclusion

Life would be simple if words had unique meanings universally acceptable. That, alas, is not the case and one has to contend with a world where impressions that words make have much to do with the context in which they are uttered. Inflation is a term which conjures up visions of different things to different people at different times at different places. We have not considered some of the more common usages of this word because they are dealt with elsewhere in this book. One may wonder how our definition squares with the conventional view: that price rises are synonymous with inflation. The significant aspect of this attitude is the following underlying assumption. If prices keep rising, insecurity, confusion and fear could set in, unleashing a spiralling process which would destroy the entire price mechanism, requiring a return to the barter system. In a sophisticated economy manufacturing all manners of goods, such a system is bound to cause chaos in production and distribution. The notion that there is something unnatural about a situation where money income and real income do not move in unison is strongly ingrained in much discussion on inflation. An increase in prices, even when real wage is going up, might tempt workers to make demands which over-compensate for price rises, thereby causing an even greater increase in prices. The clear implication of much that is written on prices is a view of human behaviour which suggests that only certain particular trajectories of real income are acceptable. What empirical reason there is to paint such a picture of human nature, perhaps some of the other chapters will tell.

In this chapter, we also make an assumption about human nature. No empirical evidence is presented because ours is a very modest claim: a sudden fall in real wages is politically less acceptable than a gradual decline. Physical constraints on production faced in a Malthusian world are different from those encountered in a Ricardian situation. The former model leads to an abrupt jump in wages; whereas the latter is a more gradual process. In the first case the competition to maintain total real income, total real expenditure and/or total output is more probably going to be physically impossible to sustain. The Ricardian model provides a more continuous picture, possibly politically more viable. According to the definition of inflation adopted in this chapter constraints on production placed by the scarcity of natural resources are more likely to lead to inflation in a Malthusian world than in a Ricardian scenario. The question as to which model is closer to reality is a matter of fact that we have not made any attempt to ascertain here. Exactly how many years there remain before the onset of declining wages owing to difficulty in extracting minerals and cultivating the soil are questions of measurement that we have not attempted to undertake. Nor do we know for sure that such measurements are indeed possible.

It may reasonably be asked what all this has to do with policy. Nothing directly. Policies must emerge through discussion and debate about priorities and possibilities. To the extent that by sharply focusing on alternatives open to us, we improve the quality of such debates, a model-building exercise is helpful.

If there is anxiety that perhaps oil would run out in the next forty years, decisions would be required about substitutes to be developed. Suppose the alternative is shale oil costing $5 per barrel as opposed to the 10–50 c. a barrel extraction cost (not the posted price) of fossil fuel oil from the Middle East. In a Malthusian world the production cost of fossil fuel would not go up until almost the very last moment when this resource suddenly runs out. There are two possibilities: (a) either the price of present fossil fuel oil should equal the marginal cost of extraction, or (b) it should include a royalty element to reflect expected appreciation in the price of oil left in the ground. In the former case an investor in shale oil would be at a disadvantage until present sources almost dry out. In the latter situation, expected appreciation in the price of oil left in the ground would depend on whether alternative sources are developed. It would, therefore, be an attractive proposition for present owners of this resource to drive competition away by foregoing their own royalty for a period of time. In either event, probably no one would risk money on developing the necessary plant and machinery to make oil from shale. This could lead to an abrupt transition with undesirable consequences. Government policy providing a minimum floor price to encourage a smoother transition may be called for. In a Ricardian scenario, the extraction cost of fossil oil would gradually rise as reserves dwindle. There would come a time before fossil oil runs out when the shale substitute should become competitive. The policy implications are clearly different.

Much depends on (a) the exact nature of the Ricardian scenario, (b) the time delay involved in fabricating commercial plants for squeezing out oil from shale, and (c) the degree of tolerance obtaining in society for dislocation entailed in the changeover period. Our discussion cannot resolve all these issues but it can provide an approach, a framework, for partial analysis.

Appendix

Table 4.1 Time series for l_1, *Wage* and P_b for slow and sudden decline in labour productivity.

Time	l_1		Wage		P_b	
	Slow	Sudden	Slow	Sudden	Slow	Sudden
1	1·00	1·0	0·622	0·622	0·006	0·006
5	1·48	1·0	0·403	0·622	0·058	0·006
9	1·96	1·0	0·298	0·622	0·083	0·006
13	2·44	1·0	0·236	0·622	0·098	0·006
17	2·92	1·0	0·196	0·622	0·107	0·006
21	3·40	1·0	0·167	0·622	0·114	0·006
25	3·88	1·0	0·146	0·622	0·119	0·006
29	4·36	1·0	0·129	0·622	0·123	0·006
33	4·84	1·0	0·116	0·622	0·126	0·006
37	5·32	1·0	0·105	0·622	0·129	0·006
41	5·80	1·0	0·097	0·622	0·131	0·006
45	6·28	1·0	0·089	0·622	0·133	0·006
49	6·76	1·0	0·083	0·622	0·134	0·006
53	7·48	9·0	0·075	0·062	0·136	0·139
57	8·28	15·0	0·067	0·037	0·138	0·145
61	9·08	50·0	0·061	0·011	0·139	0·151
65	9·68	100·0	0·056	0·001	0·140	0·153
69	10·68	100·0	0·052	0·001	0·142	0·153
73	11·48	100·0	0·043	0·001	0·142	0·153
77	12·28	100·0	0·045	0·001	0·143	0·153
81	13·08	100·0	0·042	0·001	0·144	0·153
85	13·88	100·0	0·040	0·001	0·144	0·153
89	14·68	100·0	0·038	0·001	0·145	0·153
93	15·48	100·0	0·035	0·001	0·145	0·153
97	16·28	100·0	0·034	0·001	0·146	0·153

Table 4.2 *NREM* as a function of *NRFR* (Figs. 4.4 and 4.10)

NRFR	NREM		NREM	
	Malthusian	Ricardian	MLTHUS 1	MLTHUS 2
0·0	0·0	0·0	0·0	0·0
0·1	0·84	0·05	0·84	0·04
0·2	1·0	0·11	1·0	0·80
0·3	1·0	0·21	1·0	1·0
0·4	1·0	0·36	1·0	1·0
0·5	1·0	0·50	1·0	1·0
0·6	1·0	0·64	1·0	1·0
0·7	1·0	0·78	1·0	1·0
0·8	1·0	0·88	1·0	1·0
0·9	1·0	0·94	1·0	1·0
1·0	1·0	1·0	1·0	1·0

Table 4.3   *NRMM* as a function of Y/P (Fig. 4.5)

Y/P	$NRMM$
0·0	0·00
0·1	1·00
0·2	1·80
0·3	2·40
0·4	2·90
0·5	3·30
0·6	3·60
0·7	3·80
0·8	3·90
0·9	3·95
1·0	4·00

Table 4.4   Time series for *PRNR/PRCAP*, *Wage* and *NRFR* in two cases: Malthusian and Ricardian (Figs. 4.6–4.8)

Time	PRNR/PRCAP		Wage		NRFR	
	Malthusian	Ricardian	Malthusian	Ricardian	Malthusian	Ricardian
1	0·610	0·610	0·239	0·239	1·00	1·00
5	0·678	0·678	0·275	0·275	0·996	0·998
9	0·678	0·678	0·352	0·351	0·995	0·995
13	0·678	0·678	0·451	0·448	0·991	0·992
17	0·678	0·678	0·577	0·570	0·987	0·987
21	0·678	0·678	0·739	0·724	0·980	0·980
25	0·687	0·680	0·943	0·917	0·971	0·971
29	0·731	0·723	1·17	1·12	0·960	0·960
33	0·770	0·760	1·44	1·37	0·945	0·946
37	0·804	0·791	1·78	1·65	0·927	0·929
41	0·878	0·838	2·13	1·95	0·905	0·909
45	0·951	0·900	2·53	2·25	0·879	0·884
49	1·03	0·955	2·96	2·56	0·848	0·856
53	1·12	1·01	3·43	2·88	0·812	0·824
57	1·23	1·07	3·93	3·16	0·771	0·788
61	1·33	1·11	4·45	3·38	0·725	0·748
65	1·47	1·14	4·98	3·55	0·673	0·704
69	1·61	1·14	5·51	3·59	0·615	0·658
73	1·77	1·13	6·02	3·51	0·553	0·609
77	1·94	1·10	6·52	3·35	0·485	0·559
81	2·13	1·05	6·99	3·10	0·413	0·508
85	2·33	0·383	7·45	2·78	0·336	0·458
89	2·54	0·917	7·88	2·42	0·259	0·410
93	2·61	0·838	8·05	2·01	0·170	0·366
97	2·04	0·768	6·80	1·60	0·081	0·325
101	0·742	0·727	1·42	1·25	0·012	0·290
105	0·651	0·685	0·051	1·01	0·001	0·260
109	0·651	0·657	0·002	0·799	0·000	0·234
113	0·651	0·657	0·001	0·619	0·000	0·213
117	0·651	0·660	0·000	0·486	0·000	0·195
121	0·651	0·659	0·000	0·401	0·000	0·181
125	0·651	0·659	0·000	0·331	0·000	0·168

Table 4.5   (Fig. 4.11)

Time	Wage	
	MLTHUS 1	*MLTHUS 2*
1	0·239	0·239
5	0·275	0·275
9	0·352	0·352
13	0·451	0·451
17	0·577	0·577
21	0·739	0·739
25	0·943	0·943
29	1·17	1·17
33	1·44	1·44
37	1·78	1·78
41	2·13	2·13
45	2·53	2·53
49	2·96	2·96
53	3·43	3·43
57	3·93	3·93
61	4·45	4·45
65	4·98	4·98
69	5·51	5·51
73	6·02	6·02
77	6·52	6·52
81	6·99	6·99
85	7·45	7·45
89	7·88	7·42
93	8·05	5·83
97	6·80	1·58
101	1·42	0·446
105	0·051	0·344
109	0·002	0·268
113	0·001	0·210
117	0·000	0·166
121	0·000	0·132
125	0·000	0·106

Table 4.6 Primary fuel input and index of industrial production (Fig. 4.12)

Year	INDPRINOX	FUEL INPUT
1948	50·5	215·4
1949	53·8	220·4
1950	57·1	224·5
1951	58·4	232·6
1952	56·6	231·6
1953	60·2	235·3
1954	63·1	245·6
1955	66·4	249·9
1956	66·9	253·6
1957	68·1	246·9
1958	67·5	248·6
1959	70·9	246·1
1960	75·8	265·2
1961	76·7	265·5
1962	77·4	274·1
1963	79·7	284·8
1964	86·5	286·7
1965	89·1	298·5
1966	90·6	298·3
1967	91·7	297·5
1968	97·2	308·7
1969	99·8	320·3
1970	100·0	331·4
1971	100·4	325·7
1972	102·7	332·7
1973	110·2	347·9
1974	106·3	332·2
1975	101·0	319·7

References

1. **Barnett, H. J. and Morse C.,** *Scarcity and Growth.* Johns Hopkins Univ. Press, Baltimore, 1977.
2. **Baumal, W. J.,** *Economic Theory and Operations Analysis,* 3rd edn. Prentice-Hall, London, 1972.
3. **Central Statistical Office,** *Economic Trends* Supplement, HMSO, London, 1975.
4. **Central Statistical Office,** *Economic Trends* Supplement, HMSO, London 1976.
5. **Chakravarty, S. P.,** 'Econometric models: mathematical expressions of personal prejudices?' *IEEE Transactions on Systems Man and Cybernetics,* SMC, 7, 462–5, June 1977.
6. **Forrester, J. W.,** *World Dynamics.* Wright-Allen Press, Cambridge, Mass. 1971.
7. **Kahn, H.,** *The Next 2000 Years.* William and Morrow, New York, 1972.
8. **Macdonald, D.,** *Against the American Grain.* Vintage Books, New York, 1962.
9. **Meadows, D. et al.,** *The Limits to Growth.* Earth Island, London, 1972.
10. **Malthus, T.,** *An Essay on Population,* 6th edn. Ward Lock, London, 1862.
11. **Malthus, T.;** *An Essay on the Principle of Population,* 7th edn. Reeves and Turner, London 1872.
12. **New York Times,** 'The real economic threat', *New York Times,* 22.9.1974.
13. **New York Times,** *New York Times Magazine,* 15.12.1974.
14. **Radner, R.,** 'Equilibrium under uncertainty', *Econometrica,* **36,** 31–58, 1968.
15. **Revelle, R.,** 'Food and population' *Scientific American,* **231,** 161–70, Sept., 1974.

16. **Ricardo, D.,** *Principles of Political Economy and Taxation.* Bell, London, 1925.
17. **Robinson, C. and Crook, E. M.,** 'Is there a world energy crisis?', *National Westminster Bank Review*, May 1973.
18. **Roscoe, T.,** *The Work of Jonathan Swift*, Vol. 2. Bolan, Covent Garden, 1859.
19. **Shubik, M.,** 'The general equilibrium model is incomplete and not adequate for the reconciliation of micro and macroeconomic theory', *Kyklos*, **28**, 545–73, 1975.
20. **Smith, A.,** *The Wealth of Nations.* Penguin, Middlesex, 1970.
21. **Turvey, R.,** 'Some aspects of the theory of inflation in a closed economy', *Economic Journal*, 534–5, 1951.
22. **Zinn, H.,** *The Politics of History.* Beacon Press, Boston, 1970.

Chapter 5

International aspects of inflation

George McKenzie

Over the past several years the preponderance of theoretical and empirical investigations into the causes of inflation have emphasized the role of monetary factors. This methodological bias is particularly apparent in discussions of the transmission of inflation from one country to another. In a world of free trade and unrestricted capital flows, it is argued that an increase or decrease in the money supply in one country will have secondary financial implications in other nations, and as a result affect the level of economic activity and prices worldwide. There is no doubt that there is much truth in this proposition, as I shall argue below. Indeed, the laws of supply and demand which every novice economics student learns are sufficient to show that if there is an increase in consumer spending power due to an increase in the money stock, and if the world economy is operating at full capacity, then prices will invariably rise.

However, as I plan to argue in this paper, while money matters in a very fundamental sense, it is not the only factor which influences the rate of inflation throughout the world. We must also consider real variables such as: (a) the rate of change in productivity; (b) the state of economic activity at any point in time, i.e. whether there is full or excess capacity; (c) variations in tariffs or import quotas; (d) exogenous shocks to the system such as the policy-induced increases in the price of petroleum or 'acts of God' which cause various crop shortages. Only when such events are fully considered can the process of inflation be properly understood and the requisite policy responses properly formulated. As we shall see the so-called monetary approach does not offer this possibility since its proponents claim to offer the 'only' explanation of worldwide inflation. However, having said this, I do not propose to provide a detailed survey of the rapidly growing body of literature on this subject. Useful surveys are referred to in the Reference Section at the end of this chapter (cf. [1, 8, 9, 14, 15, 17]). My aim, in contrast, will be to examine some of the analytical problems inherent in the study of inflation and how it may be transmitted from one nation to another.

A simple monetary model

The virtue of starting our discussion with an explanation of the monetary approach is that it forces us to focus our attention on the operation of the foreign exchange market. This, to my mind, is the key pedagogic message of this approach. The market for foreign exchange provides a significant channel through which the monetary policies of one country may be transmitted worldwide. Let us examine the processes whereby this may occur within the following simple framework.

Let us suppose that there are two countries, Europa and America, whose currencies are, respectively, the denero and the dollar. Each country produces a specific commodity, say cloth in Europa and wine in America, and prices always adjust so that full employment is maintained. Neither country has a very sophisticated banking system: the denero and the dollar are the only financial assets and these are always minted in gold. However, there does exist a foreign exchange market where specialist dealers buy and sell dollar and denero coins for a commission.

Let us further suppose that the authorities in both countries do not allow the exchange rate between deneros and dollars to vary. In order to achieve this result, the authorities in each country are obliged to maintain inventories of the other's currency. For example, suppose that there is an excess supply of dollars on the foreign exchange market. The American authorities will then purchase this excess in exchange for gold deneros. The result is a decrease in the number of dollars in the hands of the public but an increase in the quantity of deneros in circulation. The overall picture is that of a gold-specie flow exchange rate system which modern monetary economists have argued forms the historical basis for their approach (cf. [5,6]).

Now let us examine a particular case in order to see how inflationary pressures may be transmitted from one country to another. Assume initially that the world economy is in complete equilibrium, in particular that there are no international trade imbalances. Then suppose that the authorities in Europa mint coins from some recently mined gold and that they place these in circulation by making lump-sum payments to each European citizen. As a result each person will be wealthier and thus will attempt to increase his or her consumption of both home-produced cloth and imported wine. This has two implications. First, since the output of both commodities is already at the full employment level, any increased demand will lead to higher prices worldwide. Second, the increased spending in Europa will produce a balance-of-payments deficit: that is, its citizens will be spending more on goods produced abroad than foreigners will be spending on goods produced in Europa. The result is an excess supply of deneros on the foreign exchange market. Under the assumed institutional arrangement, this excess will be melted down and reminted into dollars. The result is a decrease in the wealth of Europeans but an increase in the wealth of Americans. This development then sets in motion a secondary adjustment process. Spending on all goods, including importables, will fall in Europa but increase in America, a process which will continue until finally the trade imbalance is completely eliminated and full equilibrium fully restored.

The above analysis can be better understood if we set out a simple algebraic model (this is a special case of the more general model described in [13]). Suppose that the structure of the European and American economies can be described by the following six equations:

Europa	America
$E_{11}(t) = m_{11}[W_1(t-1)]$	$E_{21}(t) = m_{21}[W_2(t-1)]$,
$E_{12}(t) = m_{12}[W_1(t-1)]$,	$E_{22}(t) = m_{22}[W_2(t-1)]$,
$M_1(t) = m_{13}[W_1(t-1)]$,	$M_2(t) = m_{23}[W_2(t-1)]$,

where $E_{ij}(t)$ is the expenditure by country i on the goods produced by country j in period t (Europa=1; America=2), $M_i(t)$ the demand for cash balances by country i in period t, and $W_i(t)$ the total wealth of country i at the end of period t equals the value of income received during the period plus the stock on money held:

$$W_1(t)=p_1(t) . S_1 + M_1(t), \tag{1}$$

$$W_2(t)=p_2(t) . S_2 + M_2(t), \tag{2}$$

where S_1 and S_2 are the full-employment outputs of cloth and wine and $p_1(t)$ and $p_2(t)$ their respective prices during period t. Consumer decisions are thus relatively simple within this model. Consumer expenditure on wine and cloth and their holdings of money during period t depend simply upon the holdings of wealth held at the end of the previous period.

Now if commodity prices always adjust so that there is no excess supply or demand for cloth or wine, then the following two equations must always hold:

$$E_{11}(t)+E_{21}(t)=p_1(t) . S_1, \tag{3}$$

$$E_{12}(t)+E_{22}(t)=p_2(t) . S_2. \tag{4}$$

As indicated earlier, the key aspect of the monetary approach is the relationship between activity in the foreign exchange market, changes in wealth and thus spending patterns. Consider the following. Substitute Europe's balance of trade:

$$B(t) = E_{21}(t) - E_{12}(t)$$

into the expression for the current value of its output:

$$p_1(t) . S_1 = E_{11}(t) + E_{21}(t) \tag{5}$$

to obtain:

$$B(t)=p_1(t) . S_1 - E_{11}(t) - E_{12}(t). \tag{6}$$

This expression is the well-known relationship between a country's balance of trade, value of output and expenditure (i.e. absorption). (cf. [5]). We also know that current total expenditure on commodities plus the current demand for nominal cash balances $M(t)$ equals the nominal value of wealth inherited from the previous period:

$$M(t)+E_{11}(t)+E_{12}(t)=M(t-1)+S_1 p_1(t-1). \tag{7}$$

Equations (5)–(7) can now be combined to yield:

$$B(t)=M(t)-M(t-1)+p_1(t)S_1-p_1(t-1)S_1$$
$$=W(t)-W(t-1). \tag{8}$$

That is, changes in Europa's wealth equal its balance of trade surplus or deficit.

Finally, it is useful to define a variable called world wealth $W_w(t)$ which equals:

$$[W_1(0)+A_1]+[W_2(0)+A_2]=W_1(t)+W_2(t)$$

where $W_1(0)+W_2(0)$ is the initial, equilibrium value of world wealth and A_i represents the discretionary increase in i's money stock carried out by its authorities.

We are now in a position to construct a model consisting of three equations and three unknowns, $p_1(t)$, $p_2(t)$ and $W_1(t)$:

$$p_1(t).S_1=(m_{11}-m_{21})W_1(t-1)+m_{21}[W_1(0)+W_2(0)+A_1+A_2], \tag{9}$$

$$p_2(t).S_2=(m_{12}-m_{22})W_1(t-1)+m_{22}[W_1(0)+W_2(0)+A_1+A_2], \tag{10}$$

$$W_1(t)=(1-m_{12}-m_{21})W_1(t-1)+m_{21}[W_1(0)+W_2(0)+A_1+A_2]. \tag{11}$$

This system may now be solved for the short-run and long-run effects of changes in Europa's money supply. Let us examine the latter first since it is primarily the long run with which the monetary approach is concerned. As shown in the appendix to this chapter, the full-equilibrium effects of variations in A are as follows:

$$p_1=(m_{21}m_{12}+m_{21}m_{11})[W_1(0)+W_2(0)+A_1+A_2]/S_1, \tag{12}$$

$$p_2=(m_{22}m_{12}+m_{21}m_{12})[W_1(0)+W_2(0)+A_1+A_2]/S_2, \tag{13}$$

$$W_1=[m_{21}/(m_{12}+m_{21})][W_1(0)+W_2(0)+A]/S_2. \tag{14}$$

In other words, any increase in A will lead to proportional increases in p_1 and p_2: both countries are inextricably linked. Even though Europa increased its national money stock, the institutional framework supporting the fixed-*exchange* regime guarantees that the American money stock must increase as well. Inflationary pressures are thus transmitted from one country to another. This has led Laidler and Parkin, in their recent survey of the inflation literature, to conclude that the only way adequately to study a worldwide inflation is via an aggregate worldwide model. They write [8]:

> In a world of fixed exchanges the closed economy of the quantity theory models . . ., in which the time path of prices is determined in the long run by the time path of the money supply, is not an individual country. Its appropriate empirical analogue is the aggregate of all

those individual countries that are linked to one another by fixed exchange rates. Thus the relevant money supply, as far as the determination of prices is concerned, is the sum of the domestic money supplies of each national economy (converted to a common unit at the fixed exchange rates); its time path is determined as a result of the combined monetary policies of the individual countries.

The role of other variables

However, there may be many slips between cup and lip. For one thing, as Scandinavian economists have frequently emphasized (cf. [8]), changes in productivity will affect the rate of inflation. For example, let us re-examine equations (12) and (13). If output per worker in both countries increases at the same rate as $[W_1(0) + W_2(0) + A]$, then p_1 and p_2 will be constant in the long run and will appear completely independent of changes in the money stock. Or, as another example, assume that output per worker in Europa and $[W_1(0) + W_2(0) + A]$ increase at the same rate. The price of European output will remain constant, but as can be seen from equation (13), the price of American output will increase. In other words we have paradoxical result that America will appear as the source of inflationary pressures, even though the money stock in Europa has increased. More sophisticated versions of this model would distinguish between three sectors: those producing exportable commodities, importables and non-traded goods. If each had different rates of productivity change, then it would, of course, be extremely difficult to separate the influence of real from monetary factors.

This conclusion becomes even more apparent if we return again to our simple model and examine the *short-run* implications of an increase in Europa's money stock. From equations (9)–(11) we may derive the short-run effects of an increase in A_1 as follows:

$$p_1(1) = \{m_{11}[W_1(0)+A_1]+m_{21}[W_2(0)+A_2]\}/S_1, \tag{15}$$

$$P_2(1) = \{m_{12}[W_1(0)+A_1]+m_{22}[W_2(0)+A_2]\}/S_2, \tag{16}$$

$$W_1(1) = (1-m_{12})[W_1(0)+A_1]+m_{21}[W_2(0)+A_2]. \tag{17}$$

Unlike the long-run results discussed above, in the short run rates of inflation may differ in the two countries. To determine this let us examine the effect of alternate increases in A_1 and A_2 on the Laspeyres price index for Europa.

$$CPI_1 = \frac{p_1(1)X_{11}(0)+p_2(1)X_{12}(0)}{p_1(0)X_{11}(0)+p_2(0)X_{12}(0)}, \tag{18}$$

where $X_{ij}(0)$ represents the initial quantity of commodity j consumed by country i and serves as the 'weight' for the appropriate price in the index. If we assume that the initial prices $p_1(0)$ and $p_2(0)$ are both one, then

$$CPI_1 = \frac{m_{11}p_1(1) + m_{12}p_2(1)}{m_{11} + m_{12}}. \tag{19}$$

It should be noted that $m_{11}/(m_{11} + m_{12})$ and $m_{12}/(m_{11} + m_{12})$ are, respectively, country one's propensities to consume cloth and wine out of total wealth. Then, by substituting equations (15) and (16) for $p_1(1)$ and $p_2(1)$, we obtain:

$$CPI_1 = \frac{m_{11}}{S_1(m_{11} + m_{12})} \{m_{11}[W_1(0) + A_1] + m_{21}[W_2(0) + A_2]\} +$$
$$+ \frac{m_{11}}{S_2(m_{11} + m_{12})} [m_{12}(W_1(0) + A_1) + m_{22}(W_2(0) + A_2)]. \tag{20}$$

If we differentiate equation (20) with respect to A_1 and then with respect to A_2, we obtain:

$$\frac{\partial CPI_1}{\partial A_1} = \frac{m_{11}}{S_1(m_{11} + m_{12})} m_{11} + \frac{m_{12}}{S_2(m_{11} + m_{12})} m_{12}, \tag{21}$$

$$\frac{\partial CPI_1}{\partial A_2} = \frac{m_{11}}{S_1(m_{11} + m_{12})} m_{21} + \frac{m_{12}}{S_2(m_{11} + m_{12})} m_{22}. \tag{22}$$

If $m_{11} < m_{21}$ and $m_{12} < m_{22}$, we find that an increase in Europa's money stock will lead to a lower rate of European inflation (in the short run) than an equal increase in the American money stock. The same result would have occurred if we had examined the American price index CPI_2. In other words, in order to study the process of international inflation, we need to have information about structural parameters relating to the real sector.

Although our analysis so far has been extraordinarily simple, it does enable us to cast doubts on the approach which a number of economists have taken to the study of inflation. For example, Brunner and Meltzer [2] have argued that it is useful to decompose any price change into two components:

1. a *persistent* component, which they claim arises from financial shocks arising from fiscal and monetary actions;
2. a *transitory* component, which arises from changes in real variables.

However, this fails to recognize that each country may experience persistent changes in its productivity and, as we have already seen, this possibility will influence the rate of inflation. It should be pointed out that changes in productivity may not be positive but could be negative over prolonged periods if there exist poor industrial relations and, as a result, increasing worker dissatisfaction.

Furthermore, the emphasis of the monetary approach on inflation as purely a long-run phenomena needs to be questioned. For example, consider the definition presented by Laidler and Parkin [8] in the first sentences of their survey article: 'Inflation in a process of continuously rising prices, or equivalently of a continuously falling value of money.

Its importance stems from the pervasive role played by money in a modern economy.' While I do not deny the potential importance of monetary factors in the generation and transmission of inflation, defining inflation as involving only *continuously* rising prices appears to me to be highly dubious. In practice, we only know the short-run. There is at any point of time such a great lack of information about the operation of any national economy that it is virtually impossible to distinguish between price rises which ultimately turn out to be transitory from those which are persistent. From a practical point of view it would be rare if we were able to experience periods over which monetary or productivity growth were continuous enough to generate continuous and uniform price rises. The implications of this can easily be seen if we return to equations (15) and (16) which indicated the short-run price effects of an increase in Europa's money stock. Without knowledge of the parameters, policy makers, seeing the inflation rate higher in America than Europa, might conclude that the problem really is due to events in the former country, not the latter. The proper approach to the study of inflation should be concerned with the sources of rising prices and not solely those adjudged to be persistent in some sense.

Let us pursue this analysis a bit further by introducing two additional, essentially short-run factors which affect the rate of inflation: (a) expectations as to future commodity prices, and (b) the market environment in which firms set their prices.

Suppose that we find ourselves in a position where prices have been rising at a faster rate than in the past. This may be due to either a monetary expansion or perhaps an increase in the price of some basic raw material such as petroleum. At this stage consumers and producers will begin to wonder whether the rate of price increase will continue into the future. Most likely, they will form their expectations by extrapolating from recent events and as a result they will begin to adjust their behaviour to take into account even higher prices (they believe) in the future. As a result both consumers and producers will increase their current expenditure by reducing their stock of saving in an attempt to buy goods and services before prices rise even further. However, this process is self-reinforcing; at least in the short run the increased demand will force prices up at a faster rate.

There is a limit to the extent that expectational influences can have their effect on the rate of inflation. Individuals and firms have only limited stocks of saving which they can draw upon to purchase goods and services now before prices rise. Unless the authorities increase the money stock over time, demand will ultimately decline.

However, this does not mean that commodity prices will necessarily fall. In the face of falling demand, firms will face reduced profit levels and may therefore attempt to raise their mark-ups. Prices may therefore rise even in the face of reduced demand, at least in the short run. As Wachtel and Adelsheim [18] have argued, this is more likely to be the case the more concentrated are the industries involved. The higher the level of concentration, they argue, the more likely will the demand facing the firms in the particular industry be inelastic – thus higher mark-ups mean higher profits in the aggregate.

In summary, we have two more reasons why inflation rates, at least over the short to medium term, may bear little resemblance to monetary rates of expansion. Further comparative international studies are therefore called for in an attempt to identify how the formation of expectations and degree of industrial concentration may cause different rates of inflation throughout the world.

Foreign exchange markets and central bank intervention

Although the above discussion is essentially pedagogic in nature, it does capture some of the main elements of modern monetary discussions of inflation. In particular it implicitly assumes:

1. that prices adjust relatively quickly to changes in excess demand or excess supply: the period of adjustment is not so long that there will be queues in the case of excess demand or unemployment in the case of excess supply;
2. that there is a stable relationship between the quantity of money and the level of consumer expenditure.

The major difference between the gold standard, which we have just been discussing, and recent discussions of the monetary basis for inflation centres on the nature of money itself and the processes whereby it is created. We no longer use gold as the basis for our currency. Instead there has developed over the past several hundred years a complex set of financial institutions who create assets which individuals and firms treat as money. These institutions, in turn, are influenced by the actions of central banks (such as the Bank of England, the Federal Reserve System in the US or the Deutsche Bundesbank in Germany) whose role it is to ensure stability in various financial markets, including the foreign exchange market, and to undertake various monetary policies with the aim of achieving national economic objectives such as price stability and full employment.

However, as before, the key to understanding the international transmission of inflation involves an understanding of the operation of foreign exchange markets. Therefore, let us examine in greater detail how these actually work. In all countries there exist foreign exchange dealers, usually commercial banks, who, as part of their services, buy and sell foreign currency on behalf of their customers. The latter may simply be tourists purchasing foreign currency for their holidays or large corporations settling accounts abroad. In order to meet the needs of these customers, dealers must maintain deposits of foreign currencies with correspondent banks abroad. The procedure is completely analogous to that of the shop-keeper who maintains an inventory of goods on his shelves in order to meet the potential requirements of his customers. Thus, when one of the bank's customers desires to buy foreign currency for business purposes abroad, the bank will ask that funds be transferred from its account at the correspondent bank to an account in the customer's name. Conversely, the dealer bank's deposits at the correspondent will increase when someone sells him foreign currency.

However, it should be emphasized that the inventory of foreign currency held by dealers is not a passive variable depending simply on the net demand or supply of foreign currencies. At any point in time the bank will have some idea of a desired level of these foreign correspondent deposits. The size of this desired inventory will depend on a number of factors: (a) the probability that customers will want to make large purchases of foreign exchange at any point in time; (b) the profits made by the bank from commissions; and (c) the alternative return which the bank could earn if it reinvested some of its foreign currency in other assets.

Now if the actual stock of foreign currency held by the bank is greater than the desired level, it will attempt to sell off the excess. This it does by contacting other dealer banks or perhaps a foreign exchange broker to ascertain whether there is anyone who desires to purchase the excess. But suppose there is no potential buyer. What happens then? There are a number of possibilities.

1. In order to dispose of the excess supply of foreign currency, the dealer could lower the price, or exchange rate, at which he is willing to sell. The aim here is to induce potential buyers to come forward at an exchange rate which would be more attractive to them. This possibility would exist under a perfectly flexible exchange rate scheme. Further to appreciate what is involved, let us consider Fig. 5.1. Here are depicted the demand and supply schedules for dollars on the foreign exchange market. The higher the denero–dollar exchange rate, the greater will be the price of American goods (wine) relative to European goods (cloth). In *normal* circumstances, this will mean that the quantity demanded of American-produced wine will decline and hence fewer dollars will be demanded on the foreign exchange market. This explains the negatively sloped demand schedule *DD*. Similarly, the demand for products manufactured in Europa will increase as will the quantity of dollars supplied to the foreign exchange market in order to buy the desired pounds. Hence, the positively sloped supply schedule *SS*.

   Thus, if the exchange rate is at the level indicated by *B*, there is an excess supply of dollars on the foreign exchange market. Dealers will lower the price of dollars thereby reducing their supply and increasing demand for them until finally the exchange rate indicated by *A* is achieved. At this point the foreign exchange market is in equilibrium.

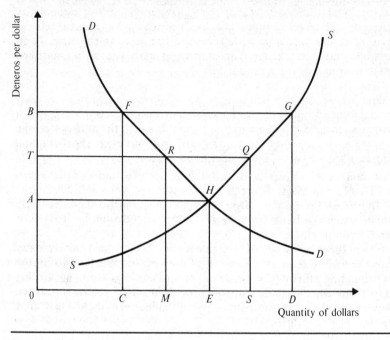

Fig. 5.1

2. At the opposite extreme, the authorities, in this case the central banks, could maintain fixed exchange rates by agreeing to intervene to eliminate any excess demand or supply of foreign currency. In the example under consideration, the central bank of Europe could purchase the excess supply of dollars FG ($= CD$). This sequence of events would have occurred under a fixed exchange rate scheme such as the Bretton Woods System in operation from 1944 to 1972.

3. In between these two polar cases is what has been frequently been referred to as a 'dirty float'. In this instance, the central bank will still intervene but not to such an extent as to maintain a fixed exchange rate. In other words, the price of the foreign currency will be allowed to decline, but not to the level which a perfectly flexible rate system would bring about. For example, in Fig. 5.1 the European central bank might purchase RQ ($=MS$) dollars but this would also imply that the exchange rate would have to fall from B to T.

A second important difference between the simple gold-standard model discussed earlier and the real world is that there is not only international trade in goods and services but also in financial items, i.e.

bonds, shares, time deposits, etc. This means that just as the pattern of international trade will respond to changes in relative commodity prices, so will the make-up of investors' portfolios change as the relative rates of return available on alternative financial assets varies. This possibility must be taken into account when analysing the international inflation transmission mechanism.

Now let us suppose that the countries involved in our earlier pedagogic example possess the more sophisticated and complex financial institutions that we have just been discussing. As a result, it turns out that there are a variety of ways in which the authorities of a country may vary its money stock, each with different short-run and long-run implications. We shall examine two cases here.

Case I

As before, assume that Europa increases its money stock by simply making lump-sum payments to its citizens. This time, however, this objective is achieved by distributing paper currency not gold coins. As these funds are spent some proportion will be deposited in commercial banks and in turn lent out. There will be a multiple expansion of the money stock. Wealth will increase, but as a result European consumers will attempt to purchase not only more home- and foreign-produced commodities (cloth and wine, respectively), they will also increase their demand for securities. The sequence of events emanating from this increased stock of money is depicted by the flow chart of Fig. 5.2.

As European wealth increases, the demand for securities will also increase and as a result, this will drive the price of European securities up and simultaneously lower yields. Investors, both European and American, will then be encouraged to rearrange their portfolios so as to include a higher proportion of American securities. As a result, such investors will increase their demand for dollars. At the same time adjustments will also be taking place in the real sector, much the same as in our discussion of the gold standard. The increased expenditure on the goods of both countries will drive commodity prices up. In addition, Europa will experience a trade deficit. Overall, then, there will be a net excess demand for dollars.

At this point, the European central bank is obliged to sell dollars for deneros in order to keep the exchange rate constant. This results in a reduction in European wealth but a corresponding increase in America's and sets in motion a further sequence of events. Spending falls in Europa but rises in America, thereby reducing the former's overall deficit until there arises a final equilibrium with higher prices and lower interest rates.

Case II

In this instance let us suppose that the European central bank increases its money stock via open-market operations: it buys securities in exchange for a cheque written on itself. The money stock can be

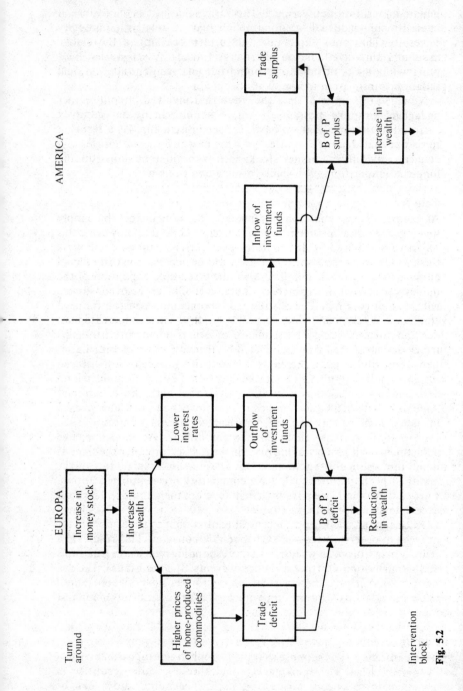

Fig. 5.2

increased by the same amount as the previous case, but unlike that example there will also be a reduction in the stock of securities held by the public. Thus there is no net change in the wealth of European consumers, unlike the first case. In the short run, at least, the sequence of events will be similar to that of case I: a European deficit on trade and capital accounts, a reduction in wealth in Europe but an increase in American wealth and so forth. This will continue until a full equilibrium is reached with increased world money stock, decreased stock of securities and a higher level of prices though probably not as high as in the first instance.

Under modern institutional arrangements, many countries will attempt to offset or neutralize the financial implications of balance-of-payments deficits or surpluses. However, the outcome of such attempts will depend in large measure on the nature of the resulting disturbances. For example, let us consider the possible reactions of the American monetary authorities to the American surplus, depending on whether it was generated as in case I or case II.

The American treasury could raise a lump-sum tax on consumers equal in amount to their balance-of-payments surplus. The funds would be deposited with the American central bank, thereby withdrawing them from circulation. The net result is a constant American money stock. To the extent that there remains a net increase in money and wealth in Europa, even after its deficit, they will continue to experience further deficits which could be neutralized in turn by America until finally an equilibrium is restored which is identical to the position before Europa initially attempted to increase its money stock. Any inflation which initially occurred as a result of the actions of the European monetary authorities would be unsustainable and prices (at least in the long run) would have to fall back to their initial levels.

However, the result is somewhat different if the American authorities attempt to neutralize their international payments imbalance via open-market operations. In this instance, America's central bank would sell securities, thereby reducing the amount of funds available for banks to lend out. However, wealth in America would still have increased due to the exchange of money for interest-bearing financial assets. This means that subsequently consumers will desire to increase their expenditure, thereby inducing a trade deficit. But the sale of securities by the American central bank will have the effect of driving interest rates up and this will cause a capital inflow. Obviously, the net effect on each country's balance of payments at any point in time will depend crucially on the speeds of adjustment in commodity and financial markets to relative price and interest rate variations.

When final equilibrium is restored the net effect would be to leave the world stock of money unchanged. However, consumers in both countries would now hold additional stocks of wealth and as a result their consumption levels will still have increased, thereby pushing prices up.

In actual practice, neutralization of the monetary effects associated with international payments imbalances is undertaken through a myriad of different institutional arrangements. And in some countries it is only possible to a limited extent. Therefore, it is useful briefly to examine a number of examples.

The United States In the case of a balance-of-payments deficit or surplus in the US, the Federal Reserve System is in a position to offset the effect on the monetary base through offsetting open-market operations. This, however, is a discretionary act. If, for example, there was an international payments deficit at the same time that the Federal Reserve System desired to follow a restrictive monetary policy, then there might be no neutralization of the payments deficit.

The United Kingdom In this country, neutralization of payments imbalances is an automatic action. For example, suppose that the UK was experiencing a balance-of-payments deficit. In this instance the Exchange Equalization Account would supply the necessary amount of foreign exchange (say dollars) to the foreign exchange market by purchasing pounds. In turn the Account would use the newly acquired pounds to buy Treasury bills. The sellers of these securities, whether banks or the public would thus obtain additional cash balances and, as a result, the reduction in the money stock arising from the balance of payments deficit would be offset.

Other countries In many other important nations, notably Germany and Japan, the act of neutralizing international payments imbalances is not an easy one. The reason for this is that neither country has a large enough stock of widely acceptable, marketable assets (such as government debt) which can be bought or sold by the central banking authorities in such a way as to offset the wealth effects of a payments imbalance. The result is that in large measure the international payments positions of these countries determined their domestic money supplies in much the same way as a gold standard would operate.

The role of the eurocurrency system and international financial intermediation

In our previous discussion we have assumed that all transactions in a particular currency were undertaken through financial institutions in the country whose currency was involved. For example, European banks held their dollar deposits at an American bank. However, over the past twenty years there has developed the widespread practice of banks located in one country accepting deposits denominated in the currency of another country. The banks carrying out such transactions are frequently called Euro-banks and are said to operate in the Euro-currency system. The bulk of such deposits are denominated in dollars, but over recent years the Deutsche Mark, Swiss franc and French franc have become increasingly important. A full and formal analysis of the system is beyond the scope of this paper – and besides suitable discussions are provided elsewhere (cf. [10, 11, 12]). However, it is necessary for us to examine whether the development and operation of the Euro-currency system has affected the rate of world inflation. Specifically, two points need to be examined. First, Euro-banks are international financial intermediaries and as a result have the potential of increasing demand and output, even though the money supply of any or all countries remain constant. Secondly, many central banks have used the Euro-currency system as a repository for a portion of their international reserves. This has had the effect of increasing the liquidity available to banks and hence their ability to encourage an expansion of economic activity. To the extent that the international economy is operating at or near full capacity, both of these developments will lead to increased prices. Let us examine these two points in turn.

Before actually considering the intermediating activities of the Euro-currency system, it is helpful to understand the process of intermediation as carried out by domestic financial institutions. At any point of time there may exist firms and households who are short of cash and desire to borrow the required amount from other firms and households who have savings and are thus looking for profitable investment opportunities. For example, consider the case of a household with excess funds which it desires to spend in a month's time. It could keep these funds either in an ordinary chequing account or in the form of a savings or time deposit. In either case, however, the commercial bank may loan the funds either to another household or to a business. A direct loan of this would probably not be contemplated by the surplus household at all. First, it would be highly risky. Even if the borrower was the epitome of honesty, he could very well lose his job because of poor health or bad business conditions or, in the case of a firm, become bankrupt. In any case, a substantial and costly credit check would be required to establish whether or not the potential borrower was honest and reliable. In addition, the required loan (say, for building a house or factory) might be for a longer period than the lender would like. Unless a market developed for the purchase and sale of such loans, there would be no means for the lender to cash in his investment if he needed to. For these reasons, he may insist upon a high rate of interest to compensate him for these undesirable aspects of the loan. Indeed, this rate could be so high as to be prohibitive. As a result, in the absence of financial intermediaries the efficient distribution of savings is likely to be impaired and the level of economic activity could be adversely affected.

In contrast, banks are normally in a position to *diversify* their portfolio of assets in such a manner that they do not have 'all their eggs in one basket'. As a result, the risk element is significantly reduced: the probability that all borrowers will default at the same time is also rather small. The placement of funds in a large number of investments means that the probability of the bank or intermediary's entire stock of assets being wiped out is rather low. Thus, there is greater certainty as to the value of the intermediary's liability and the income stream that they generate than if funds had been placed entirely in one investment.

Furthermore, such institutions are in a position to provide fairly liquid liabilities. Because each bank will have a large number of individuals or firms which place funds with it, the probability that everyone will want to withdraw their funds is, in normal times, quite small. Finally, financial intermediaries are in a position to take advantage of certain technical economies of scale. Because they will possess a full-time, expert staff, they will easily be in a position to evaluate the creditworthiness of potential borrowers. This will be even more the case, the more the intermediary specializes in loans to certain groups of individuals or firms or in certain types of securities. Furthermore, to the extent that intermediaries are enabled to undertake relatively large transactions, they can usually keep the level of transactions costs lower than that available to individual investors.

The operation of the Euro-currency system falls within the rubric which we have outlined above. First, the system operates on a wholesale basis involving deposits and loans of large size. This means that any fixed costs of processing transactions can be spread out so as to enable low profit margins. Thus, Euro-banks are in a position to be highly competitive with alternative financial instruments on both the loan and deposit sides. Second, Euro-currency transactions are carried out within the foreign exchange departments of banks and this means that transactions costs can be lowered by eliminating any duplication of paperwork that might occur if bank loan departments were also involved. Third, the fact that only the dollar and a few other currencies account for the bulk of Euro-currency activity means that banks need hire only specialists in these currencies. Fourth, typically Euro-banks tend to specialize in their operations, dealing only with customers well known to them and hence possessing well-established credit ratings. Thus the risk of default on loans is less than it might otherwise be. In fact, many Euro-banks do not require any collateral for their loans, a situation which, of course, is advantageous to potential borrowers.

The Euro-currency system also offers a number of technical advantages to international borrowers and lenders. Even though the number of currencies denominating international financial transactions is relatively small, there are a number of technical disadvantages to maintaining deposits outside one's own country. For one thing, there is a considerable time difference between New York, on the one hand, and London and continental financial centres on the other. It is therefore not surprising that many individuals and firms would prefer to maintain their foreign currency holdings in their own country at a bank whose business hours are roughly parallel to their own. In addition, European residents may simply prefer to deal with banks where a personal working relationship is easily assured. If an individual or firm maintains all of its funds at one bank, the latter is in a much better position to assess the creditworthiness of its customer. Should the time arise when that individual or firm needs to borrow funds, it will thereby be much better placed to draw on the bank's resources and to obtain a favourable borrowing rate. While possible, it is more difficult for borrowers or lenders to establish good working relationships with banks that are located several thousand miles away.

While the above factors have undoubtedly accounted for much of the innovative activity in the Euro-currency system, many economists believe that the prime cause for its development and growth has been differences in national economic policies and in banking regulations. Many commentators trace the origin of the system back to the years following the Second World War when many Eastern European countries drew down their dollar deposits in the US (for fear of expropriation) and deposited them with banks in Western Europe. These banks then would invest the dollars received in the US. However, an important stimulus to the growth of the system occurred in 1957 when the Bank of England placed restrictions on the granting of sterling credits with a view to limiting the availability of funds for speculation. At the time the expectation was that the pound would be devalued, and hence there was an incentive for foreign traders to increase their sterling liabilities. Restricted in the amount of sterling trade credits which they could grant, UK banks then resorted to lending dollars to those traders who otherwise would have purchased pounds. These traders were not necessarily Americans, but Europeans, and thus for the first time dollar assets were widely placed *outside* the United States.

Perhaps more important to the development of the system were three banking regulations of the Federal Reserve System in existence in the 1960s:

1. Interest payments are (still) prohibited on time deposits of less than thirty-day maturity. In contrast, interest is paid even on overnight Euro-currency deposits.
2. US banks could borrow from their overseas branches, particularly those in London, but did not have to hold any reserves against them.
3. Regulation Q placed a ceiling on interest payments by US banks which at various times made it difficult for them to compete for funds. However, their foreign branches were not subject to such regulations and as a result there was an additional important incentive for US banks to encourage depositors to place funds with these branches.

Neither of these latter two regulations are in effect today. However, their existence encouraged banks to expand their activities in the Euro-currency system with the result that they gained valuable information about its potential for international financial intermediation. The result has been a more efficient allocation of savings internationally, and as a result a greater level of economic activity. However, this has taken place at a time when the world was already experiencing inflation and thus

Table 5.1   Euro-currency deposits (billions of US dollars)

End of year	Dollars			Other currencies		
	Total	Banks	Non-banks	Total	Banks	Non-banks
1968	30·4	25·3	5·2	7·3	6·0	1·2
1969	47·6	41·5	6·1	10·5	8·3	2·2
1970	60·4	48·5	11·9	17·9	13·2	4·7
1971	71·5	57·1	14·4	28·6	21·9	6·8
1972	98·0	79·3	18·3	33·8	25·8	8·0
1973	132·1	107·4	24·7	55·5	41·5	14·0
1974	156·2	121·3	34·9	58·9	40·9	18·1
1975	190·2	149·3	40·9	68·0	47·5	20·5
1976	224·0	173·2	50·8	81·3	58·6	22·7

Source: Bank for International Settlements, *Annual Reports*, various years.

undoubtedly added to the pressure of demand at a time when available supply was not keeping pace.

The recent growth and size of the Euro-currency system may be ascertained by examining Table 5.1. If we look at the net size of the system – deposits held by non-banks – then it amounted to 73·5 billion dollars at the end of 1976. Of this amount 50·8 billion was denominated in US dollars whereas the remainder, 22·7 billion was denominated in various European currencies: the Deutsche Mark, Swiss franc, pound, guilder and French franc. However, the bulk of activity in the system is due to inter-bank operations. At the end of 1976 these totalled 231·8 billion dollars: 173·2 billion in US dollars and 58·6 billion in the various European currencies noted above. This inter-bank depositing offers us a good idea of the nature of the intermediating activities of the Euro-currency system and how Euro-banks tend to specialize. Suppose, as is indeed the case, that lenders have a very strong preference for keeping funds liquid, whereas borrowers want to obtain funds for a longer period of time. Thus the opportunity for financial intermediation exists, as discussed above. In many cases, only one bank or financial institution might be interposed between original lender and ultimate borrower. However, in the case of the Euro-currency system many banks may be involved. For example, the bank with an original Euro-currency deposit may not desire to lend it at the terms required by ultimate borrowers. As a result, this bank may lend the funds to another Euro-bank willing to undertake the loan. More banks could be involved, depending on the maturity associated with the final loan and the risk attached to it. Each bank will borrow the funds and lend them out at a higher interest rate to compensate for the longer maturity involved at each step.

As we discussed earlier in this chapter, under a fixed exchange rate system or even under a 'dirty float', all countries are obliged to maintain stocks of international reserves, or foreign currencies, which can be used to intervene in the foreign exchange markets in order to establish the

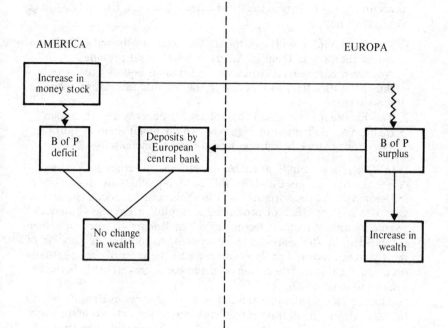

AMERICA

EUROPA

Increase in money stock

B of P deficit

Deposits by European central bank

B of P surplus

No change in wealth

Increase in wealth

Fig. 5.3

desired rate. When such actions were undertaken, the result was a decline in the money stock in deficit countries and an increase in surplus countries. This was the fundamental message of the monetary approach to the study of the balance of payments and inflation.

However, over the past decade, surplus nations, particularly the oil-producing countries, have been very concerned with receiving the maximum return possible on their reserve assets which otherwise would remain idle. As a result, these countries have placed some of their reserve funds both in the domestic financial institutions of the countries whose currencies are held and also directly in the Euro-currency system. But this action has had the effect of offsetting the adjustment process of the gold-standard/monetary approach. Consider Fig. 5.3. Suppose that our hypothetical country America increases its money stock, thereby experiencing an international payments deficit. There is, of course, a corresponding surplus in Europa. If the adjustment process were allowed to operate in the manner described earlier there would be an induced decline in America's money stock and an increase in Europa's. However, suppose that the European central bank decides to redeposit its accumulating dollars in the Euro-currency system. One of two things would then happen.

1. The Euro-bank could loan the dollars to a firm or individual who would then spend them in America. This would provide American commercial banks with additional liquidity and would thus have the effect of amplifying the original increase in the money stock.
2. The Euro-bank could sell the dollars for deneros and then loan them to an individual or firm who would spend them in Europa. The money stock in Europa would then be increased.

In either case, funds available to citizens, whether in Europa or America, have increased and this will, of course, add to the international inflationary pressures originally set in motion in America. The second case also has the effect of producing a surplus in Europa's balance of payments and a further accumulation of dollars. If these are then redeposited in the Euro-currency system, a continuous process of money creation would.be set in motion. This sequence of events actually occurred as a result of the actions of a number of central banks in the late 1960s and early 1970s.

Although a considerable amount of research remains to be done into the ultimate impact of this central bank depositing of funds in the Euro-currency system, it is my opinion that they are extremely significant. As can be seen from Table 5.2, at the end of 1975 identified official holdings of Euro-currencies stood at 55·9 billion dollars.

Simplicity versus reality

In the previous discussion of the international transmission inflation mechanism, our aim was to take a rather eclectic approach towards analysing the factors which influence the rate at which prices increase.

Table 5.2 Identified official holdings of Euro-currencies, end of years, 1969–75 (in billions of dollars)

	1969	1970	1971	1972	1973	1974	1975
1. Euro-dollars	4·9	10·4	11·2	19·3	25·1	41·4	48·2
Industrial countries	2·2	5·1	3·7	6·1	8·8	7·7	7·6
Primary producing countries	2·7	5·3	7·5	13·2	16·3	33·7	40·6
Major oil producers of primary producing countries	0·8	1·6	3·0	4·2	4·9	21·5	28·3
2. Other Euro-currencies	–	0·3	1·1	3·3	5·7	6·5	7·7

We emphasized the central role that the foreign exchange market plays in transmitting disturbances in one country to others. While we have emphasized the significance of monetary factors in this process, financial innovation, productivity changes and other variables are also seen to be important in affecting the rate of inflation throughout the world.

In other words, we have taken a very 'Keynesian' view which emphasizes the causal relationships which determine price increases, rather than the 'black box' approach which many modern monetary economists have taken. For them, only the influence of monetary factors should be considered – all others are irrelevant.

However, a number of economists have argued that only the influence of monetary factors should be considered – all others are irrelevant. Therefore, it is of some importance to examine this methodological position in detail. Perhaps the best way to do this is to look at the discussions which have taken place at the 1971 and 1974 Paris–Dauphine conferences [3, 4] on economic policy. In 1971 Assar Lindbeck warned the conference 'against simplistic explanations for complex problems'. 'I'm more impressed', he said, 'by the complexities of the world than by simplicity. In Chicago, the tendency is to over-simplification.' To this Robert Mundell, then of Chicago replied, 'Newton didn't have to invent a great many explanations for the falling apple', thereby implying a very strong belief in persistent regularities in patterns of human behaviour. In 1974, Lindbeck defended his eclectic position by arguing that 'a lot of factors [income freezes, price freezes, elections, aggressiveness of labour unions, etc.] introduce noises in equations which try to explain inflation through a limited number of factors, and the weight of these noises are different according to the length of time one considers'. This immediately brought forward several challenges which I now quote:

> Michael Parkin: . . . while it is a good thing to be eclectic – open-minded – when formulating assumptions, it is intellectually criminal to remain eclectic in the face of empirical evidence. Thus, economists must stop saying that all inflation explanations are equal since certain models explain remarkably well quarterly variations in the rate of change of money wages and money prices.
> Alexander Swoboda: There is a risk with eclecticism, namely to end up describing reality and to explain only divergences, while forgetting the central phenomenon.
> David Laidler: . . . good science implies the simplest explanation. Eclecticism prevents from looking for the simplest explanation.

From a logical point of view, these statements by Parkin, Swoboda and Laidler are unsound. There are two issues involved. First, a simple explanation is not necessarily a logical one. Two series of data may move very closely together and yet there may be no causal relationship between the two at all. Furthermore, even if there is a relationship between the two, the world is a sufficiently complex place, as Lindbeck argued, that it is unlikely that the relationship is monistic – other variables may be involved. Second, even if there is a causal relationship between two variables, it is not simply enough to say that there is a 'high correlation'. We must also ask in which direction the causation goes.

Indeed, if we look at the experience of the past decade, it is possible to raise several questions, which remain unanswered.

First, it is possible to argue that expectations of continuing price rises were enhanced if not created by exogenous shocks emanating from the real sector:

1. The war in Indo-China which expanded dramatically in the mid-1960s created a heavy demand for basic raw materials.
2. The failure of wheat crops in the Soviet Union plus a policy of reducing grain stores in the United States created an environment in which even the slightest demand increase could have a marked effect on prices.
3. The increase in the price of petroleum by the oil-producing countries in the early 1970s further contributed to higher consumer prices and producer costs. In addition, the policy of these countries has been to increase prices on an annual basis, contributing further to fears of future inflation.

With higher prices in the real sector, reduced output is the only alternative, unless the authorities increase the money stock. In other words, changes in monetary variables may be induced by events in the real sector. Indeed in the short run at least, even if the authorities had not increased the money stock, one would expect that firms would continue to increase prices in an attempt to maintain profits in the face of rising costs.

Financial variables also figure prominently in two other ways, although these are not core to the monetary theory of inflation. First, as discussed earlier, institutional arrangements are such that the two major countries with significant balance-of-payments surpluses are not in a position to neutralize fully the monetary effects of such surpluses. In contrast, those countries suffering international payments deficits such as the US and UK do neutralize them. The results of this asymmetric behaviour is an automatic upward bias in the world money stock.

Secondly, there has been a vast increase in the amount of international financial intermediation in the 1960s and 1970s. The result, we argued above, is that a given money stock can support a higher level of economic activity. In a sense, the financial sector of the international economy has become more productive.

In conclusion, we must agree with the 1970 Nobel Laureate in Economics, Paul Samuelson [16] who argues that no monistic theory of inflation can be validly maintained. He writes: 'One is forced by the facts of experience into an eclectic position. It is not a case where intellectual indecision or uncertainty leads to a hedged position of eclecticism. It is rather that explanation of the varied pattern of ongoing experience calls for bold combination of causation.'

The one problem with this approach, of course, is that it is 'messy'. A lot of hard work is involved in carrying out the analysis. And clearly, in this instance, a lot more research still needs to be undertaken into the causes of the worldwide inflation of the 1970s.

Appendix

Equations (12)–(14) may be obtained by solving the set of equations (9)–(11) for the equilibrium values of p_1, p_2, W. This may be achieved by rewriting (9)–(11) in matrix notation as

$$A \cdot X(t) = B \cdot X(t-1) + C,$$

where

$$A = \begin{bmatrix} S_1 & 0 & 0 \\ 0 & S_2 & 0 \\ 0 & 0 & 1 \end{bmatrix}, \qquad B = \begin{bmatrix} 0 & 0 & m_{11} - m_{12} \\ 0 & 0 & m_{12} - m_{22} \\ 0 & 0 & 1 - m_{12} - m_{21} \end{bmatrix},$$

$$X(t) = \begin{bmatrix} p_1(t) \\ p_2(t) \\ W_1(t) \end{bmatrix}, \qquad C = \begin{bmatrix} m_{21} \\ m_{22} \\ m_{21} \end{bmatrix} [W_1(0) + W_2(0) + A_1 + A_2].$$

In equilibrium (provided that the system is stable)

$X(t) = X(t-1) = X$. Therefore:
$AX = BX + C$ implies $X = [A - B]^{-1} C$.
It is then an easy matter to rewrite this last expression as equations (12)–(14).

The short-run effects described by equations (15)–(17) can be obtained in a similar manner as follows:

$$X(t) = A^{-1} B X(t-1) + A^{-1} C.$$

References

1. **Branson, W. H.**, 'A "Keynesian" approach to worldwide inflation', in L. Krause and W. Salant, eds, *Worldwide Inflation: Theory and Recent Experience*. The Brookings Institution, Washington DC, 1977.
2. **Brunner, K. and Meltzer, A. H.**, 'The explanation of inflation: Some international evidence', *American Economic Review*, **67**, 148–154, Feb., 1977.
3. **Claasen, E. and Salin, P.**, *Stabilization Policies in Interdependent Economies*. North-Holland, Amsterdam, 1972.
4. **Claasen, E. and Salin, P.**, *Recent Issues in International Monetary Economics*. North-Holland, Amsterdam, 1976.
5. **Johnson, H.**, (ed.) 'Towards a general theory of the balance-of-payments', in *International Trade and Economic Growth: Studies in Pure Theory*, 153–168. Harvard Univ. Press, Cambridge, Mass., 1961.

6. **Johnson, H.,** 'The monetary approach to balance-of-payments theory', in Michael Connolly and Alexander Swoboda, eds., *International Trade and Money*, 206–224. Allen and Unwin, London, 1973.

7. **Krause, L. and Salant, W.,** *Worldwide Inflation: Theory and Recent Experience.* The Brookings Institution, Washington DC, 1977.

8. **Laidler, D. and Parkin, M.,** 'Inflation – a survey', *The Economic Journal*, **85,** 741–805, Dec., 1975.

9. **Laidler, D. and Nobay, A. R.,** 'International aspects of inflation: a Survey', in E. Claasen and P. Salin, eds., *Recent Issues in International Monetary Economics*, 291–307. North-Holland, Amsterdam, 1976.

10. **McKenzie, G.,** 'The oil cartel and international financial stability', *Resources Policy*, **2,** 106–117, June 1976.

11. **McKenzie, G.,** *The Economics of the Eurocurrency System.* Macmillan, London, Wiley, New York, 1976.

12. **McKenzie, G.,** 'Economic interdependence and the Eurocurrency system', *British Journal of International Studies*, **3,** 26–38, Apr., 1977.

13. **McKenzie, G.,** 'Devaluation and the real-balance effect', *Zeitschrift für Nationalökonomie*, **37,** 109–122, 1977.

14. **Parkin, M.,** 'A "Monetarist" analysis of the generation and transmission of world inflation: 1958–1971', *American Economic Review*, **67,** 164–71, Feb., 1977.

15. **Salant, W. S.,** 'International transmission of inflation', in L. Krause and W. Salant, eds., *Worldwide Inflation: Theory and Recent Experience.* The Brookings Institution, Washington DC, 167–236, 1977.

16. **Samuelson, P. A.,** 'Worldwide stagflation', *The Morgan Guaranty Survey*, June 1974, 3–9, adapted from a memorandum prepared for the West German Council of Economic Advisers.

17. **Swoboda, A.,** 'Monetary approaches to worldwide inflation', in L. Krause and W. Salant, eds., *Worldwide Inflation: Theory and Recent Experience*, 9–60. The Brookings Institution, Washington DC, 1977.

18. **Wachtel, H. and Adelsheim, P.,** 'How recession feeds inflation: price markups in a concentrated economy', *Challenge*, Sept./Oct., 1977.

Chapter 6

Inflation: A disaggregated model approach

David F. Heathfield

Introduction

Of the many possible definitions of inflation the most widely accepted is undoubtedly that of increasing aggregate price level. Even then there are many possible candidates – are we referring to the aggregate of imports or exports or final goods produced or final goods consumed or gross output or consumer goods consumed? Furthermore, are we referring to the wholesale price or retail price or factor costs? In order to focus our minds we will consider the 'cost of living' by which we mean the price paid by the household sector for all the goods and services it consumes whether home produced or imported. This is the retail price index and would be used to index link pensions or to argue for higher wage rates – it is not necessarily relevant for balance of trade or investment models.

Retail prices are made up of four principal components; ex-works or wholesale prices, ex-docks or import prices, distribution margins and final taxes. The contribution of each of these to the total value of final sales may be judged from Table 6.1. Of these four items this chapter

Table 6.1 The composition of consumers' expenditure

	Consumers' expenditure (%)			
	Home products (wholesale)	Imports (ex-docks)	Distribution	Tax
1968	53·6	16·6	12·4	17·4
1970	52·7	17·6	11·6	18·1
1971	54·0	17·8	11·2	17·0

Source: Economic Trends, No. 258, Apr. 1975.
Note 12% distribution costs represents a 17% mark-up on pre-tax, pre-margin supply price.

examines only wholesale prices and distribution margins. The remaining two items, import prices and final taxes, are taken as given, but that is not to say that their influences on retail price level are ignored, indeed insofar as exchange rates and final tax rates are instruments of policy it is necessary to see how changes in them work their way through to retail prices.

The most casual of casual empiricism suggests that, in this country at any rate, prices are decided by those who sell (higgling is rare and negligible) and hence to explain price changes it is necessary to describe the behaviour of those who make price decisions. It is the purpose of this chapter then to look at wholesale and retail price decisions, albeit in a somewhat truncated and simplified model, so as to investigate the possible effects on prices of various spontaneous and contrived events.

Wholesale prices

The typical elementary theory of the firm suggests that in a perfectly competitive market, prices are 'given' as far as the producer is concerned and in the long run will equal minimum short-run average costs. For the imperfect competition case the producer may decide either price or quantity but not both. Again with free entry, in the long run, price equals average cost. In either case an increase in costs or an imposition of a final tax leads unambiguously to an increase in price. It is, however, observed that producers set prices and publish price lists no matter whether competition is more or less perfect. Evidently some modification of the elementary theory is required.

If demand curves facing firms and their costs curves were as stable as supposed in the standard elementary analysis then prices and quantities would indeed be fixed, possible for all time, and the scope of economics would be greatly reduced. In fact, of course, demand curves (defined narrowly here as the relationship between price and quantity demanded) are not fixed. Cost curves are also subject to both regular and random movements. The problem now is how should the entrepreneur behave in the face of such movements?

For goods which cannot be stored (e.g. services) it must be the case that without free disposal the quantity produced must exactly equal the quantity sold. Unless the fluctuations in demand exactly match those in supply then either demand is left unsatisfied or prices must change to stifle any excess demand. For most goods, however, it is possible to hold inventories (thereby temporarily separating production from demand) and the entrepreneur can decide not only on prices but also on production and inventories.

Production and prices can be decided by the entrepreneur directly, but sales (and hence inventories) are decided by the demanders. The dialogue between sellers and buyers would be in terms of sellers setting prices and buyers setting quantities. With a downward-sloping demand curve the quantity sold will depend on prices and hence, with a given demand curve, an output decision and a price decision together imply an inventory. Thus, production, price and inventory decisions are to some extent interrelated.

Despite this, inventory decisions are often treated quite separately from those of price and output (see Hilton [17], Trivedi [42]) not in the sense that prices do not influence inventories or that output is independent of inventories, but in the sense that the entrepreneur takes prices and sales as 'given' and, in this rather restricted setting, has only to decide optimum inventories. It may seem strange to begin a chapter on prices with a model in which prices are taken as given but, as will become clear, it does provide a convenient starting point for more general models.

A simple inventory model

With demand and prices given the fluctuations in demand (and/or supply), necessary for the existence of inventories, is brought about by production being done in batches and by deliveries from and to the plant being in batches. The batch sizes are decided by the entrepreneur and this, together with the given average rate of production, determines the frequency with which batches are produced. If, for example, the average rate of production (or demand) is 200 units per month and the optimum batch size turns out to be 50 units then there must be four batches per month.

Although the entrepreneur, in these models, is unable to control the average level of demand he can control the size of batches and thereby the size of the inventories. He does so with a view to minimising the costs associated with holding inventories and costs associated with setting up a batch for production (or of arranging for an extra delivery or despatch). This yields the well-known square-root relationship between the average level of inventories and the square root of the average level of demand (production).

Frequently, when these optimum inventory rules are used in more complete models, a linear relationship is assumed between optimum inventories and demand. This linearity can arise when the relationship is in terms of an aggregate over several 'lines', or plants (for each of which the square-root formula holds) if the size distribution of lines (or plants) if lognormal (see Hilton and Cornelius [17]).

This is, of course, a particularly simple version of the truncated model of inventory behaviour and does not yet include our original problem of price determination. It is simply the 'transactions' demand for inventories analogous to the quantity theory of money equation. If prices are beyond the control of entrepreneurs, as we have assumed, then there may well also be a speculative demand for inventories so that if prices are expected to rise the demand for inventories will also increase. Now the benefits (or capital gains) associated with these price changes will accrue to the *owners* of the inventories, but the transaction demand outlined above is determined not by ownership but by possession of inventories. If sales occur after despatch then ownership and possession of finished goods stocks for example amount to the same thing, but sales often precede despatch (indeed sometimes sales precede production); and in this case ownership differs from possession and it is necessary to consider not only inventories but also orders on hand. Industries which produce to order will have no incentive to hold speculative stocks (unlike those which produce to stock). If prices are generally expected to rise, the production to order industry would be reluctant to extend its order books, but its customers would be keen to place their orders before prices rose. The cost to the producer of not accommodating customers is the possible loss of sales. Customers may also go elsewhere if order books are too long since, with a given rate of production, long order books imply a long wait for delivery. There are therefore no simple explanations of speculative demands for inventories, but the transaction demand is well established.

In this 'truncated' model, then, the optimum level of inventories depends upon expected prices, expected output, the costs of holding inventories, the costs of disappointing customers and the cost of despatching and producing a batch. Orders on hand occur when changes of ownership precede changes in possession and may be used to 'signal' future demand. They would then moderate the demand for inventories by reducing both the speculative and the precautionary demands for them.

A more general model

A somewhat less truncated model may recognise that the entrepreneur has some control over both production and prices and allow for the interrelated nature of prices, production and inventories, mentioned earlier. Mills [25] sets up such a model and, by assuming that the entrepreneur maximises some discounted value of future expected profits, derives a set of decision rules about production and price. The entrepreneur is assumed to know the shapes of his demand curve and the cost curve, but not the position of the demand curve which is subject to short-run changes. It may also be subject to some secular changes, but consideration of these require long-run cost curves and capacity decisions to be introduced and this chapter is concerned only with the short run.

This dismissal of capacity or investment decisions by relegating them to the long run may have powerful precedents, but sits uneasily in a model which has as its maximand not this period's profits but some discounted value of an expected future profit stream. Nevertheless, we will confine ourselves to output, price and inventory decisions as if capacity is 'given' or decided elsewhere.

Introducing the future in this way will give rise to further difficulties since the decision maker cannot know what the future holds and is therefore obliged to form expectations of future demand and future costs. In order to describe his behaviour it is necessary then to know, not what the future actually turned out to be, but what the entrepreneur expected it to be at the time of his decision. Expectations are dealt with at some length by Mills [25] and a brief survey seems called for here too.

Expectations

As foretold by Keynes [19] expectations are among the most troublesome of problems in empirical work, and although the models outlined below pretend to treat expectations, they very rarely do more than suggest some combination of actual historical values.

Lovell [21] posits a general form which is not claimed to represent any expectation-forming equation, but which will nevertheless capture the outcome of any such equation. If the entrepreneur uses the best possible model he will predict the change exactly; if he uses the most naive model he will predict no change, hence the outcome of whatever model he uses must lie between these extremes. Thus:

$$\Delta x_{et} = \lambda(x_t - x_{t-1}), \tag{1}$$

where Δx_{et} is expected change in demand at time t (*N.B.* $x_{et} - x_{t-1}$ not $x_{et} - x_{et-1}$) x_t is actual demand at time t and λ is a constant such that $0 \leqslant \lambda \leqslant 1$.

Lovell is careful to suggest that this applies to an aggregate of firms some of which might use naive forecasting procedures ($\lambda = 0$ and $x_{et} = x_{t-1}$) and some of which use perfect forecasting procedures ($\lambda = 1$ and $x_{et} = x_t$). If it were to apply to one firm it would imply that the entrepreneur consistently underpredicts the actual change in demand by $(1 - \lambda) \times 100$ per cent and one doubts that such consistency of error would not be noticed and corrected (cf. rational expectations below) (although there is some evidence to suggest that expectations underestimate actual changes (Theil [39]). Much more likely is the Mills view that sales expectations deviate from actual sales by a random variable with a mean of zero. To estimate λ as if it were constant would therefore show only general tendencies to over- or underpredict by a group of firms.

If 'no change' represents the most naive predictor then the next naive predictor would be a simple extrapolation of a trend.

$$\Delta x_{et} = \Delta x_{t-1}. \tag{2}$$

This would clearly be unsuitable for a cyclical pattern, and a far more common approach would be the adaptive expectations model of Nerlove [27]. This posits that current expected sales are last period's predicted sales less some proportion of last period's prediction error. Thus:

$$x_{et} = x_{et-1} + \delta(x_{t-1} - x_{et-1}). \tag{3a}$$

As has been pointed out elsewhere (Lawson [20]) this form is incapable of capturing a simple trend since it may be written:

$$(x_{et} - x_{et-1}) = \delta(x_{t-1} - x_{et-1}), \tag{3b}$$

hence, if it correctly predicts in time $t-1$, then $x_{t-1} = x_{et-1}$ and the LHS $= 0$. Therefore the change in expected value ($x_{et} = x_{et-1}$) is zero. In the next period then ($x_t - x_{et}$) is non-zero and the model would correctly predict the next periods change only if $\delta = 1$. The problem is not quite as intractable as it may appear since a constant term added to the RHS of equation (3) would resolve the matter (Turnovsky [43]). This rather simple form of expectation-forming equation may be developed in two ways Trivedi in Pearce [30] retains the same set of variables (lagged actual values of the variables and past error terms) but uses a much more general form of time dependence (this is a slight modification of the Trivedi equation since his model caters for seasonal patterns which is an unnecessary complication here):

$$(1-B)^d(1-\Phi B - \ldots \Phi_p B^p)\ (x_t - \Phi_0) = (1 - \theta_1 B \ldots - \theta_q\ B^q)\ (e_t - \theta_0), \quad (4)$$

where:

B is a lag operator,

d is the number of differences,

p is the number of autoregressive parameters,

q is the number of moving average parameters, and

Φ_0 and θ_0 are constants.

In fact the scheme used by Trivedi is of the form $\Phi_0 = 0, \theta_0 = 0, p = 0, d = 1$ and $q = 2$ so that equation (4) becomes:

$$x_t - x_{t-1} = \varepsilon_t - \theta_1\ \varepsilon_{t-1} - \theta_2 \varepsilon_{t-2}. \tag{5}$$

Since $x_t + \varepsilon_t = x_{et}$ we have:

$$x_{et} = x_{t-1} + \theta_1(x_{t-1} - x_{et}) + \theta_2(x_{t-2} - x_{et-1}).$$

The choice of model from the very wide range contained in equation (4) is a matter of trying various combinations of p, d and q and comparing residual correlograms.

The essential element of all the foregoing models is that expectations are expressed as more or less complicated functions of past values. It seems unlikely that entrepreneurs would ignore all other variables, some of which are known (or at least believed) to be related to or even to influence the value of the predicted variable. Muth [26] argues that the entrepreneur would be rational in this as in any other of his activities and would make use of all the information at his disposal in making his predictions. To include other variables is to construct an economic model (no matter how simple) and hence entreprenurial expectation-forming equations are econometric models. Muth illustrates his approach with a simple three-equation model of the form:

$$C_t = -\beta p_t \qquad \text{(demand)} \tag{6}$$

$$P_t = \gamma p_t^e + u_t \qquad \text{(supply)} \tag{7}$$

$$P_t = C_t \qquad \text{(equilibrium)} \tag{8}$$

(all variables expressed as deviations from some equilibrium). Only the supply equation is stochastic, but Grossman [12] has shown the complication of allowing both supply and demand to be stochastic – a more interesting case. From equations (6)–(8) we have:

$$p_t = \frac{\gamma}{\beta} p^e_t + \frac{1}{\beta} u_t. \tag{9}$$

If firms use this model to predict price, then

$$p^e_t = p_t \quad \text{thus} \quad p^e_t = \frac{-1}{(\beta + \gamma)} u_t, \tag{10}$$

where u_t is the random component of supply. We are once again reduced to analysing systematic components of errors (or shocks) except that unlike the Trivedi model we are here confined to a stationary series only, so that using Trivedi's notation $d=0$.

Rather than impose the constraint that $p_t = p^e_t$ we could begin by using a more general relationship comprising systematic and unsystematic parts (cf. Theil's U statistic):

$$p_t = \alpha_0 + \alpha_1 p^e_t + v_t. \tag{11}$$

Muth's assumption amounts to $\alpha_0 = 0$, $\alpha_1 = 1$ and $E(v_t) = 0$, and rationality in this context is that 'the expectations and the realizations follow the same autoregressive pattern' (Turnovsky [43, p. 1445]).

Expectation-forming equations are rarely tested directly since there are so few actual observations of expectations. This results in expectation variables being replaced by the generating equations, the parameters of which are estimated from reduced-form equations. An exception is the paper by Turnovsky [43] which, using the well-known survey data of Livingston, tests some of these equations directly. He concludes that in the recent past, at any rate, expectations have been rationally formed. This essentially redeems the Trivedi approach while concluding that the standard expectations hypotheses (extrapolative and adaptive expectations) tend to be inconsistent with the assumption of rationality.

Carlson and Parkin [1] construct a series of expected inflation rates from a UK survey which asked 1000 persons if prices would rise, fall or remain constant. This series was then used to see if simple error learning models performed better than those with economic variables such as unemployment and devaluation, as independent variables. They conclude that of these only devaluation affects expectations, and that for mild inflation an autoregressive scheme works better than the second-order error learning process. These results, of course, span more than the entrepreneurial class and may reflect less sophisticated expectation-forming models than would normally be used by that class alone in regard to their own products.

Expected values have been so far treated like single numbers, but clearly they are not held with certainty. The subjective probability distribution is rarely considered. The models are usually constructed to meet the certainty equivalence requirements (see Simon [37]) but Muth [26] introduces a non-linear utility function in expected future profits and this non-linearity requires not only the first but the second moments of the distribution to be considered. In the model outlined below only the first moment is used and often expected values are simply replaced by actual values.

Some further problems

Apart from the expectations difficulties arising when the maximand is discounted future profits, there is also the difficulty of choosing a time horizon. Much of course depends on the rate at which future profits are discounted. With a high rate of discount only the first few terms into the future need be considered.

A somewhat more fundamental problem arises from the 'as if' assumption upon which many of the very complicated decision models are justified. The extremely complicated nature of Mills' model, for example, can only be justified on the ground that although it does not represent the actual decision-making process it must describe the outcomes of that process if entrepreneurs do in fact manage to maximise profits, no matter how they do it. In a single-period model (or an unchanging state representable by a one-period model) the 'as if' arguments may be convincing, but it is difficult to see how they can be applied to multiperiod models. Darwinism may allow only the survival of 'those fittest to survive', but in a changing environment 'those fittest to survive' may comprise a very wide range of species indeed.

This background to the models used for pricing behaviour, though now fairly complicated, is not yet complete. It is necessary to consider not only the costs associated with given levels of production and inventory but also to consider those costs associated with changes in output and changes in price. Thus, even when the costs recognised by a purely static model may suggest a change in output or price, the dynamic adjustment costs modify or prevent altogether any such changes. Adjustment cost functions are rarely explicitly introduced, but nevertheless lie behind most partial adjustment models. When they are explicitly introduced they usually take the form of a quadratic in which the cost associated with changing a variable is proportional to the square of the rate of change. The choice of such a functional form is dictated by the need for symmetry (changes up or down both incur cost), partly for its generality, partly for its mathematical tractability and partly because it gives rise to the linear decision rules necessary for certainty equivalents to replace distributions of variables.

Models

In this section we shall look in some detail at two models and glance at some others. The two models are chosen to illustrate what seem to be the two main approaches to describing entrepreneurs' behaviour. The first is the explicit maximising approach in which the entrepreneur is assumed to be maximising some well-specified objective function subject to some well-specified constraint. Decision roles are derived mathematically and are often too complicated to lend themselves to empirical testing, hence some simplification is usually made between the pure theory and the equations actually estimated. This approach will be referred to as the Mills approach and illustrated principally by the model of Hay [13]. The second approach is rather heuristic. The behavioural equations are written linearly and include those variables believed by the model-builder to be likely to influence the outcome. We will take up the methodological problems associated with this approach when we come to consider the model of Courchene [2] which will be used to illustrate what we will call the Liu [22] approach. Finally, we look at some price equations specified as part of more general econometric models – one for the UK and one for the US.

Hay's model

Hay [13] claims to use Mills' model to derive an exact set of decision rules. His model is as follows:

Desired level of orders on hand (U_t^*) is some function of the rate of production (x_1):

$$U_t^* = C_{13} + C_{14}x_t. \tag{12}$$

The cost of deviating from desired orders on hand (F_{ut}) is proportional to the square of the deviation:

$$F_{ut} = C_{11} + C_1(U_t - U_t^*)^2. \tag{13}$$

Desired inventories (H_t^*) is a linear function of sales (S_t):

$$H_t^* = C_{23} + C_{22}S_t. \tag{14}$$

The cost of deviating from desired finished goods inventories (F_{ht}) is proportional to the square of such deviations:

$$F_{ht} = C_{21} + C_2(H_t - H_t^*)^2. \tag{15}$$

The short-run average cost curve is assumed to be flat which may not conform to the usual assumption of the 'U' shape short-run average cost curve, but which perhaps conforms better to reality – at least up to that level of output regarded as short-run capacity. (Capacity variables are discussed below.) It should also be noted that although flat the cost curve can change its position as input prices change (see below).

New orders (O_t) is a function of price (P_t):

$$O_t = Q_t - {}^{bP}{}_t, \tag{16}$$

where Q_t is an intercept term subject to random shocks.

The costs of changing prices are divided into those induced by cost changes and those induced by demand changes. The former will elicit no penalty from competitors on the assumption that they suffer similar cost changes and do not interpret cost-induced price changes as a hostile act. Other price changes do, however, bring about retaliation by competitors, hence the cost of changing prices (F_{pt}) is

$$F_{pt} = C_4 |(P_t - V_t) - (P_{t-1} - V_{t-1})|, \tag{17}$$

where V_t is direct unit costs of production.

The following identities hold. New orders less shipments equal change in orders on hand:

$$O_t - S_t = U_t - U_{t-1}. \tag{18}$$

Output less shipments equal change in inventories:

$$X_t - S_t = H_t - H_{t-1}. \tag{19}$$

Future profits are discounted at a rate λ over a time horizon of N periods yielding the following Lagrangian equation to be maximised:

$$L = \sum_1^N \lambda^{t-1} \left\{ P_t Q_t - b P_t^2 - C_{11} - C_2 (U_t - C_{13} - C_{14} X_t)^2 - C_{21} - \right.$$
$$- C_2 (H_t - C_{23} - C_{24} S_t)^2 - \gamma_t X_t - C_3 (\gamma_t - X_{t-1})^2 -$$
$$\left. - C_4 |(P_t - V_t) - (P_{t-1} - V_{t-1})|^2 \right\} - \delta_t (Q_t - b P_t - S_t - U_t + U_{t-1})$$
$$- \gamma_t (X_t - S_t - H_t + H_{t-1}), \tag{20}$$

where δ_t and γ_t are the Lagrangian multipliers associated with the accounting identities, equations (18) and (19). Maximixing equation (20) yields the following decision rules:

$$P_t = A_{21} X_{t-1} + A_{22} P_{t-1} + A_{23} H_{t-1} + A_{24} U_{t-1} + A_{25} Q_t +$$
$$+ A_{26} Q_{t+1} \ldots + A_{27} V_t + A_{28} V_{t+1} \ldots + K_2. \tag{21}$$

Decision rules for X_t and H_t are similar to equation (21), having identical explanatory variables.

Hay begins by exploring the sensitivity of these reduced-form parameters to changes in the structural parameters. He chooses some appropriate values for the structural parameters and calculates the parameters of equation (21). The levels chosen are as follows:

$$C_{11} = C_{13} = C_{21} = C_{23} = 0, \qquad b = 0 \cdot 05, \qquad \lambda = 0 \cdot 99,$$
$$C_{14} = C_{24} = 0 \cdot 6, \qquad C_1 = 150, \qquad C_2 = 100,$$
$$C_3 = 35 \quad \text{and} \quad C_4 = 5.$$

The resulting parameters of equation (21) are shown in the first row of Table 6.2. As might be expected, prices rise with current costs (V_t), increased unfilled orders (U_t) and increases in demand (Q_t). They fall as inventories (H_t) increase. Less obviously, prices fall as production increases (X_{t-1}) and when past and future costs (V_{t-1}, V_{t+1}) go up. Each of the structural parameters is then altered in turn and the resulting changes in the reduced-form parameters of equation (21) are also

Table 6.2 The influence of structural changes on the reduced form equation.

	X_{t-1}	P_{t-1}	H_{t-1}	U_{t-1}	Q_t	Q_{t+1}	Q_{t+2}	V_{t-1}	V_t	V_{t+1}	V_{t+2}
Original structure	−0·169	0·903	−0·058	0·066	0·156	0·106	0·081	−0·903	1·028	−0·010	−0·008
$\lambda = 0.89$	−0·013	+0·032	+0·001	+0·002	+0·005	−0·004	−0·008	−0·032	−0·017	0	+0·001
$C_1 = 300$	−0·004	0	−0·003	+0·006	+0·007	+0·001	0	0	0	0	0
$C_2 = 200$	−0·009	−0·001	0	+0·002	+0·002	+0·001	0	+0·001	0	0	0
$C_3 = 70$	−0·135	−0·005	−0·039	+0·040	+0·039	+0·014	+0·004	+0·005	−0·004	−0·002	−0·001
$C_4 = 10$	+0·079	+0·030	+0·031	−0·035	−0·079	−0·052	−0·038	−0·030	−0·005	+0·005	+0·004
$C_{14} = 1.2$	−0·050	−0·001	+0·024	−0·024	−0·027	−0·005	0	+0·002	0	0	0
$C_{24} = 1.2$	+0·035	+0·001	+0·001	+0·002	+0·002	−0·005	−0·004	−0·001	−0·003	0	0
$b = 0.10$	−0·135	−0·052	−0·051	+0·060	+0·045	+0·011	−0·006	+0·007	−0·007	−0·012	−0·007

shown. The changes in structural parameters are quite large – all save γ are doubled and γ is reduced from 0·99 to 0·89.

It will be evident from Table 6.2 that the parameters of equation (21) are largely insensitive to changes in structural parameters. The exception being C_3 (the cost of changing the rate of production) and b (the slope of the demand curve).

The sensitivity of price to changes in b opens up a completely different approach to pricing policy, and inflation, b being the inverse of the slope of the firm's demand curve, may be viewed as a measure of market imperfection. Decreasing b implies a greater degree of monopoly. Cowling and Waterson [3] show that, for durable goods, the price–cost margins increase with the degree of industrial concentration. Any steady trend towards greater concentration would therefore induce a trend in prices, even with constant costs. Hay shows that the effects of aggregate demand variables (H_{t-1}, U_{t-1} and Q_t) on prices are doubled when b moves from 0·5 to 0·1. Cowling and Waterson claim that the degree of concentration has changed very little in the US and hence Hay's results may hold but in the UK his model may be less acceptable. Domberger [5, p. 30], concludes that: 'Market power can contribute to inflation though the speed with which cost changes are passed on and the link between market power and inflation is worthy of further research.'

Hay nevertheless argues that his results are encouraging for empirical work, particularly time series work, since changes in structural parameters over time do not invalidate the assumed constancy of the parameters of equation (21). In order for equation (21) to be tested empirically it becomes necessary to replace future values of Q_t and V_t by their expected values – expected, that is, by the entrepreneur who, when deciding on P_t, cannot know future values of Q_t or V_t. Having no information about expectations, Hay uses actual values for Q_{t+n} and V_{t+n}, thus assuming that expectations are at any rate unbiased, (as rational expectations would require). However, his assumption severely limits our ability to assess the role of expectations in explaining price changes.

The data used are monthly from March 1953 to August 1966 for two industries in the US – Lumber and Woods and Paper and Allied Products. The price equations are as follows:

	X_{t-1}	P_{t-1}	H_{t-1}	U_{t-1}	Q_t	Q_{t+1}	Q_{t+2}	V_{t-1}	V_t	$\bar{R}^2$	DW
lumber $P_i =$	−0·261	0·914	−0·318	0·063	0·130	0·172	0·366	−0·012	0·002	0·947	
	(2·73)	(39·26)	(2·65)	(0·72)	(1·21)	(1·62)	(4·13)	(0·47)	(0·07)		1·42
paper $P_i =$	−0·019	0·970	−0·554	0·123	0·086	−0·026	0·049	−0·031	0·046	0·981	
	(0·31)	(49·20)	(2·90)	(1·48)	(1·32)	(0·42)	(0·89)	(0·80)	(1·12)		1·80

These results conform well with those of arbitrarily selected structural coefficients. However, in terms of the significance of the explanatory variables, it is surprising that costs seem to be insignificant in both industries (at the 5% level). Both price series seem to be dominated by lagged price which may mean that prices remain unchanged for long periods of time – possibly due to the costs of changing price or some institutionalised price-changing procedure as described by Steuer and Budd [38]. Demand (Q) does have an impact on prices but not a particularly large one. 'The full effect of price increases is to absorb 11, 4 and 7 per cent of the demand increase in lumber, paper and the sample experiment respectively.' Hay [13, p. 543].

The results for price equations of lumber based on monthly data from January 1933 to December 1940 reported by Mills [25, p. 180] are as follows:

$$P = \underset{(0.062)}{0.764Q_t} - \underset{(0.063)}{0.572X_t} - \underset{(0.021)}{0.286H_{t-1}} + \underset{(0.034)}{0.910P_{t-1}} \quad \begin{array}{cc} R^2 & DW \\ 0.980 & 1.57 \end{array}$$

the notation is that of Hay rather than Mills, but the figures in parentheses are standard errors rather than 't' statistics reported by Hay.

Lagged prices again dominate but demand (Q), output (X) and inventories (H) each have a role to play in ways similar to the results of Hay. Steuer and Budd [38] use the Mills model to estimate price and output equations for some UK companies and conclude that it works better for output than for price. Wallis [44] subsequently concluded that the model as a whole should be rejected on the Steuer and Budd data. These data were of particular products rather than industry or even firm aggregates (Remington Typewriters, Echo Margarine, Nescafe, etc.). A feature of the price changes was the rather sharp step changes in price, 'typically, prices hold for a year, two years, five years' (Steuer and Budd [38, p. 16]). It would be possible to argue that Mills' model, like that of Marshall, applies to the 'representative' firm and hence to apply it to a particular decision maker is hardly a fair test. It is unlikely that one would want to reject consumer demand theory because some individuals were observed to behave differently. Nevertheless, as Steuer and Budd point out, the theory omits much: there is no advertising, no capacity decisions and no financing problems. They conclude [38, p. 20]: 'It is difficult really to regard equations like [these] as 'decision' rules in a boardroom sense. If this were firm procedure, a low grade clerk could announce price and output each quarter.'

The justification for this approach seems to be that it describes the day-to-day decisions of firms in general as if in the main they were maximising profits.

Courchene's model
It is arguable that in view of the simplifications forced on the theoretician by mathematical and empirical limitations it is hardly worth spending any great effort in deriving sets of decision rules from well-specified premises. The same end result may appear if the decision-making process is treated like a black box. The workings of the box are forever a mystery, but by examining its input variables and comparing them with its output variable(s) some systematic relationship (or transfer function) may be discovered between them. Although this approach is well known in the physical sciences (where perhaps inputs

170   Perspectives on inflation

and outputs can be better identified) its application to 'free will' subjects of the social sciences may cause misgivings. These misgivings may perhaps best be eased by regarding the specification of inputs and

Table 6.3 Simple regressions of price changes on alternative measures of demand or excess demand, 1956–62. $\triangle P_t = \hat{a} + \hat{B}X_t$ or $\triangle P_t = \hat{B}X_t$ (all value variables are in nominal terms, except for those in row 11; intercept coefficients are not shown)

Where the variable X_t is represented by:	Various manufacturing industries (dependent variable is the relevant industry selling-price index, 1956=100)			
	Heavy transportation	Heavy electrical equipment	Iron and steel	Textiles
Row				
1. Unemployment rate	−0·2798	−1·056	−0·3000	−0·0478
	(3·19)	(4·62)	(6·25)	(0·60)
2. $\dfrac{1}{\text{Unemployment rate}}$	7·478	25·73	8·140	0·7320
	(3·57)	(4·47)	(8·34)	(0·37)
3. New orders (NO_t)	0·0348	1·194	−0·1360	0·1271
	(2·10)	(3·72)	(0·82)	(3·30)
4. Unfilled orders (U_t)	0·0182	0·2531	0·0421	0·2340
	(2·40)	(2·25)	(6·52)	(3·03)
5. H_t^{aE}	0·0299	0·5211	0·0333	0·1810
	(1·99)	(1·45)	(3·29)	(3·63)
6. H_t^{fE}	−0·3177	12·46	−0·0988	0·4540
	(1·01)	(0·87)	(1·23)	(3·63)
7. $H_t^{aE} - H_t^a$	0·1086†	1·750†	0·0356	0·1881†
	(2·60)	(3·68)	(3·50)	(3·18)
8. $H_t^{fE} - H_t^f$	−0·3238	3·337	0·1375	0·3140
	(1·01)	(1·44)	(1·79)	(1·87)
9. H_t^{aE} −H_t^a	0·0998	1·750	0·0358*	0·1850*
	(2·26)	(3·53)	(3·54)	(3·11)
	0·0877†	1·758	0·0323	0·1962
	(1·74)	(3·19)	(3·10)	(3·04)
10. H_t^{fE} −H_t^f				0·2723*
				(1·66)
				0·2882
				(1·60)
11. $H_t^{aE} - H_t$ (real terms)	0·1217†	1·711	0·0424	0·1595
	(2·76)	(3·61)	(2·95)	(2·45)
Elasticity at sample mean	(1·48)	(0·77)	(0·07)	(4·29)
12. $X = \triangle WPH_t$	0·2529	1·429	0·4297	0·3574
	(1·83)	(2·81)	(2·74)	(1·56)
13. Average value of NO_t	18·9	5·86	72·3	20·4
Relative value of NO_t	0·117	0·030	0·449	0·127
14. Value for $\dfrac{H_t^f}{U_t}$	0·014	0·159	0·324	1·04

Notes:
Explanation of variables given in text, p. 172.
Figures in parentheses are 't' statistics.
* Estimated without an intercept term.
† The actual inventory variable is for period $t-1$ rather than for period t, i.e. $H_t^{aE} - H_{t-1}^a$ rather than $H_t^{aE} - H_t^a$.
‡ No $H_t^{aE} - H_t^a$ series appears to work for this industry. In its place we have used H_t^f, actual finished goods inventories. Hence the negative coefficient.

Table 6.3 (continued)

Where the variable X_t is represented by:	Various manufacturing industries (dependent variable is the relevant industry selling-price index 1956=5 100)		Total manufacturing where dependent variable is:	
	Leather	Refrigerators, vacuum cleaners and appliances	Wholesale price index, 1939=100	Aggregate selling price index, 1956=100
Row				
1. Unemployment rate	−0·0466 (0·26)	0·0789 (0·61)	−0·1340 (0·60)	−0·1231 (3·34)
2. $\dfrac{1}{\text{Unemployment rate}}$	−0·2630 (0·05)	−1·530 (0·48)	3·812 (0·77)	3·259 (3·68)
3. New orders (NO_t)	0·4319 (0·94)	0·1418 (0·95)	0·0110 (1·43)	0·0060 (0·04)
4. Unfilled orders (U_t)	−0·2895 (0·26)	−2·131 (1·87)	−0·0029 (0·35)	0·0036 (2·25)
5. H_t^{aE}	0·5803 (0·96)	0·1462 (0·86)	0·0175 (1·40)	0·0031 (1·10)
6. H_t^{fE}	0·9234 (0·98)	0·1878 (0·52)	0·0312 (1·28)	−0·0012 (0·22)
7. $H_t^{aE} - H_t^a$	3·466† (5·61)	0·2288 (1·65)	0·0346 (2·16)	0·0106 (2·81)
8. $H_t^{fE} - H_t^f$	4·989 (4·63)	0·4190 (1·66)	0·0800 (1·80)	0·0243 (2·78)
9. $\dfrac{H_t^{aE}}{-H_t^a}$	3·321 (3·48) / 3·333 (3·38)	0·2072* (1·47) / 0·4015 (2·53)	0·0346 (2·11) / 0·0376 (1·56)	0·0101 (3·18) / 0·0154 (3·29)
10. $\dfrac{H_t^{fE}}{H_t^f}$	4·970 (5·03) / 6·873 (5·35)	0·3217* (1·26) / 0·7121 (2·59)	0·0858 (1·96) / 0·0682 (1·48)	0·0218 (2·50) / 0·0288 (3·14)
11. $H_t^{aE} - H_t^a$ (real terms)	4·137† (3·84)	−1·189‡ (2·58)	0·0197 (1·52)	0·0178 (2·68)
Elasticity at sample mean	(0·54)	(N/A)	(0·27)	(0·33)
12. $X = \Delta WPH_t$	0·3544 (0·52)	−0·092 (0·60)	0·1853 (1·04)	0·0787 (0·78)
13. Average value of NO_t	6·52	3·91	161·0	161·0
Relative value of NO_t	0·040	0·024	1·0	1·0
14. Value for $\dfrac{H_t^f}{U_t}$	1·08	2·08	0·58	0·58

Rows 13 and 14 do not contain regression coefficients. In row 13, the average value of quarterly new orders over the period 1955–62 is given for each industry, so as to give an indication of the relative weight of each industry in total manufacturing. In row 14 the values for $\bar{H}_t^f/\bar{U}_t$ (a measure of the degree of PTO versus PTS), are the means of quarterly observations from 1955 to 1962.

output(s) as a reduced form of some (albeit unspecified) structure of equations in the mind of the experimenter. Under such circumstances it is difficult to regard empirical work as hypothesis testing, since without a well-specified structure it is impossible to advance hypotheses about the parameters of the reduced form. This 'black box' approach then implies that empirical work is a method of discovery or quantification rather than of proof or hypotheses falsification.

This approach has been adopted by Liu [22] on an aggregate level, and subsequently by Courchene [2] who applied a version of Liu's model to a disaggregated industry data. Courchene, seeking to explain price changes in terms of excess demand, regresses price change on a number of alternative excess demand indicators for the Canadian economy using quarterly data from 1956 to 1962 (see Table 6.3) where:

H_t^{aE} are equilibrium aggregate inventories,
H_t^{fE} are equilibrium finished goods inventories,
H_t^a are actual aggretate inventories,
H_t^f are actual finished goods inventories, and
$\triangle WPH_t$ is the change of hourly wage rate.

Unemployment is 'general' unemployment, but all other variables (e.g. inventories) apply only to the industry whose price is being explained. Rows (1) and (2), unlike row (12), are not therefore unambiguously supply cost influences on price since they are indicators of the aggregate level of demand. Row (12) again demonstrates the weakness of cost influences on prices.

In the demand side, deviations of inventories from their equilibrium levels are marginally better than the actual or equilibrium levels on their own and aggregate inventories (raw material and fuel plus work in progress plus finished goods) work better than do finished goods alone. Equilibrium inventories are estimated from equations taken from Courchene's unpublished Ph.D. thesis and it may be the different estimates of equilibrium levels of aggregate and finished goods inventories (see Appendix A of Courchene [2]) which give rise to these differences. Courchene claims, however, that the results for aggregate inventories are not particularly sensitive to changes in the specification of equilibrium inventories. Perhaps shortfalls of aggregate inventories imply a more sustained period of excess demand than do shortfalls of finished goods alone and hence are more likely to provoke a change in price rather than a change in supply. Furthermore, finished goods inventories are unlikely to reflect demand for industries which produce to order (PTO) rather than produce to stock (PTS). Of course, even in a pure PTO industry there will be a 'transactions' demand for finished goods inventories, but the level of inventories held will not reflect excess demand.

Splitting the excess demand variable $(H_t^E - H_t)$ into its two components H_t^E and H_t does not much alter the results – the coefficients being very similar on both components.

Extending his model somewhat, Courchene uses both excess demand and cost variables to explain price changes (see Table 6.4). This form works well for all the industries considered. Excess demand always plays the dominant role, but it is clear that raw material and labour costs also contribute to price.

Table 6.4 Some final extensions. $\triangle P_t = a + b(H_t^{aE} - H_t^a) + c\triangle WPH_t + d\triangle USP_t + e\triangle RMP$

Industry	a	b	c	d	e	R DW
Heavy transportation	−0·6204 (1·74)	0·1238* (3·04)	0·2616 (2·17)		0·0976 (1·10)	0·60 2·67
Heavy electrical machinery	−1·586 (3·10)	1·577* (3·86)	0·9065 (2·23)		0·4636 (2·45)	0·73 2·05
Iron and steel	−0·1315 (0·99)	0·0359 (3·65)	0·3751 (3·58)		0·1670 (3·52)	0·80 1·19
Iron and steel	0·0181 (0·15)	0·0266 (2·98)	0·1896 (1·75)	0·1831 (3·01)	0·1363 (3·28)	0·86 1·30
Textiles	−0·5704 (2·18)	0·1666 (2·70)	0·3844 (1·86)		0·0030 (0·94)	0·50 1·86
Leather †	−0·2532 (0·55)	2·364* (2·13)	0·5953 (1·32)		0·0563 (3·10)	0·73 1·64
Leather †	0·0189 (0·03)	1·574* (1·37)	0·3206 (0·70)	0·1353 (1·80)	0·0326 (1·50)	0·76 1·34
Total manufacturing	0·1273 (1·92)	0·0169 (2·64)			0·0780 (1·66)	0·48 2·00
Total manufacturing	0·0998 (1·44)	0·0117 (1·54)		0·1612 (1·23)	0·0963 (1·97)	0·50 2·09

Notes
Explanation of variables given in text, p. 000.
Figures in parentheses are 't' statistics.
*$(H_t^{aE} - H_{t-1}^a)$ is used in place of $(H_t^{aE} - H_t^a)$. The latter also 'works'.
† If we define equilibrium minus actual inventories for this industry in terms of finished-goods inventories rather than aggregate inventories, this variable performs much better and still remains significant when the US price variable enters the equation.
USP = relevant US price index.
RMP = relevant raw-material price index.

Finally, Courchene examines the possibility that there is some asymmetry in response to excess demand. Prices may be more flexible upwards than downwards or stock depletion may be viewed with less concern than stock build-up. The excess demand variable $(H_t^E - H_t)$ is therefore split into two components: $(H_t^E - H_t)^+$ when positive (excess demand) and $(H_t^E - H_t)^-$ when negative (deficient demand), see Table 6.5. It is evident that excess demand has a much greater influence on prices than does deficient demand, implying that prices are much more flexible upwards than downwards. This clearly has implications for inflation in that asymmetry produces a rachet effect whereby fluctuations in demand cause successive increases in price but not the offsetting decreases, thereby cranking up the average price level over time.

This result is similar to that of Heathfield and Pearce [15] whose price equations derive from Pearce [29]. In their model the entrepreneur is assumed to be unable to predict with any accuracy the positions of his cost and demand curves but is aware of their shapes. At the beginning of each market 'day' he knows past periods sales and costs and the current

Table 6.5 Some estimates of price flexibility, real terms, 1956=62. $\Delta P_t = a + b_1(H_t^{aE} - H_t^a)^+ + b_2(H_t^{aE} - H_t^a)^- + e_t$

Industry	Where $H_t^{aE} - H_t^a$ is split into two series; one containing the positive values of $H_t^{aE} - H_t^a$ and the other containing the negative values							Where $H_t^{aE} - H_t^a$ is split into two series; one containing the actual values of $H_t^{aE} - H_t^a$ whenever these values are above the mean of $H_t^{aE} - H_t^a$, and the other containing the values of $H_t^{aE} - H_t^a$ below the mean						
					Estimated without the intercept							Estimated without the intercept		
	a	b_1	b_2	R/DW	b_1	b_2	R/DW	a	b_1	b_2	R/DW	b_1	b_2	R/DW
Heavy transportation								−0·6090 (0·91)	0·1658 (2·20)	0·1528 (1·48)	0·38 (1·83)	0·1003 (4·78)	0·0594 (2·28)	0·40 (1·86)
Heavy electrical machinery	−0·1047 (0·14)	1·523 (1·63)	2·045 (1·36)	0·53 (1·71)	1·423 (2·48)	2·215 (2·66)	0·55 (1·70)							
Iron and steel	−0·0338 (0·19)	0·1034 (3·53)	−0·0260 (0·81)	0·58 (1·28)	0·0989 (5·81)	−0·0211 (1·08)	0·61 (1·25)							
Textiles								−0·1683 (1·22)	0·1634 (2·35)	0·1326 (0·87)	0·32 (1·64)	0·1050 (2·09)	0·0890 (0·60)	0·28 (1·47)
Leather	0·4100 (1·00)	4·625 (2·43)	3·099 (1·33)	0·52 (1·65)	5·806 (3·87)	1·537 (0·89)	0·52 (1·71)							
Total manufacturing	0·0544 (0·44)	0·0353 (3·26)	−0·0289 (1·18)	0·51 (2·36)	0·0313 (5·24)	−0·0205 (1·36)	0·54 (2·33)							
Heavy electrical machinery*	−0·9462 (1·36)	1·819 (2·54)	0·0358 (0·04)	0·46 (1·63)	1·099 (2·24)	1·049 (1·05)	0·42 (1·63)							

Notes

* For this equation, b_1 and b_2 refer to $(H_t^{aE} - H_{t-1}^a)^+$ and $(H_t^{aE} - H_{t-1}^a)^-$ respectively, rather than to $(H_t^{aE} - H_t^a)^+$ and $(H_t^{aE} - H_t^a)^-$.
Explanation of variables given in text, p. 172.
Figures in parentheses are 't' statistics.

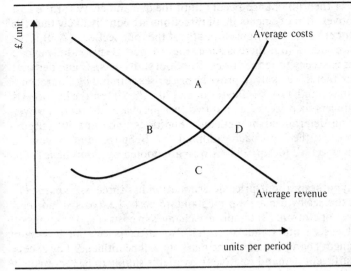

Fig. 6.1

inventory level; he is searching for a price–output combination for the coming period which equates output with sales and which avoids losses. In terms of the standard diagram (Fig. 6.1) the two curves divide the quadrant into four parts (A, B, C and D). The entrepreneur can choose any point in the quadrant (price–output decision). If the point lies in A then price lies above cost and profits are made. Similarly, output is greater than sales and hence inventories build up. In B price still lies above costs and hence profits are positive, but sales exceed production and inventories fall. In C inventories fall and profits are negative. In D inventories rise and profits are negative. In order to meet our minimum requirements the entrepreneur must avoid C and D since they are loss making. Thus, the boundary between A and B is the set of possible combinations of price and output which satisfy the no loss and steady inventories requirements. To get on to this line from somewhere in A, prices may be reduced and/or output cut.

From somewhere in B prices may be increased and/or output increased;
From somewhere in C prices increase and/or output cut;
From somewhere in D prices increase and output cut;
Each of these will bring the entrepreneur towards the A/B boundary.

The Pearce hypothesis is then that the entrepreneur decides price and output changes by observing excess inventories or excess profits. As always the difficulty is to decide what is 'normal' inventories or 'normal' profits.

If the entrepreneur chooses a point in the quadrant which does satisfy his criteria then no change occurs until the demand curve (or the cost curve) moves. If movements in all directions are equally likely then the entrepreneur could find himself in any of the four sections (A, B, C or D). In three out of four there is a tendency to increase price, only in one is there a tendency to reduce price. Random shifts of costs and demand curves are therefore likely to provoke price rises as found by Courchene.

Stromback and Trivedi (Pearce et al. [30, Ch. 5]) test the hypothesis that producers fix prices on a modified cost-plus basis, the mark-up over costs being determined by demand conditions and capacity output. This, too, is the approach adopted by Schultze and Tryon in Duesenberry et al. [6, pp. 284–5] who are quoted by Courchene [2, p. 328] thus:

> Our hypothesis about price determination has three basic parts: (1) prices are set by a mark up on standard costs, i.e. costs at 'normal' levels of operation; (2) temporary changes in costs (i.e. deviations of actual costs from standard costs) also affect prices but less than permanent changes; and (3) the mark up will be influenced by excess or insufficient demand relative to available supply to be represented by a capacity utilization variable or the deviation from a straight line trend of the ratio of inventories to output. T.C.J.

It matters little whether the argument is couched in terms of mark-up or as straight price decisions; the basic ingredients are cost influences due to labour and raw materials and demand influences representable by inventory disequilibria or expected excess demand. What is new is the introduction of an explicit capacity variables. The short-run average cost curve is no longer flat but rises sharply at some 'capacity' output. These are costs associated with movements along the short-run cost curve rather than movements of the short-run cost curve (wage and material costs). Capacity is usually represented by the Wharton measure which simply identifies peaks in the output series of any particular industry or group of industries and, by joining up peaks with straight lines, determines capacity output. Deviations of actual output from this capacity is called capacity utilization. For a survey of such measures see Hilton [16].

A further influence on cost curves is of course technical progress or factor productivity change. This is computed by examining the inputs and production levels. Stromback and Trivedi use the output–employment ratio divided by its own time trend.

Both capacity and productivity measures, then, use actual output in their construction and actual output may be demand determined – i.e. the influence of neither capacity variables nor productivity variables is unambiguously a cost influence. To quote Stromback and Trivedi [30, p. 126]:

> Partly for reasons to do with the limitations imposed by the available data and partly because of the inherent conceptual difficulties in measuring variables such as CM (raw material costs), CL (labour

costs) and $H(D)$ (a function of capacity usage) we have not entirely succeeded in satisfactorily disentangling the respective roles of these variables in price determination. It seems that complex econometric problems arise when we try to replace 'unobservables' by their measurable counterparts. . . . However, it is clear that the costs of materials and labour as well as fluctuations in demand affect prices in a distinct way and that none of these influences can be safely neglected.

Schultze and Tryon [6, pp. 290–1] conclude that:

1. Normal costs, measured by normal unit labour costs or in a few industries by the sum of normal unit labour costs and normal depreciation costs, are the dominant influences on prices.
2. Temporary cost changes, measured by deviations of actual from normal unit labour costs, in some industries have an effect on prices, but this influence, where it exists, is much less than changes in normal costs.
3. Raw material prices, where raw materials are an important element of cost, exercise a significant influence on prices. . . . Thus short-run variations in raw material prices appear to be passed on more consistently than short-run labor cost variations.
4. In many industries, but not all, markups over normal costs are modified by excess or deficient demand relative to supply. In far too many cases the capacity utilization variables proved disappointing . . . the inventories/output measure of relative supply pressure yielded a better fit. . . . In those industries where capacity utilization ratio appeared to be significant the positive deviations of the utilization ratio were generally more important.

Thus, it seems that while there are difficulties associated with empirical work of this kind, it is possible to say something about the principal determinants of wholesale prices and to indictate some asymmetries and some high-inertia variables and some low-inertia variables. Information of this kind can obviously be used to advantage when formulating anti-inflation policies. Stability of (or smooth changes in) aggregate demand and raw material prices are clearly as important as controlling the mean rate of growth of them. For labour costs, however, the high-frequency fluctuations are smoothed out.

Before concluding this section on wholesale prices it would seem appropriate to point out that many studies of price formation (including Stromback and Trivedi [30] and Schultze and Tryon [6]) seek also to explain changes in labour costs and changes in material prices. The latter in Stromback and Trivedi involve the use of an input–output matrix to translate prices of some industries' output into costs for other industries. For aggregate study this is clearly not necessary, but if wage rates are influenced by price level and prices are in turn influenced by wages then some simultaneous-equation system must be used. See for example, Dicks Mirreaux [4], Espasa [8]. It has not been intended that this chapter should look behind the price decision since costs are explained elsewhere in this book. What has been offered in this section is an indication of some of the work which has been done on price decision of producers. The difficulties faced and the results achieved have been illustrated by taking examples from one or two pieces of work in this field.

The distributive trades

Wholesale prices are undoubtedly an important element in costs of goods bought by industry and by households (or more generally final demanders), but for many goods, particularly those bought by households, retail prices rather than wholesale prices are appropriate. Increases in retail prices may arise by imposing taxes or by increasing wholesale prices or by increasing the mark-up of the distributive trades. This latter is a very large element of retail prices (as indicated in the introduction) and this section is concerned with explaining how distribution margins change over time.

Most work on this topic is couched in terms of mark-ups and how they vary. The simplest approach would be to assume fixed or simple time trend mark-ups, but Heathfield and Evans [14] show that the variation across industries is large (from 70% for chemicals to 20% for food, drink and tobacco) and variations over time are also large, having strong seasonal patterns – chemicals, for example, declining from 75 per cent in 1960 to 46 per cent in 1966. This, it seems, is something to be explained.

Timbrell, in an unpublished paper [41], quotes Mill [24, p. 532], Marshall [23, p. 396] and Wicksell [45, p. 86], each of whom argues that distribution requires separate treatment.

Mill [24]:

> Hence it is that, the price paid by the consumers, so large a proportion is absorbed by the gains of Retailers; and anyone who enquires into the amount which reaches the hands of those who make the things he buys, will often be astonished at its smallness. . . . Retail prices do not follow with all the regularity which might be expected the action of the causes which determine wholesale prices.

Marshall [23]:

> It stands to reason that retail prices follow wholesale prices the less closely the larger elements of partial monopoly and of expenses of working that enter into them; . . . So small alterations in wholesale prices (or in cost, for the retailer is often an agent of the producer), including those due to taxation, work themselves out in changes in quality, unless it happens that a change in nominal price had already been impending.

Wicksell [45]:

> To a considerable extent the apparent divergence of retail prices from
> the law of costs and from wholesale prices is to be regarded as an
> example of joint supply.

Much later George [10] examined the efficiency of distributive trades,
using as a measure of output the quantity of goods sold. No allowance is
made for the fact that distributors provide a service and it is this service
rather than simply the quantity of throughput which constitutes the
'output' of the distributive trades: they are a service industry. Hence,
although volume of throughput has been increasing per unit of input (as
George suggests) the service elements may well have been decreasing.
Indeed Schwartzman [35], using Canadian data for the years 1929–63,
estimates that the service element per transaction has been decreasing to
the extent that it explains away more than half the apparent
productivity changes.

Schultz and Tryon in Duesenberry et al. [6] treat aggregate wholesale
and retail trade in a similar manner to that which deals with other
industries' price equations, the dependent variable being the value added
per unit of real throughput. The explanatory variables are unit labour
costs and inventories – the latter being used as a measure of excess
demand. It is of course a measure of demand for commodities rather
than a demand for 'value added' by the distributive trades. The use of
unit labour costs as an explanatory variable implies that the production
function for the distributive trades is known (or is explained elsewhere
in the model) otherwise wage rates could not be translated into labour
cost per unit of output. The problem is that distributive trades have very
flexible production functions – if indeed one can speak of production
functions in this context. What is being supplied is a joint good–part
commodity, part service. The commodity cannot be bought without
buying the service and the service is not paid for unless the commodity is
bought. The service/commodity mix can be changed by changing the
level of stocks or the number of employees. The mix can also be changed
by changing the level of demand. When demand increases less service is
given per customer. If service is provided but not bought, then it flows
to waste since service cannot be stored.

The approach used by Heathfield and Evans [14] is a simple one. They
assume that distributors use a rule-of-thumb mark-up to spread their
expected costs evenly over the commodities they sell. Thus, they
estimate their total costs and total sales and spread the former over the
latter in a uniform way. This mark-up is held until losses (or very low
profits) cause it to be revised upwards. The problem is therefore to
specify the principal influences on retailers' profits.

Mark-up is defined as

$$d = \frac{P_r q - P_h q_h - P_m q_m}{P_h q_h + P_m q_m}$$

where: P_r is retail price net of taxes,
    P_h is ex-works price of home-produced, home-consumed goods,
    P_m is ex-docks price of imports,
    q_m is the quantity of imports,
    q_h is the quantity of home-produced, home-consumed goods, and
    $q = q_h + q_m$.

Here, d would be set to yield normal profits on some expected level of sales, q.

If sales fall below the expected level, the mark-up will be insufficient to cover normal profits and will be forced up. If sales are above expectations, then excess profits are earned and other cost increases may be absorbed into the existing mark-up. Expected sales are estimated by regressing actual sales on a quadratic time trend and seasonal dummies. The residuals of these equations were used as abnormal sales. In other words, distributors have successfully predicted the main systematic parts of future sales (although it is not known how).

Low profits may also be due to increased costs, but this would be so only if the costs in the distributive trade changed at a rate different from those in the manufacturing sectors. For example, if all labour costs rose by 10 per cent and productivity was everywhere the same, then the mark-up would yield 10 per cent more revenue since the supply price (of which it is a proportion) had risen by 10 per cent. This would be sufficient to absorb the 10 per cent rise in costs and maintain profits. If, however, costs or productivity in the manufacturing sector changes at a rate different from that in distribution, then the mark-up would have to change to maintain normal profits. It is impossible to measure productivity in the distributive trades since their output cannot be measured, hence it is assumed that any difference between costs in manufacture and costs of distribution may be approximated by a quadratic time trend. The signs which their coefficients will take in the explanatory equation would indicate the relative rates of technical progress in manufacturing and distribution and cannot be assessed *a priori*. It is of course impossible to distinguish between changes in distributive efficiency and changes in commodity/service mix, hence the quadratic time trend is a catch-all for both these effects.

Purchase tax and duties may also influence the mark-up. This may be simply due to timing otherwise inevitable mark-up changes to coincide with changes in tax or due to the increased costs of holding retail stocks when taxes are increased. Some trades may typically set their mark-ups on gross of tax supply prices while others use net of tax supply prices. Heathfield and Evans include a tax variable in their explanatory equation.

Seasonal dummies were included since some industries' products are subject to seasonal 'sales'. This is particularly so for textiles, leather and clothing and mining and quarrying products. There may also be some seasonal influence due to changing product mix over quarters.

During the sample period the UK legislation against Resale Price

Maintenance was enacted and this clearly may have some influence on distribution margins. Resale Price Maintenance has provoked an extensive literature on the distributive trades. See, for example, Reddaway [33] Pickering [31] Gould and Preston [11]. The Act was passed in the fourth quarter of 1964, but it may have been anticipated in some cases while in others its impact was postponed by appeals to the Restrictive Trades Practices Court. It is difficult to estimate the point in time when the Act became effective. The solution was simply to insert a dummy variable which took the value 0 up to 1964. iii, then took the values 1, 2, 3, . . . up to the end of the sample period. This trend was thought to be the best way of representing the gradual impact of the Bill subsequent upon its being enacted. This is not an entirely defensible approach, but seemed the best which could be done with the data available.

Finally, they investigated the possibility that imported commodities were treated differently from home-produced commodities, i.e. if the mark-ups on imports were similar to those on the home-produced equivalents.

If mark-ups on imports are typically higher than those on home produce it would be expected that overall mark-up increased as imports become a bigger proportion of total throughput. The ratio of imports to home products was therefore entered as an explanatory variable, and its coefficient will be positive if imports are subject to a higher mark-up than home produce and negative if lower.

Furthermore, if imports and home produce are substitutes there will be a tendency for them to have similar retail prices irrespective of their supply prices. If, for example, retail prices are fixed by the supply price and mark-up on home produce, then the mark-up on imported commodities will be determined by their supply prices. If this is so then:

$$D = q_m(P_r - P_m) + q_h(P_r - P_h),$$

but

$$P_r = M_h P_h,$$

where M_h is the percentage mark-up on home goods, therefore

$$D = q_m M_h P_h - q_m P_m + q_h P_h M_h - q_h P_h,$$
$$D = M_h P_h(q_m + q_h) - q_m P_m - q_h P_h = M_h P_h q - P_s q$$

and

$$d = \frac{D}{q_m P_m + q_h P_h} = \frac{D}{P_s q},$$

therefore

$$d = M_h \frac{P_h}{P_s} - 1.$$

That is to say if margins on imports are determined by their supply prices and by the mark-up on home produce (i.e. there is a common retail price) then the overall margin (d) will be a function of the relative price of home to total supplies. Conversely, if the mark-up on imports is the same as the mark-up on home produce then:

$$D = q_m P_m M_h + q_h P_h M_h,$$

therefore

$$D = M_h / q_m P_m + q_h P_h /,$$

then

$$d = \frac{D}{q_m P_m + q_h P_h} = M_h,$$

in which case distribution margins are unaffected by price ratio of home produce to imports. If margins are sensitive to the ratio of import price to total supply price it can be concluded that there is a tendency for retail prices to be similar as between imported goods and home-produced goods, even though supply prices differ.

The final explanatory equation estimated by Heathfield and Evans for each of their six commodity groups was therefore:

$$d = \alpha_1 + \alpha_2 t + \alpha_3 t^2 + \alpha_4 T + \alpha_5 R + \alpha_6 V + \alpha_7 P + \alpha_8 D + \alpha_9 \sigma_1 + \alpha_{10} \sigma_2 + \alpha_{11} \sigma_3,$$

where: α_1 is the mark-up if all other exogenous variables are at their mean values,

t is time,

T is implicit (tax and duty) rate,

R is abnormal sales,

V is the ratio of the value of imports to the value of home produce,

P is the ratio of the price of imports to the combined supply price,

D is the Resale Price Maintenance dummy, and

σ_1, σ_2 and σ_3 are seasonal dummies.

The results of these regressions are shown in Table 6.6.

A general comment which may be made about these results is the regularity with which the abnormal sales variable appears. In every case it is significant (at the 5% level) and in every case it has a negative coefficient. The implication is that when an economic squeeze is imposed so as to depress sales below their 'expected' or 'normal' level, distributors increase their margins. Any gains which the squeeze may achieve by depressing manufacturing costs are therefore offset to some extent by the reactions of distributors. This offsetting effect is of course a once and for all change, whereas the squeeze may be intended to reduce the rate of change of manufacturing prices. Nevertheless, in the short run a squeeze may have an inflationary rather than a deflationary effect on retail prices.

In order to estimate the extent of this offsetting reaction it is necessary to consider some actual cases. For each group of industries the greatest R experienced over the sample period yield the following corresponding changes in retail prices:

Table 6.6 Estimated mark-up equations

Chemical and allied

$$d = 1.16 \ - 0.489T + 0.0093t - 0.0001t^2 - 0.0085R + 0.074P$$
$$ (6.81) \ \ (-4.84) \ \ (3.39) \ \ (-1.48) \ \ (-1.82) \ \ (1.51)$$
$$R^2 = 0.89 \qquad\qquad DW = 1.82$$

Food, drink and tobacco

$$d = 0.61 \ - 0.483T + 0.0001t^2 - 0.002R + 0.166P + 0.018\sigma_1 - 0.008\sigma_2 - 0.016\sigma_3$$
$$ (3.26) \ \ (-3.70) \ \ (2.01) \ \ (-5.12) \ \ (1.69) \ \ (1.07) \ \ (-1.18) \ \ (-1.33)$$
$$R^2 = 0.62 \qquad\qquad DW = 1.33$$

Mining and quarrying

$$d = 0.47 \ + 0.007t - 0.0001t^2 - 0.004R + 0.04\sigma_1 - 0.018\sigma_2 - 0.04\sigma_3 + 0.0078D$$
$$ (19.9) \ \ (2.65) \ \ (-2.21) \ \ (-1.92) \ \ (3.5) \ \ (-1.56) \ \ (-3.54) \ \ (1.11)$$
$$R^2 = 0.49 \qquad\qquad DW = 0.64$$

Engineering and allied

$$d = 0.53 \ - 0.0001t^2 - 0.17T - 0.0012R + 1.21\ V + 0.196P - 0.02\sigma_1 - 0.018\sigma_2 + 0.01\sigma_3$$
$$ (4.92) \ \ (-1.81) \ \ (-1.93) \ \ (2.70) \ \ (1.84) \ \ (3.09) \ \ (-2.16) \ \ (-1.99) \ \ (1.60)$$
$$R^2 = 0.68 \qquad\qquad DW = 1.82$$

Textiles, leather and clothing

$$d = 0.36 \ - 0.0002R - 0.0039D - 0.24\ V + 0.019P - 0.0097T$$
$$ (14.32) \ \ (-2.19) \ \ (-3.08) \ \ (-1.31) \ \ (1.33) \ \ (-1.05).$$
$$R^2 = 0.89 \qquad\qquad DW = 1.45$$

Other manufacturing

$$d = 0.42 \ - 0.0009R - 0.177\ V + 0.01\sigma_1 + 0.005\sigma_2 - 0.005\sigma_3$$
$$ (8.18) \ \ (-1.98) \ \ (-1.19) \ \ (2.90) \ \ (1.83) \ \ (-1.88)$$
$$R^2 = 0.51 \qquad\qquad DW = 1.96$$

Notes

The figure in (parentheses) below each parameter is its '*t*' statistic. Those variables which had '*t*' values of less than unity are excluded from these results.

Chemical and allied, 3% change in Pr
Food, drink and tobacco, 9% change in Pr
Mining and quarrying, 1·3% change in Pr
Engineering and allied, 2·5% change in Pr
Textiles, leather and clothing, 0·3% change in Pr
Other manufacturing, 0·7% change in Pr

Over all these industries the maximum effect is on the food, drink and tobacco industries. These industries do, however, constitute a major part of consumers' expenditure and may have appreciable counter-productive effect on the attempts to stabilise prices by an economic squeeze.

The Resale Price Maintenance dummy variable appears significantly different from zero only in the textile, leather and clothing industries. It has the expected negative sign. The appropriateness of our form of dummy variable is of course highly questionable, but if it is accepted (and it does seem to work in one industry) then the influence of that effect on retail prices seems to have been much less than has elsewhere been supposed.

The tax term (which includes customs and excise duties) is significant in three groups of industries, chemical and allied industry, food, drink and tobacco, and engineering and allied, the first two of which bear a substantial load of customs and excise duties. The large negative coefficients on these tax variables imply the following changes in d owing to the maximum variations in T over the sample period:

Chemicals $\triangle d = 0{\cdot}45$
Food, drink and tobacco $\triangle d = 0{\cdot}25$
Engineering $\triangle d = 0{\cdot}10$

These changes in percentage mark-up are very large in the cases of chemicals and food, particularly the latter which typically has a mark-up of only about 35 per cent.

Part of these difficulties may arise owing to the unsatisfactory way in which the implicit tax variable is calculated. By dividing tax revenue by expenditure one may pick up effects other than those simply due to changing tax rates.

Apart from this it may be that on many forms of chemicals and food, drink and tobacco products, the mark-up is fixed according to the quantity sold rather than the value of the sales. This may be the case for example if petrol is retailed at 2·5p per gallon or if cigarettes are retailed at 0·5p per packet. These fixed margins would create negative changes in the 'd' variable if the manufacturing sector increased wholesale prices (P_s) by more than that due to duty or purchase tax. Thus, the wholesale value would rise with 'D' remaining fixed to yield a fall in d (since d is $(D/q_s P_s)$).

The engineering industry is rather a different case. The implication here is that some taxes (mostly purchase taxes) are absorbed by the distributive trades. The trend terms appear in most equations. Positive coefficients imply that manufacturing costs have risen less quickly than distribution costs or that the service given per unit of commodity has been increasing over time.

The ratio of the value of imports to home produce (V) is nowhere significantly different from zero, which implies that over the sample period there has been no persistent difference in mark-up as between imported and home-produced goods. The proportion of these commodities which are imported is very small and one may wish to accept these variables even at 10 per cent level of significance. If so then these results imply that, for engineering goods, imports have higher mark-ups than do home produce. For textiles and other manufacturing the reverse is the case. However, the results, when translated into the implied differences between home mark-up and import mark-up, are somewhat large.

It is known that

$$d = \frac{V_h}{V} d_h + \frac{V_m d_m}{V},$$

where: d is our estimated joint mark-up,

V_h is the supply priced value of home produce,

V_m is the supply priced value of imports,

d_h is the mark-up on home produce,

d_m is the mark-up on imports, and

V is $V_h + V_m$.

Therefore

$$d = \frac{(V - V_m)d_h}{V} + \frac{V_m d_m}{V},$$

$$d = d_h + \frac{V_m}{V}|d_m - d_h|,$$

hence the coefficient on V_m/V is $d_m - d_h$. For engineering this is $+1.21$, indicating a very large difference between import and home margins. For textiles a somewhat more credible difference of -0.24 is obtained. For other manufacturing a still smaller difference of -0.177 was found.

The ratio of import prices to home produce prices (P) is significant only in the engineering industry. (This is the industry which has the largest element of imports of consumer goods.) The significant P implies that import mark-ups are not a fixed proportion of home mark-ups. If the lower significance levels are accepted then chemicals, food, engineering and textiles all appear to have varying mark-ups as between imports and home produce. The mining industry commodity is assumed to be totally supplied from home industries for these consumer categories.

Seasonal dummies appear in food, mining, engineering and other manufacturing. Surprisingly, no seasonals appear in the textile industry: surprising because this industry traditionally holds spring and autumn 'sales'. The mining industry responds as one would expect in that typically coal is sold at lower prices in the summer than in the winter and clearly the distributors bear much of this price reduction. Food, engineering and other manufacturing are possibly explained in terms of product mix changing or that mark-ups do change, for example at Christmas, when demand is high and is expected to be high.

Conclusions

This chapter deals with prices as part of the decision-making processes of individual entrepreneurs, whether they be manufacturers or retailers. Manufacturing costs, import prices and taxes are taken as given exogenously, and the pricing behaviour of firms is derived within this somewhat truncated framework. As far as manufacturers' prices are concerned, it seems to matter very little how rigorous the derivation of the decision rules may be. The forms of the equation actually estimated are remarkably similar and usually contain measures of costs, demand

and capacity. Difficulties occur when expectations of variables over some finite time horizon are required but there are many ways of avoiding or simplifying them. Some models introduce asymmetrical responses by the entrepreneurs to one or more variables, usually on the grounds that costs of change functions ought not to be identical for increases or decreases or that dealing with excess demand is not so urgent as dealing with deficient demand.

These asymmetries give rise to a rachet effect which may jack up prices even when costs (or demand) fluctuate about some steady level. This would imply that price stabilisation policies may themselves be responsible for some price increases because of their effects on demand. It also seems that price fixers react more speedily to some cost changes than to others. Raw material price stability may be more important than wage stability if some secular rise in prices is to be avoided.

The models chosen for rather detailed treatment in this sector were those of Hay [13] and Courchene [2] which are in many ways typical or illustrative of the work done in this area.

In similar vein the somewhat sparse work done on retail mark-ups is investigated primarily through the model of Heathfield and Evans [14]; the principal cause of mark-up change seems to be unexpected changes in the volume of sales. Depressing the economy in order to contain wage costs will thereby increase retail mark-ups. This offsetting response of retailers is once and for all, whereas the decline in the rate of change in wages has a continuing effect on costs, but nevertheless in the short run depressing sales increases mark-ups.

The main policy implications of this chapter are therefore that although a comparison of two policy regimes may lead one to advise a change in policy there are often costs associated with the change of policy or the period of transition, and these costs though little understood may well argue that current policies be maintained.

References and Bibliography

1. **Carlson, J. A. and Parkin, M.**, 'Inflationary expectations', *Economica, 42,* 123–38, May 1975.
2. **Courchene, T.**, 'An analysis of the price–inventory nexus with empirical application to the Canadian manufacturing Sector', *International Economic Review, 10,* No. 3, 315–36, Oct., 1969.
3. **Cowling, K. and Waterson, M.**, 'Price cost margins and market structure'. *Economica, 43,* 267–74, 1976.
4. **Dicks Mireaux, L. A.**, 'The inter-relationship between cost and price changes 1946–1959', *Oxford Economic Papers,* **13,** 267–92, Oct., 1961.
5. **Domberger, S.**, *Industrial, market structure and the rate of price adjustment.* 'Centre for Industrial Economic and Business Research, Univ. of Warwick, Discussion Paper No. 71, 1977.

6. **Duesenberry, J., et al. (eds).** *The Brookings Quarterly Econometric Model of the United States.* Rand McNally, Chicago, 1965.
7. **Eckstein O. (ed.),** *The Econometrics of Price Determination, Chicago–Rand McNally Conference (1970),* SSRC, Board of Governors of Federal System, Washington DC, 1972.
8. **Espasa, A.,** 'A simultaneous dynamic equation model for wages and earnings and price inflation in the U.K. 1944–1970', contributed paper at the European meeting of the econometric Society, Oslo, 1973.
9. **Fuchs V. R. (ed,),** *Production and Productivity in the Service Industries, NBER Studies in Income and Wealth,* Vol. 34, Columbia Univ. Press, New York, 1969.
10. **George, K. D.,** 'Productivity and the distributive trades', *Bulletin of the Oxford University Institute of Economics and Statistics,* **31,** 61–75, May, 1969.
11. **Gould J. R. and Preston L. E.,** 'Retail price maintenance and retail outlets' *Economica,* **32,** 302–12, 1965.
12. **Grossman, S.,** 'Rational expectations and the econometric modelling of markets subject to uncertainty', *Journal of Econometrics,* **3,** 255–72, 1975.
13. **Hay, G. A.,** 'Production, price and inventory theory', *American Economic Review,* **60,** 531–45, Sept., 1970
14. **Heathfield, D. F. and Evan G. J.,** 'Distribution margins in the U.K.: a quarterly analysis', *Applied Economics,* **3,** 205–17, 1971.
15. **Heathfield, D. F. and Pearce, I. F.,** 'A view of the Southampton econometric model of the U.K. and its trading partners', in [34], 83–128, 1975.
16. **Hilton, K.,** 'Capital and capacity utilization in the U.K.: their measurement and reconciliation', *Bulletin of the Oxford University Institute of Economics and Statistics,* **32,** 187–217, 1970.
17. **Hilton, K. and Cornelius, D. J.,** 'Planned stock holding. Evidence from British company data', *Oxford Bulletin of Economics and Statistics,* **36,** 247–65, Nov., 1974.
18. **Hilton, K. and Heathfield, D. F., (eds,),** *The Econometric Study of the U.K.* Macmillan. London 1970.
19. **Keynes, J. M.,** *Collected Works,* Vol. XIV, Macmillan. London 1973.
20. **Lawson, T.,** 'Adaptive expectations and uncertainty', mimeograph, Cambridge, DAE GPP 448, 1977.
21. **Lovell, M. C.,** 'Manufacturers' inventories, sales expectations and the acceleration principle', *Econometrica,* **29,** 293–314, July 1961.
22. **Liu, T. C.,** 'An exploratory quarterly econometric model of effective demand in the postwar U.S. economy', *Econometrica,* **31,** 301–48, July 1963.
23. **Marshall, A.,** 'Retail prices' from an undated manuscript in [32], 356, 1956.
24. **Mill, J. S.,** *Principles of Political Economy with some of their applications to Social Philosophy,* Vol. 1., fifth edition, 532. Parker, Son and Bourne, London, 1862.
25. **Mills, E. S.,** *Price, Output and Inventory Policy.* Wiley, New York, 1962.
26. **Muth, J. F.,** 'Rational expectations and the theory of price movements', *Econometrica,* **29,** 315–35, 1961.
27. **Nerlove, M.,** 'Adaptive expectations and cobweb phenomena', *Quarterly Journal of Economics,* **72,** 224–40, May 1958.
28. **Nerlove M.,** 'On the structure of serial dependence in some U.S. price series', in [7].
29. **Pearce, I. F.,** 'The Southampton econometric model of the U.K. and its trading partners', in [18], 29–52, 1970.
30. **Pearce, I. F. et. al.,** *A Model of Output, Employment, Wages and Prices in the U.K.* Cambridge Univ. Press, 1976.
31. **Pickering, J. F.,** *Retail Price Maintenance in Practice.* Allen and Unwin, London, 1956.
32. **Pigou, A. C. (ed.),** *Memorials of Alfred Marshall.* Kelly and Millman, New York, 1956.
33. **Reddaway, W. B.,** 'Effects of the Selective Employment Tax', *First Report: The Distributive Trades,* HMSO, London, 1970.
34. **Renton, G. A.,** *Modelling the Economy.* Heinemann, London 1975.
35. **Schwartzman, D.,** 'The growth of sales per man hour in retail trade 1929–1963', in [9], 1972.

36. **Silberston, A.,** 'Surveys of applied economics: price behaviour of firms', *Economic Journal*, **80**, 511–82, 1970.
37. **Simon, H. A.,** 'Dynamic programming under uncertainty with a quadratic criterion function', *Econometrica*, **24**, 74–81, Jan., 1956.
38. **Steuer, M. D. and Budd, A. P.,** 'Price and output decisions of firms – a critique of Mills' theory', *Manchester School*, **36**, 1–25, 1968.
39. **Theil, H.,** *Economic Forecasts and Policy*, North-Holland, Amsterdam, 2nd ed., 1961.
40. **Theil, H.,** *Optimum Decision Rules for Government and Industry*. North-Holland, Amsterdam, 1964.
41. **Timbrell, M.,** 'On retail prices and distribution margins' (mimeo), Univ. of Exeter, 1977.
42. **Trivedi, P. K.,** Inventory behaviour in U.K. manufacturing 1956–67', *Review of Economic Studies*, **37**, 517–36, 1970.
43. **Turnovsky, S. J.,** 'Empirical evidence on the formation of price expectations', *Journal of the American Statistical Association*, **65**, 1441–1454, Dec., 1970.
44. **Wallis, K.,** 'Output decisions of firms again', *Manchester School*, **38**, 163–5, 1970.
45. **Wicksell, K.,** *Lectures in Political Economy*, Vol. 1. 86. Routledge, London, 1934.

Chapter 7

A Keynesian approach to inflation theory and policy

J. A. Kregel

Introduction

Students who have been introduced to Keynes' theories by means of the familiar 45° line diagram or the IS–LM curve approach may consider an analysis of prices and inflation based on the *General Theory* a contradiction in terms. Indeed, these simplified representations of Keynes' theories are usually presented in real terms or without any explicit reference to prices or price determination. Since Keynes' approach is classified as 'macroeconomic' it is often argued that it need not deal directly with such factors which are normally considered as 'microeconomic'. The discussion of prices is thus carried out under a different analytical framework (as well as in a different course of lectures). This reasoning is supported by the widely held view, recently echoed by a Nobel prize-winner (in economics), that Keynes proposed no explanation of prices and did not even discuss such problems (see Friedman [7], p. 222).

Yet, Keynes' analysis was expressly monetary, and he expressly rejected any analytical separation between microeconomic and macroeconomic theory (or between the theory of value and distribution, and money and prices). Thus, while it is true that there is no separate, independent analysis of prices in the *General Theory*, the analysis of prices forms an integral part of the overall analysis of output and employment considered as a whole. It is within the perspective of the analysis of the determinants of the level of output and employment that Keynes develops his views on the determination of prices and inflation.

Given this widely accepted (but erroneous) view that such topics are not discussed in Keynes' work, and in order to demonstrate more clearly how such analysis is integrated into Keynes' particular analysis of the levels of output and employment, it is useful to look carefully at the historical development of Keynes' work for, perhaps surprisingly to some, Keynes' early interests were in monetary theory, and more particularly, concerned to give a more detailed explanation of the determination of money prices than that found in the traditional (i.e. what Keynes defined as classical) determination of prices by means of the Quantity Theory of Money. Indeed, in *A Tract on Monetary Reform*, [19] Keynes was basically preoccupied with the effects of post-war inflation on the economic and social structure of Europe. In this sense Keynes' early writing can be considered as directly addressing the problems of the determination of prices and inflation. How this interest evolved into the analysis of output and employment in the *General Theory* will be the subject of the next section and will, perhaps, help to explain why some economists consider Keynes to have abandoned the analysis of prices.

From prices to output, from the Treatise to the General Theory

In the *Tract on Monetary Reform* [19] Keynes provided an exposition and explanation of inflationary conditions in the period following the First World War from a quantity theory viewpoint. The explanation of variations in the general level of prices (the purchasing power of money) remained as one of the basic objectives of Keynes' *Treatise on Money* [20]. The theory that Keynes developed in that book was considered by its author to be one of a number of possible 'versions of the Quantity Theory of Money' (Keynes [20], Vol. I, p. 138). Within the framework of the fundamental equations of the *Treatise*, which determined the prices of consumption and investment goods in terms of efficiency wages and the difference between savings and investment, Keynes identified three different types of inflation. Income inflation and profit inflation referred to price changes generated by changes in the two terms of the first of his fundamental equations. Income inflation referred to a rise in 'efficiency earnings', i.e. money wages per unit of output. Profit inflation was divided into two separate types: commodity inflation and capital inflation. The first referred to increases in the prices of consumption goods and raw materials relative to costs, the second, to increases in the prices of capital goods [20, Vol. I, p. 155].

In the *Treatise*, one of the basic objections that Keynes made to the Quantity Theory was that it failed in 'separating out those factors through which in a modern economic system, the causal process actually operated during a period of change'. While 'the real task . . . is to treat the problem dynamically, analysing the different elements involved, in such a manner as *to exhibit the causal process by which the price level is determined* and the method of transition from one position of equilibrium to another' ([20], Vol. I, p. 133, emphasis added).

In discussing the role of money and credit in the cycle Marshall [28, p. 250] had written: 'as credit by growing makes itself grow, so when distrust has taken the place of confidence, failure and panic breed panic and failure. The commercial storm leaves its path strewn with ruin. When it is over there is a calm, but a dull heavy calm'. In discussing the effect of changes in the value of money (i.e. the general price level) due to changes in the quantity of money on the long-run prospects of the US economy after the Civil War, Keynes [19, p. 65] comments: 'But this *long-run* is a misleading guide to current affairs. *In the long run* we are all dead. Economists set themselves too easy, too useless a task if in tempestuous seasons they can only tell us that when the storm is long past the ocean is flat again.'

Patinkin [29] distinguishes between the classical Quantity Theory and that more recently proposed by Friedman. Keynes' objections are clearly aimed at the 'classical' or long period version of the Quantity Theory.[1] Keynes instead seems to favour a 'Cantillon'-style Quantity Theory which would explain short-period adjustment processes. Compare the description given in Cantillon's *Essai* [1, pp. 162 ff.]:

> M. Locke lays it down as a fundamental maxim that the quantity of produce and merchandise in proportion to the quantity of money serves as the regulator of market prices. I have tried to elucidate this idea in the preceding Chapters: he has clearly seen that the abundance of money makes everything dear, but he has not considered how it does so. The great difficulty of this question consists in knowing in what way and in what proportion the increase in money raises prices.

But this desired change in the application of the Quantity Theory in fact represents a change in the questions to be analysed by the theory. This shift emerges fully in the *General Theory*. The transition from the *Treatise* to *The General Theory* has often been represented as a shift from the analysis of those factors which explain changes in the general price level to those factors which explain changes in the aggregate level of output and employment. As Joan Robinson [32, p. 55] has aptly described this transition:

> . . . the experts in the Quantity Theory of Money certainly avoided crude errors, but when they recognised that their equations were tautologies without causal significance they were beset by an uneasy feeling that their theory only provided them with wisdom after the event. Anything that had happened could always be explained in terms of their truisms, but they were never very confident in predicting what would happen next. Moreover, their methods condemned them to discuss the price level; when what they had really at heart was the volume of employment.
>
> Now, once Mr. Keynes has shown us how to crack the egg, it appears the most natural thing in the world to attack the interesting part of the problem directly instead of through the devious route of the Quantity Theory of Money. If we are interested in the volume of output, why should we not try what progress can be made by thinking in terms of the demand for output as a whole; and its cost of production, just as we have been taught to think of the demand and cost of a single commodity?

Thus, the analysis that Keynes proposes in the *General Theory* not only attempts to determine directly the level of output and employment, it changes the method used in the analysis. The method of analysis used

---

1. It is interesting to note that Keynes' position here corresponds closely with Friedman's dissatisfaction with the 'classical' version of the theory.

by the Quantity Theory is jettisoned at the same time as the Quantity Theory itself. This also implies that the concept of a *general price level* as an economic entity ceases to have objective meaning and the analysis of prices becomes a secondary by-product of the analysis of the level of output. In particular, it means that the theory of output and employment replaces the Quantity Theory of Money, while the focus of the determination of individual prices is referred to the level of the theory of individual firms. As Keynes [21, pp. 292–3] put this shift:

> So long as economists are concerned with what is called the Theory of Value, they have been accustomed to teach that prices are governed by the conditions of supply and demand; and in particular, changes in marginal cost and the elasticity of short-period supply have played a prominent part. But when they pass in volume II, or more often in a separate treatise, to the Theory of Money and Prices, we hear no more of these homely, but intelligible concepts and move into a world where prices are governed by the quantity of money, by its income-velocity, by the velocity of circulation relatively to the volume of transactions, by hoarding, by forced saving, by inflation and deflation *et hoc genus omne*; and little or no attempt is made to relate these vaguer phrases to our former notions of the elasticities of supply and demand,. . . One of the objects of the foregoing chapters has been to escape from this double life and to bring the theory of prices as a whole back to close contact with the theory of value.[2]

Thus the recognition that the level of output will not tend to full-employment output makes a theory to explain the level of output necessary and implies that the Quantity Theory of Money and the direct analysis of the general price level can be abandoned; the analysis of particular prices or the aggregate of these prices can be treated in terms of the traditional Marshallian theory of value. The quantity of money, the general price level, the velocity of circulation all become redundant concepts for the analysis of prices when the Quantity Theory is replaced by the *General Theory of Employment, Interest and Money*.

The behaviour of costs as output changes

It seems clear that in rejecting the Quantity Theory approach to the determination of price, Keynes believed that he was simply generalising what he considered to be the traditional analysis of prices, although he

2. Keynes [23, p. 39, n. 1] credits this approach to R. F. Kahn: 'It was Mr Kahn who first attacked the relation of the general level of prices to wages in the same way as that in which that of particular prices has always been handled, namely as a problem of demand and supply in the short period rather than as a result to be derived from monetary factors.' Compare Kahn [14, p. 177]: 'The price-level and output of home produced consumption-goods, just like the price and output of any single commodity, are determined by the conditions of supply and demand.' (Compare also [14], pp. 179, 181–2.)

also suggested that some modification might be required if such analysis were to be made compatible within an attempt to provide a theoretical explanation of the level of output and employment. There was perhaps a tendency to play down the actual differences and modifications that were required, so that it would not be correct to say that Marshall's theory of price determination was adopted completely, and uncritically, for Keynes' overall approach required that the traditional theory be modified substantially:

> The fact that the assumptions of the static state often underlie present-day economic theory, imports into it a large element of unreality. But the introduction of the concepts of user cost and of the marginal efficiency of capital, as defined above, will have the effect, I think, of bringing it back to reality, whilst reducing to a minimum the necessary degree of adaptation. (Keynes [21], p. 146.)

In line with his initial criticisms of the Quantity Theory, Keynes' primary concern was to analyse changes in prices in relation to changes in the level of output. In order to do this several modifications of substantial importance in the traditional theory were required. Keynes accepted the traditional view on diminishing returns, indeed he considered it as one of the few real 'laws' that prevailed generally in economics: 'I have always regarded decreasing physical returns in the short period as one of the very few incontrovertible propositions of our miserable subject' (Keynes [26], Vol. XIV, p. 190).[3] Yet Keynes' explanation of diminishing returns departs radically from that found in traditional theory.

Non-homogeneous labour

First of all, Keynes considers the skill–quantity of labour to be non-homogeneous. Thus, for any given firm operating a process of production requiring given particular amounts of skilled labour, its supply curve for a given money wage rate and no labour supply constraint, might look like the solid line in Fig. 7.1. However, if the general level of employment, N, rises with output, Q, the firm might have to accept labour with a lower than required skill level. The labour-cost curve faced by the firm would then take on a more traditional shape, as given by the dotted line. The position of any firm (and thus its ability to draw on supplies of skilled labour) must be considered within the general context of the overall level of activity rather than in the

---

3. Kahn is again cited as support for this assumption, (cf. Keynes [23], pp. 39, 44) which Keynes justifies 'on common-sense grounds, surely beyond reasonable question'. Kahn [14, p. 182]: 'It should now be clear that the whole question [of the influence of public works on prices] ultimately turns on the nature of the supply curve of consumption goods. At normal times, when productive resources are fully employed, the supply of consumption-goods in the short period is highly inelastic . . . for the short-period supply curve is concave upwards.'

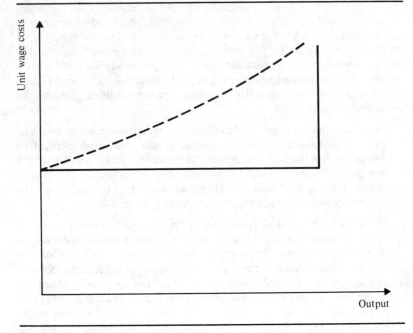

Fig. 7.1

partial context on the assumption of unlimited supplies. Keynes [21, p. 42, see also pp. 81, 114] treats the problem of differing skill levels by imputing it to capital equipment:

> . . . if as output increases, a given firm has to bring in labour which is less and less efficient for its special purposes per wage-unit paid to it, this is merely one factor among others leading to a diminishing return from the capital equipment in terms of output as more labour is employed on it. We subsume, so to speak, the non-homogeneity of equally remunerated labour units in the equipment, which we regard as less and less adapted to employ the available labour units as output increases, instead of regarding the available units as less and less adapted to use a homogeneous capital equipment.

Vintages of productive equipment

The second cause of diminishing returns thus relates directly to the non-homogeneous productive equipment: 'Moreover, if equipment is non-homogeneous and some part of it involves a greater prime cost per unit of output, we shall have increasing marginal prime costs over and above any increase due to increasing labour-costs.' (Keynes [21], pp. 299–300.)

Thus, if there are several 'vintages' of equipment (or plants

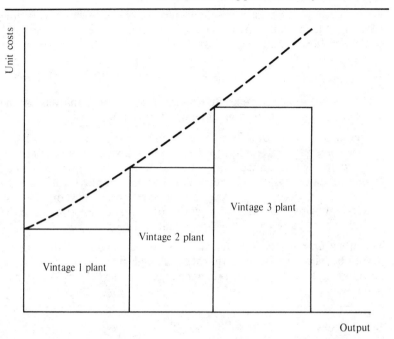

Fig. 7.2

embodying different technology) available, each showing constant costs, the cost curve of the firm might be shown by the solid line in Fig. 7.2. The dashed line shows the imputed effect of non-homogeneous labour. Thus, even if every unit of productive equipment has the technical potential of constant returns, diminishing returns, which formally resemble Marshallian diminishing returns, would still occur as a result of these two factors.[4]

Raw materials

Keynes gives a place of lesser importance to raw materials costs and overhead costs, as does Kalecki, yet he does not ignore them. Their analysis is closely linked to the behaviour of wages by the assumption that the costs 'of the different factors of production which enter into marginal costs all change in the same proportion, i.e. in the same proportion as the wage-unit' (Keynes [21], p. 295). This assumption is, however, considered as being but a 'first approximation' and 'it might be

---

4. 'But a point must surely come, long before plant and labour are fully employed, when less efficient plant and labour have to be brought into commission or the efficient organisation employed beyond the optimum degree of intensiveness.' (Keynes, [23], p. 44.)

better, perhaps, to take a weighted average of the rewards of factors entering into marginal prime costs, and call this the cost-unit' ([21], p. 302, cf. [23], p. 43).

User costs

The most original element in Keynes' [21, p. 302] analysis of the determinants of costs in non-static conditions and,

> Perhaps the most important element in marginal cost which is likely to change in a different proportion from the wage-unit, and also to fluctuate within much wider limits, is marginal user cost. For marginal user cost may increase sharply when employment begins to improve, if (as will probably be the case) the increasing effective demand brings a rapid change in the prevailing expectation as to the date when the replacement equipment will be necessary.

The effect on costs of this element may be independent of the scale of output but simply depend on the rate of change in the level of activity or, more precisely, the expected rate of change (see also [21], p. 55 and [23], p. 44).

Bottle-necks

In addition to the behaviour of labour, raw materials and user costs there are two additional factors that will tend to increase costs in a greater proportion than output as output increases. Not all inputs or the capacity of producing units to expand output will be in excess supply in the proportions required for expansion. As the level of output and employment expand, supply and capacity shortages may appear in particular sectors and markets, while other sectors still have the capacity to expand and other markets still have the ability to supply inputs. If the prices of inputs in short supply rise owing to production bottle-necks the cost-unit will rise as output increases. The relation, however, will not be continuous or smooth for it depends on the actual conditions at hand and the actual character of the expansion process. Furthermore, this relation will also affect the determination of the aggregate supply curve when adjustment lags are taken into account (cf. Keynes [21], p. 288).

The wage unit

Finally, Keynes [21, p. 301] notes 'that the wage-unit may tend to rise before full employment has been reached, requires little comment or explanation. Since each group of workers will gain, *cet. par.*, by a rise in its own wages, there is naturally for all groups a pressure in this direction, which entrepreneurs will be more ready to meet when they are doing better business'.

This factor will also not be a stable function of the rate of expansion, but will vary 'discontinuously'.

These points of discontinuity are determined by the psychology of the workers and by the policies of the employers and trade unions. In an open system, where they mean a change relatively to wage-costs elsewhere, and in a trade cycle, where even in a closed system they may mean a change relatively to expected wage-costs in the future, they can be of considerable importance. . . . But they do not readily lend themselves to theoretical generalisations (Keynes [21], pp. 301–2).

Thus, even if firms were using equipment whose technical coefficients of production were such as to produce constant returns their cost curves would tend to rise with output. Even in the case of constant input costs (Keynes' initial simplifying assumption [21], p. 55, n. 2) there should be a tendency for rising supply price (marginal prime costs of production) to be associated with technically constant-cost systems.

The relation of costs to price change

The factors that have just been described all deal with costs in the short period. To make the transition from costs to prices it is necessary to refer to Keynes' [21, p. 245] assumption of a given degree of competition in the short period (which may range from prices equal to marginal prime costs to pure monopoly to oligopoly with fixed percentage mark-up pricing). On the basis of this assumption Keynes [21, p. 296] reached the conclusion that, 'we have in fact a condition of prices rising gradually as employment increases'. Thus, prices and outputs would both rise as employment was increased. Such changes in prices as would accompany an expansion in output Keynes considered as quite normal phenomena associated with the natural adjustment of the economy to changing levels of production and employment. Such changes in prices could certainly not be considered as inflationary ('unless we mean by inflationary merely that prices are rising' (Keynes, [21], p. 304)) since they are associated with the natural response of the economic system to a change in the level of output.

Thus, in contrast to the *Treatise*, inflation could no longer be considered as those cases where either (a) the costs of factors, labour or other raw materials caused prices to rise ('incomes inflation'), or (b) prices of outputs were rising relative to costs of production ('commodity inflation' for consumption goods, 'capital inflation' for investment goods). These cases were rather classified, by imperfect analogy, as 'semi-inflation' in relation to a newly defined concept of 'absolute inflation'.

Since the point of reference of the analysis had shifted from the study of prices to the study of output and employment as a whole, Keynes found that the definition of inflation had to be changed and formulated with respect, not to prices, but to the level of output, when output was the variable subject to determination and not given at some undefined level (as in the *Treatise*) or at the full-employment level (as in the traditional quantity theories).

The General Theory definition of inflation

A new definition was thus required by the shift in the emphasis of the analysis between the two books. The change in the explanation of the price level required a change in the definition of inflation. In this new explanation, the price level, 'Given the state of technique and equipment, will depend partly on the cost-unit and partly on the scale of output, increasing where output increases, *more* than in proportion to any increase in the cost-unit, in accordance with the principle of diminishing returns in the short period.' (Keynes [21], pp. 302–3). Changes in the level of output will thus normally be associated with rising prices owing to the rising supply prices caused, first, by the falling productivity of the various productive units brought into service, the non-homogeneity of labour, and the non-similarity of excess supplies of inputs and productive capacity, and second, by changes in the more subjective elements of cost caused by the revision of user costs and of money wage bargains as expectations of changes in outputs and prices are affected by expansion of output and employment. Thus, in general, an increase in output caused by an 'increase in effective demand will, generally speaking, spend itself partly in increasing the quantity of employment and partly in raising the level of prices, (Keynes [21], p. 296).[5]

> When a further increase in the quantity of effective demand produces no further increase in output and entirely spends itself on an increase in the cost-unit fully proportionate to the increase in effective demand, we have reached a condition which might be appropriately designed as one of true inflation ... there is no previous point at which we can draw a definite line and declare that conditions of inflation have set in. (Keynes [21], p. 303.)

The definition of inflation that Keynes adopts is then directly linked to the analysis of output and employment: only when output is constant and only prices adjust to a change in effective demand can inflationary conditions be said to exist. When both prices and output change there is a normal process of adjustment of prices to higher levels of production, which when accompanied by increases in the wage unit can be called 'semi-inflation'.

Thus, in addition to the final critical point of full employment at

---

5. The detailed analysis of the division of a change in effective demand between price and output (and employment) changes is analysed by Keynes in terms of price, output and employment elasticities with respect to effective demand (cf. Keynes [21], pp. 250–6).

which money-wages have to rise, in response to an increasing effective demand in terms of money, fully in proportion to the rise in the prices of wage-goods, we have a succession of earlier semi-critical points at which an increasing effective demand tends to raise money-wages though not fully in proportion to the rise in the price of wage goods; . . . These points where a further increase in effective demand in terms of money is liable to cause a discontinuous rise in the wage-unit, might be deemed, from a certain point of view, to be positions of semi-inflation, having some analogy (though a very imperfect one) to absolute inflation . . . which ensues on an increase in effective demand in circumstances of full employment. [21, p. 302]

'Absolute inflation' can then be defined, in terms of supply and demand, as that position in which an increase in demand calls forth no increase in supply in the short period: the elasticity of supply is zero. There seems to be no reason why this point should correspond to full employment of labour, although in later writings Keynes explicitly defines full employment in terms of the elasticity of aggregate output such that an increase in the demand for output does not increase employment: 'If I were writing again, I should indeed feel disposed to define full employment as being reached at the same monent at which the supply of output in general becomes inelastic.' (From a letter to Hicks dated 31 August 1936 in Keynes [26], Vol. XIV, p. 71.) In general, then, if effective demand rises, and there is no adjustment either in output or employment, then demand is wasted on rising prices and increased profits that do not lead to any further expansion of the system. Below this level, or more generally for any position in which a change in demand leads to a change in output or employment *and* prices, such a situation represents the normal operation of the forces of supply and demand (except in those cases where the increase causes rises in wages which produce conditions of 'semi-inflation', but with prices rising faster than wages).

Thus, 'absolute inflation' is a most unlikely case, although *it is not the only position in which prices are likely to rise* (cf. the concept of the inflationary gap used, for example, in Samuelson's widely used text, *Economics* (Samuelson [37]) which restricts *both* price rises *and* inflation to conditions of absolute inflation, with prices assumed constant or falling below this point). It appears that many economists have been misled into the false deduction that since 'absolute' or 'true inflation' in Keynes' terminology only occurs at the full-employment level of output that prices will be unchanged (or unimportant) at positions below full employment (and further that wages can be considered as constant, or unimportant when unemployed labour exists). Keynes, however, clearly did not consider inflation and rising prices to be identical.

This may provide an explanation of why many 'Keynesian' economists using this erroneous interpretation of Keynes' analysis have given very little attention to the problems of price formation and inflation. The supposed constancy (or, simply, unimportance) of prices at less than full employment has led to a general neglect in the analysis of price change. The effects of rising prices on the operation of the economic system were also ignored for, if prices were rising (and thus, by definition, full employment prevailed) they could always be controlled, it was assumed, by a reduction in aggregate demand (e.g. by an increase in taxation), while if there was unemployment this could be treated by increasing demand without reference to any possible influence on prices. When economists started to notice the obvious fact of the coexistence of rising prices and unemployment (in recent times in the USA in the late 1950s, and more internationally from the mid-late 1960s to the present) they were faced with what appeared to be the paradoxical coexistence of an 'inflationary gap' (rising prices) and a 'deflationary gap' (falling employment). Obviously, demand could not be expanded (to increase employment) and contracted (to halt the rise in prices) at the same time. Thus the situation was considered 'paradoxical' while, in fact, it was the theoretical framework (based on the erroneous interpretation of Keynes) which provided a paradox which was more definitional than real.

Because such conditions do not meet Keynes' definition of 'absolute inflation' does not mean that they do not have serious consequences or that rising prices have no role in theoretical analysis. It does, however, mean that these conditions cannot be eliminated by policies to reduce the pressure of aggregate demand. Rather, they suggest that there has been a change in the proportion in which demand is divided between changes in price and changes in quantity, i.e. changes in the elasticities of supply of the various outputs (cf. Keynes, [21], pp. 282–6).

Thus, the current experience of rising prices and rising unemployment in many Western countries is not unambiguously one of absolute inflation. Rather, it is more closely associated with autonomous rises in the various components of the cost-unit (semi-inflation), the influence of changes in user cost on the elasticity of supply, and the operation of the forces of aggregate supply and demand to re-establish the pre-existing proportions of prices to costs (and more particularly prices to wages and wages to raw materials prices), i.e. with an adjustment of the structure of relative prices through varying rates of increase in the level of individual prices and costs, as well as a change in the value of the 'period of production' for investment goods (cf. Keynes, [21], p. 287 and Kregel [27], Appendix).

It is here that the most interesting problems of inflation within the Keynesian framework become apparent, precisely in that part of the analysis of prices that Keynes considered as given for the purposes of his analysis of the determinants of the level of employment and output: the degree of competition and the relative changes of costs and prices of the individual outputs with changes in demand and output as a whole. The various implications of these assumptions for the theory of distribution are discussed by Keynes [23, esp. section V], but he does not offer any theoretical analysis of the relation between changes in output, changes in relative prices, inflation and the distribution of income. Both Harrod [11] and Kalecki [18] did, however, directly confront these questions, although their importance has been largely overlooked in the post-*General Theory* discussions.

Long-period price changes

Keynes' analysis in the *General Theory* is strictly limited to the effects of changes in effective demand on output, employment and prices, given the productive structure of the system at any point in its development. Over time, there are continuous changes in the productive structure of the system and thus continuous changes in productivity (output per unit of labour) which will act to reduce unit labour and raw materials costs. In conditions where productivity is rising 'the long-run stability or instability of prices will depend on the strength of the upward trend of the wage-unit (or, more precisely, of the cost-unit) compared with the rate of increase in the efficiency of the productive system' (Keynes [21], p. 309).

Thus, while prices may be expected to rise in the short period, primarily, due to diminishing returns, continuously rising prices can only result when the cost-unit rises over time more rapidly than investment in productive equipment raises output per man. (This definition includes the case of absolute inflation with given capacity at full employment where 'a further increase in the quantity of effective demand . . . entirely spends itself on an increase in the cost unit fully proportionate to the increase in effective demand' [21, p. 302].) This implies that effective demand (and wages) must grow over time at just the rate of productivity growth if both price stability and full employment are to be maintained.[6]

Costs and prices, demand and prices

As mentioned above, Keynes' analysis implies or assumes a direct link between costs and prices. This position also stems from his decision to analyse the determinants of output and employment rather than considering them as given. Keynes, in fact, considered the effect of costs on prices from two different points of view. First, if the cost-unit rises autonomously, this will imply that incomes for the suppliers of

6. Joan Robinson [31, pp. 189, 195] was quick to point out how unlikely a possibility this was: . . . 'the general upshot of our argument is that the point of full employment, so far from being an equilibrium resting place, appears to be a precipice over which, once it has reached the edge, the value of money must plunge into a bottomless abyss.'' . . . Thus a policy of maintaining stable prices . . . is by no means equivalent to a policy of maintaining stable employment.' See also Robinson [32], pp. 84–8.

productive inputs, in particular wage incomes, will be increased. Given the propensity to consume out of incomes from different sources and given the distribution of income, demand should then rise by the same proportion as costs, with the degree of competition unchanged. Prices will then rise by the same proportion as costs and effective demand in wage-units would be unchanged.[7]

On the other hand, an expansion in output due to an autonomous rise in effective demand also implies that incomes expand with costs, but that output rises by a lesser proportion due to diminishing returns so that prices will be rising, given the degree of competition: 'the price-level, given the state of technique and equipment, will depend partly on the cost-unit and partly on the scale of output, increasing where output increases, *more* than in proportion to any increase in the cost-unit, in accordance with the principle of diminishing returns in the short-period' (Keynes [21], pp. 302–3). If there should happen to be increasing returns in the system, prices should be falling on this account (unless subjective factors such as user costs rise, or the wage-unit rises to offset them) by more than in proportion to the decrease in the cost-unit, the degree of competition remaining unchanged.[8]

Costs and prices, effective demand and prices

Keynes' hypothesis concerning autonomous changes in costs was that they would be reflected generally in changes in prices, in the short

7. This separation is made explicit in Keynes [23, p. 35]: 'First of all it is necessary to distinguish between two different problems. In the passage quoted above [reference is to Keynes [23, p. 10]] I was dealing with the reaction of real wages to changes in *output*, and had in mind situations where changes in real and money wages were a reflection of changes in the level of employment caused by changes in effective demand. . . . But there is also the case where changes in wages reflect changes in prices or in the conditions governing the wage bargain which do not correspond to, or are not primarily the result of, changes in the level of output and employment and are not caused by (though they may cause) changes in effective demand. This question I discussed in a different part of my "General Theory" (namely Chapter 19, "Changes in Money Wages"), where I reached the conclusion that wages changes, which are not in the first instance due to changes in output, have complex reactions on output which may be in either direction according to the circumstances and about which it is difficult to generalise.' Compare also [23, pp. 47–8]: 'Unfortunately it is often difficult or impossible to distinguish clearly between the effects of the two influences, since higher money costs and increasing output will generally go together.'
8. Compare Keynes [23]. It is in confronting questions such as this that Keynes recognises the implications for the theory of distribution and discusses the problem of whether prices rise by more or less than changes in costs when constant or decreasing costs are present, i.e. when there is a *change* in the 'degree of competition' related to a change in the level of output (cf. [23], pp. 48–50). Kalecki initiated his own analysis with the investigation of such problems and it is interesting to note that it is with respect to these themes that Keynes [23, p. 49] shows interest in Kalecki's work. Harrod [11] was also concerned with changes in the degree of monopoly as output changed and reached rather different conclusions than Kalecki. Harrod [12] has recently strongly emphasised the effects that decreasing costs have in lowering unit costs as output is expanded.

period, with little effect on the level of output, given the degree of competition. Autonomous changes in the level of effective demand would be reflected in changes in both output and prices, independently of any additional changes that might result from changes in the costs of inputs. Although Keynes held these two propositions separate from the analytical point of view, on the practical level, 'unfortunately it is often difficult or impossible to distinguish clearly between the effects of the two influences, since higher money costs and increasing output will generally go together' [23, p. 47].

The rationale behind the first hypothesis can be discerned by considering the effect of a change in costs on (a) the margin by which prices exceed direct costs of production, i.e. the mark-up representing the 'degree of competition' or the 'degree of monopoly' as Kalecki called it, or on (b) the prices that equate aggregate demand with aggregate supply, i.e. in terms of the aggregate analysis of prices equivalent to the determination of the prices of single commodities as suggested in note 2 above, with prices equal to, or greater than, marginal direct costs depending on the 'degree of competition' assumed. Both approaches can be analysed together if the value of the mark-up is thought of as taking on values from zero at the break-even point (where prices equal average direct costs) and as being independent of the level of aggregate output.[9]

Wages and prices

The effects of an autonomous change in wages sketched above can be verified by reference to a very simple equation for price determination. If wages are the only direct costs of production and λ is the 'degree of competition' the relation of unit price to unit costs can be written as

$$p = (1+\lambda)wN/Q]$$

Price per unit of output is then equal to unit costs plus λ (wN/Q) which is available to meet any indirect (overhead) cost plus profits. At this price, p, and output, Q, the propensity to consume must be such that aggregate demand is equal to pQ. If Y is total disposable income (wages + profits) and c is the propensity to consume, demand is $D = cY = pQ$

---

9. Joan Robinson [34, p. 10] suggests that Keynes 'introduced' 'user cost', (the loss of value of equipment due to using it rather than leaving it idle) to reconcile competition with the evident fact that a profit margin enters into supply price even in a deep slump'. Therefore, she argues, Keynes did not have to deal with either imperfect competition or introduce a 'mark-up' of prices over costs. It would seem that all Keynes required was that the 'degree of competition' remained constant. That he considered this in terms of a 'mark-up' can be seen from his scepticism that 'changes in the degree of the imperfection of competition should *so exactly* offset other changes' in costs due to changes in the level of output so as to leave the ratio of costs to prices unchanged. (Keynes, [23], p. 49). See also Keynes [26, Vol. XIV, p. 190]: 'Mrs Robinson, I may mention, read my proofs without discovering any connection [with Imperfect Competition].'

for a given level of output Q.[10] Keynes' assumption is that an autonomous rise in w (say by $\triangle w/w$) will cause p to rise in the same proportion (by $\triangle p/p = \triangle w/w$) leaving Q unchanged. Since wages are both a cost of production and the basis of the household incomes used to purchase output, a change in w will affect both costs and demand. With λ given, producers will want to increase prices by the same proportion as wages have risen. They can succeed only if demand rises by the same amount. Since wages are part of national income an x per cent rise in wages will increase incomes by the same proportion, as well as overheads and profits which are a given proportion, λ, of wages. Given the propensity to consume, demand will then also rise by the same proportion so that the same output may be sold at the higher price, and λ remains unchanged, implying that the distribution of income between wages and non-wage incomes (profits and overheads) is also unchanged. The propensity to consume is unchanged since real incomes have not been affected.

Raw materials costs

However, wages are not the only direct costs of production. Raw materials also form a part of direct costs. Consideration of such costs (or, more generally, of the 'cost-unit' rather than the 'wage-unit') can change the analysis of autonomous increases in costs in two different respects. To see these effects more clearly the price equation can be expanded to include raw materials costs with r the price and m the quantity:

$$p=(1+\lambda')wN/Q+(1+\lambda'')rM/Q.$$

Assuming that the mark-up is the same on both types of direct costs ($\lambda'=\lambda''=\lambda$) and that C represents the combined direct costs of wages and raw materials, gives the unit price relation $p=(1+\lambda)C/Q$

which represents unit prices as a proportion of unit direct costs or the 'cost-unit'.

Domestically produced raw materials costs and prices

If raw materials are produced domestically in the agricultural or 'primary' sector of the economy the analysis is similar to the case with

10. The 'degree of competition' as defined here can also be written as $(p-w)/w$ which corresponds directly with Kalecki's 'degree of monopoly' when raw materials are left out of account, $m = p-u/u$. For a discussion of the nature of Kalecki's measure of monopoly, see Robinson [34, pp. 10–11]: 'What it [the degree of monopoly] means is the absence of price competition. . . . The weaker is price competition in any market, the greater is the freedom of firms to set prices in excess of costs. The ratio of margins to prices is a symptom of the degree of monopoly.' (See also Feiwel [6, pp. 93–102].) Weintraub [38] produces a similar relation directly from Keynes' aggregate supply function, given the money wage rate and the level of output per man $A = Q/N$. Thus, $Z=pQ=wN+rP$ and $p=k(w/A)$, where k is the mark-up over direct costs and is equal to $1+$ the degree of monopoly.

only wage costs. From the point of view of aggregate demand the analysis is the same. Given a uniform propensity to consume out of incomes in both the primary and the manufacturing sectors, a given proportionate rise in the cost-unit will generate additional aggregate demand sufficient to cover prices that have risen by the same proportion, leaving the level of output unchanged. However, from the point of view of distribution the analysis is more complicated. While the given value of the mark-up assures a constant distribution of money incomes between profits and combined wages and primary producers' incomes, it does not determine the distribution within the latter group of non-profit incomes nor the terms of trade between primary and manufactured goods (which will also depend on r, the price of raw materials), either of which may affect demand or output. The actual proportionate rise in the cost-unit will be a weighted average (given by the unit production coefficients) of the rate of change of wages and the rate of change of raw materials prices. As already stated, if the degree of competition remains unchanged the proportionate change in the prices of manufactured goods will equal the proportionate change in the cost-unit. If the rate of change in wages is higher than the rate of change in raw materials prices then the terms of trade will move against the primary sector and real wages will rise at the expense of agricultural incomes, given r. In the opposite case, real wages will fall to the benefit of primary-product producers' incomes. Obviously, any change in either spending on consumption or spending on investment by the primary sector that results from these changes in real incomes will affect demand and thus, given the degree of competition, output and employment.

A crucial factor in determining the distribution of income between wages and primary producers will be the response of r, raw materials prices, and thus the ways in which prices are determined in the latter sector. If these prices are determined primarily by demand rather than costs at a given 'degree of competition' and money wages adjust to any reduction in real wages, a limit may be placed on the terms of trade. Thus, an improvement in the agricultural terms of trade will reduce real wages; if money wages then adapt to recover the previous position the improvement in the terms of trade will have been reversed. Alternatively, falls in primary-product prices will not bring about such counteracting forces, so that the terms of trade may be only downward flexible. If demand for manufactured goods is determined by improvements in real returns to primary production this will tend to have a cumulative dampening effect on demand by that sector for manufactured goods.[11]

---

11. The basic of this approach stems from Kalecki's early work [18, p. 43] on the relation of demand and costs to prices: 'Short-term price changes may be classified into two broad groups; those determined mainly by changes in demand. Generally speaking, changes in the prices of finished goods are "cost-determined" while changes in the prices of raw materials inclusive of primary foodstuffs are "demand-determined".' Kaldor's [17] analysis also relies on this distinction. Hicks [13] has also recently proposed such a distinction in terms of his concepts of 'fix-price' and 'flex-price'.

Imported raw materials costs and prices

But not all countries can produce their raw materials requirements domestically. If raw materials are imported, a rise in the cost-unit will not have the same influence on aggregate demand as in the analysis of a rise in the wage-unit, because domestic aggregate demand will not rise by the entire increase in costs, but only by the increase in wages. Prices could then rise in the same proportion as the cost-unit, i.e. the degree of competition could remain constant only at the expense of lower total sales, which would consequently lower output, employment and real wages to the level where incomes were again compatible with output. The only possible way of averting this result would be if the foreign countries used all their export earnings to purchase domestic goods, i.e. if the value of manufactured goods exported to the primary producing countries were equal to the value of imported raw materials. An analysis of the terms of trade between industrialised and primary producers similar to that given above for the primary and manufacturing sectors of one country could also be carried out, but in this case the assumptions that the propensity to consume is uniform for wages, or that the propensity to import is constant, appear questionable.

Autonomous changes in effective demand

For the second analytical case, where an increase in effective demand brings about an increase in output, 'common-sense' diminishing returns will apply such that as employment rises, output rises, but in a lower proportion, such that N/Q falls. Given the money-wage rate, demand then rises by the same proportion as employment ($\Delta N/N$) while output rises by a lower proportion ($\Delta Q/Q < \Delta N/N$) so that aggregate demand grows faster than aggregate supply and prices will be rising. When $\Delta Q/Q=0$ additional expansion of demand will only act to raise prices and there is 'absolute inflation'.[12]

Changes in cost and in demand

In cases where both of the two effects discussed above are at work 'the price level, given the state of technique and equipment' [which determines the ΔN required for a given ΔQ] 'will depend partly on the cost-unit' [C] 'and partly on the scale of output' [Q, so that given λ, the degree of competition, $p=(1+\lambda)\ C/Q$] 'increasing where output increases, *more* than in proportion to any increase in the cost-unit' [$\Delta'p/p=\Delta C/C$], 'in accordance with the principle of diminishing returns' [$\Delta'p/p=N\Delta Q/Q\Delta N$, where $\Delta N/N>\Delta Q/Q$] 'in the short-

---

12. This result relies as much on the assumption that money wages react to maintain stable real wages as on the assumption that prices in the primary sector are determined primarily by demand.

period'. The combined change is thus $\triangle'p/p+\triangle p/p=\triangle''p/p=(\triangle C/C)+(N\triangle Q/Q\triangle N)$ [21, 302–3].

Policies to stabilise prices

Recognition of the differing impact of the different components of costs on prices has led to a number of different policy recommendations for price stabilisation based on stabilisation of the various components of the cost-unit.

Wage stabilisation: incomes policy

Keynes, as already seen, suggested that long-period price stability would depend on the relation between the growth of wages and the growth of output per man. However, he did not use this observation as the basis for short-term policy proposals to control directly either incomes or prices.[13] In fact, Keynes was highly sceptical about the possibility or the desirability of short-period price stability given the tendency for the wage-unit to rise before full employment was reached and the potential stimulus that the expectation of prices rising relative to costs could give the marginal efficiency of capital.

If a case is to be made for a policy to link incomes to changes in productivity it can only be considered in the long-run, aggregate sense employed by Keynes, i.e. as an institutional factor in the process of overall wage determination, not as a short-period policy measure introduced in emergency conditions.

Such a policy may, however, be questionable even from a long-period perspective for, as seen above, the growth of incomes, especially wages, provides the largest part of the growth of demand for output. If full employment is to be achieved or maintained with price stability, wages must grow at least as fast as increasing productivity increases supply, but if productivity is itself determined by the growth of demand then the relation becomes indeterminate, for the growth of wages in excess of the productivity norm provokes the cost and demand conditions which make more productive techniques necessary and profitable. A long-term policy that limits wages to productivity growth may then be detrimental to the rate of growth of both real wages and of the productivity upon which they depend. These questions have been discussed, from different points of view, by both Joan Robinson [33, (Ch. 9, pp. 92–4)] and Sylos Labini [36, pp. 144–9].

Raw materials: buffer stock schemes

Keynes did, however, make explicit policy recommendations for the

---

13. With the exception of wartime. Keynes' proposals for such conditions are contained in his *How to Pay for the War* [24].

stabilisation of the prices of raw materials through the creation of an institutional mechanism of buffer stocks of primary commodities. A national or supra-national agency was to hold stocks of major raw materials and agricultural products, selling when prices tended to rise because of temporary shortfalls and buying to build up stocks when prices were falling. By such action it was hoped that supply cycles and price variations could be avoided.

However, there has been interest in such schemes only in periods when primary product prices are rising very rapidly (for the industrialised nations) or falling very rapidly (for the producing countries). Keynes' interest in the problem came from the impending shortages and speculation that were feared in the period before the outbreak of the Second World War. The problem had been all but forgotten, aside from various particular commodity agreements promoted by UNCTAD, until the rapid rise in commodity prices in the early 1970s which was sharply reinforced by the rise in the price of petroleum in late 1973.

Against this background, Kaldor [17] has recently reopened the argument in favour of buffer stock schemes. He argues that the 'primary' sector is important for the growth of the manufacturing sector, not only through the provision of raw materials but also as a source of demand for the output of the manufacturing sector. Thus, changes in the prices of primary products not only affect the costs of production of manufactures but also the primary sector's propensity to invest (buy investment goods produced in the manufacturing sector) and thus its ability to supply raw materials. Kaldor thus supports buffer-stock schemes to stabilise both productive capacity and prices of primary materials, as well as to prevent any deterioration in the primary-product producers' terms of trade which might act to depress investment and thus reduce future productive capacity, as well as the present demand for investment goods produced by the manufacturing sector.

A corollary of Kaldor's position is that policies to provide direct income supplements to primary-product producers are more efficient than policies that set minimum prices (i.e. that the Common Agricultural Policy of the Common Market based on the principle of price supports is less desirable than the previous UK policy of income supports). Kaldor extends this line of argument to the case of foreign suppliers of primary products to industrialised countries, and supports policies to increase the spendable incomes of the lesser developed countries (a variation of the 'Marshall Plan', using international purchasing power such as special drawing rights distributed to countries producing primary commodities) as the key to the continued supply of primary products at low cost and the continued expansion of demand for the outputs of the industrialised countries. (Such a policy as suggested above, would attempt to combine control of the imported component of the cost-unit with an increase in the demand for industrial outputs to offset the consequences on demand of imported inputs.)

Labour productivity

While the policy recommendations for the stabilisation of the non-labour components of the cost-unit have been primarily of a long-term, institutional nature, policies to deal with labour costs and labour productivity have been generally of a more short-term nature. Probably the best known of such policies is Kaldor's proposal, introduced by the Labour Government in 1969, for a selective tax on labour, paid for labour employed in 'low-productivity' sectors of the economy, but rebated on labour employed in 'high-productivity' sectors ('SET'). On the assumption that the growth of productivity is more rapid in the manufacturing sector than in the service sector of the economy, and assuming that labour presents a constraint on the growth of that sector, Kaldor argued that a fixed-rate tax on labour (but not wages) which was paid only for labour employed in the tertiary service sector would give a selective relative cost advantage to the hiring of labour in the manufacturing sector, as well as releasing labour from the tertiary sector.[14] Such a policy is thus meant to increase the rate at which the existing rate of productivity growth is exploited by increasing the size of the manufacturing sector. It is short term in the sense that it does little directly to affect the rate at which productivity itself grows, only the rate at which it is utilised. Only to the extent that such a policy produces a higher overall long-term rate of growth which might encourage expenditure on research and development, could it be considered directly to influence productivity growth.

Policies to control 'inflation'

In relation to the definition of 'semi-inflation' and 'absolute inflation' outlined above, policies for the short-term control of the former, which 'do not readily lend themselves to theoretical generalisations', are not directly discussed in Keynes' work for they 'are determined by the psychology of the workers and by the policies of employers and trade unions'. Keynes [21, p. 252] also refers to the 'experience of human nature' as confirming the fact that wages will tend to rise for 'the struggle about money-wages primarily affects the distribution of the aggregate real wage between different labour-groups'[21, p. 14]. Although Keynes considered that such forces would be enforced by an expansion in employment there seems to be no reason to believe that the struggle should become less intense when output is falling. It seems obvious that long-term social and institutional changes would be the only certain way

---

14. The underlying theorising for this position can be found in Kaldor's re-elaboration of Verdoorn's Law with reference to the UK (cf. Kaldor [15], but see also Rowthorn [35]).

of influencing such factors.[15]

Policies to control 'inflation' in the strict sense, on the other hand, should be concerned with the mechanisms by which supply responds to changes in the effective demand for different sectors, with the determinants of the rate of participation of the population in the active labour force, and the determinants of the changes in the rate of growth of productivity. By operating on these factors it might be possible to coordinate the broad movements in effective demand to movements in the supply of labour, raw materials and other inputs, thereby controlling the movements in costs. The introduction of the Ministry of Economic Affairs and the Economic Development Councils were meant, broadly, to deal with such problems.

Yet, even if such policies could be implemented (the lack of success of the proposals of the Labour Government in the 1960s should not be considered as definitive) there will always be changes in prices that occur as a part of a natural process of adjustment of production to changes in the level of output, the structure of demand, technical progress and changes in the cost of inputs. Such an adjustment process will take place in both periods of expansion and contraction of output, given any downward rigidity in the wage component of the cost-unit.[16]

From the point of view of short-period policy Keynes [21, p. 271], in fact, *argued in favour* of wage rigidity as a method of stabilising demand for output.[17] Such a policy would

> ... result in a fair degree of stability in the price-level: – greater stability, at least, than with a flexible wage policy. Apart from

15. The fact that Keynes did not make this consideration is linked to his belief that the presence of decreasing returns would mean that real wages moved inversely with the level of output. This belief Keynes [23, p. 40] considered as orthodox and as having no crucial role in his own theory. If real wages and output both move in the same direction then one would expect the struggle for the distribution of the aggregate real wage to become more intense when output and employment were falling, causing money wages to rise with rising unemployment and falling output. The relation indicated above, linking changes in relative prices to changes in distribution and inflation, can be seen more clearly perhaps in the context of falling output, for the changes in money wages of different groups of workers changes the distribution of labour incomes, the changes in the costs of different output changes the relative prices of final outputs and, finally, if the degree of competition is affected by these changes there will also be a change in the distribution of output between the factors covered by the cost-unit and those (profits and overheads) covered by the mark-up. There thus seems to be no reason to believe that the struggle for relative rewards that Keynes indicates as one of the major causes of rising money wages to be any more intense with rising than with falling output.

16. Periods of falling output will require the same sort of physical adjustments as rising output, but in the face of rigidity of costs they will have to take place in terms of differential rates of price rise if the degree of competition is to be maintained constant. If not, prices would be free to fall, but with even more undesirable consequences for output and employment (cf. Keynes, [21], pp. 269–70, 303–4).

17. In the light of Friedman's recent interpretation of Keynes' theory as assuming rigid prices it is perhaps necessary to stress that this was not an assumption of Keynes' theory, but rather a policy proposal, desirable for the reasons set out in the text, as well as others which are detailed in Davidson [2].

'administered' or monopoly prices, the price-level will only change in the short period in response to the extent that changes in the volume of employment affect marginal prime cost, whilst in the long period they will only change in response to changes in the cost of production due to new technique and new or increased equipment.

Thus with a rigid wage policy the stability of prices will be bound up in the short period with the avoidance of fluctuations in employment. In the long period, on the other hand, we are still left with the choice between a policy of allowing prices to fall slowly with the progress of technique and equipment whilst keeping wages stable, or of allowing wages to rise slowly whist keeping prices stable. On the whole, my preference is for the latter alternative, on account of the fact that it is easier with an expectation of higher wages in future to keep the actual level of employment with a given range of full employment. . . .

In addition, taking the existence of shifts in the structure of demand, bottle-necks in production and the tendency for the wage-unit to rise 'perfect stability of prices is impossible in an economy subject to change' [21, p. 288]. In contrast, then, with the *Treatise*, stable prices are not only undesirable but unattainable in the face of continuous change in an expanding (or contracting) economy. The *General Theory* definition of 'inflation' thus excludes such changes in prices and concerns only those positions in which prices change without any change in the level of output or employment. The control of such inflation is then reduced to policies for the control of the elasticity of supply and the control of unit costs (productivity). Autonomous changes in the cost-unit due to the prices of productive inputs when supply elasticity is not zero are classified as 'semi-inflation', and are due as much to psychology, human nature and political causes as anything else. Social and political institutional changes are more appropriate to their control. From this point of view, more is to be gained in controlling prices by increasing the elasticity of output to changes in demand and increasing productivity than by the introduction of short-term controls over wages and prices.

International price stability

As is well known, Keynes was actively involved in the post-war reform of international monetary relations. In this respect it is perhaps interesting to note that he did not consider internal price stability to be within the realm of international controls [25, pp. 186–7]:

For prices can only be stabilised by first stabilising the relation of money-wages (and other costs) to efficiency. . . . The fundamental reason for . . . limiting the objectives of an international currency scheme is the impossibility, or at any rate the undesirability, of imposing stable price-levels from without. The error of the gold-standard lay in submitting national wage-policies to outside dictation. It is wiser to regard the stability (or otherwise) of internal prices as a matter of internal policy and politics.

Some countries are likely to be more successful than others in preserving stability of internal prices and efficiency wages. ... A communist country is in a position to be very successful. Some people argue that a capitalist country is doomed to failure because it will be found impossible in conditions of full employment to prevent a progressive increase of wages. According to this view, severe slumps and recurrent periods of unemployment have been hitherto the only effective means of holding efficiency wages within a reasonably stable range. Whether this is so remains to be seen. The more conscious we are of this problem, the likelier we shall be to surmount it.

The control of prices on the international level

... is to deal with the problem of members getting out of step in their domestic wage and credit policies. To meet this it can be provided that countries seriously out of step (whether too fast or too slow) may be asked in the first instance to reconsider their policies. But, if necessary (and it will be necessary, if efficiency wage-rates move at materially different rates), exchange-rates will have to be altered so as to reconcile a particular national policy to the average pace. If the initial exchange-rates are fixed correctly, this is likely to be the only important disequilibrium for which a change in exchange-rates is the appropriate remedy. [25, p. 186]

The new international monetary arrangements, just as the gold-standard that they were designed to replace were not to be considered as a means 'to confine the natural tendency of wages to rise beyond the limits set by the volume of money' because this can only be done by 'deliberately creating unemployment' [25, p. 186]. Keynes thus rejected both internal and international policies for control of the money supply as a means to contol 'the natural tendency' for wages to rise before full employment because both types of monetary control rely on 'severe slumps and recurrent periods of unemployment' as 'the only effective means of holding efficiency wages within a reasonably stable range'. 'This weapon', Keynes claims, 'the world, after a good try, has decided to discard.' [25, p. 186] From this point of view the recent post-Bretton Woods policy of the International Monetary Fund to impose internal monetary targets and to impose exchange-rate policy on countries with balance of payments deficits due to a rate of increase of efficiency wages 'seriously out of step' with their trading partners, represents the exact opposite of the policy Keynes prescribed for such an international organisation. It should not then be too surprising if the results of these policies are large-scale increases in unemployment. The United Kingdom and Italy stand as examples of this result. What is more surprising is that the IMF has been able to use 'this weapon' which Keynes believed right-thinking men to have discarded. It may be that only international sanction is enough to encourage the economic groups which determine the movements of the cost-unit and thus of prices to 'reconsider their policies'. Keynes' faith that reason might prevail internally seems to have been misplaced. There seems to be no one willing to argue his point of view internationally.

Appendix

From the argument presented above it does not seem possible to maintain, as Professor Friedman, for example, has, that the basis of Keynes' analysis of prices is 'arbitrary' and has 'no underpinning in economic theory' because it employs the 'deus ex machina of a rigid price assumption' (Friedman, [7], p. 222). Such a view either represents a complete ignorance of Keynes' written work or a desire to create an exaggerated difference between Keynes' theory and the so-called 'new monetarism'. The latter chooses to emphasise the relation between changes in the quantity of money and changes in the level of the value of output. In particular, Friedman, as well as others of like persuasion, does not accept that 'progress can be made by thinking in terms of the demand for output as a whole, and its cost of production, just as we have been taught to think of the demand and cost of a single commodity'. Instead, this approach has placed emphasis on the demand for a different aggregate, the quantity of money, and its cost of production, in an attempt to formulate a demand function for money which, by some 'devious route' influences the demand for nominal output. But, this way of approaching aggregate analysis has made the separate analysis of prices and quantities of individual outputs impossible, leaving a theory that is only capable of dealing with 'nominal incomes' (Friedman [7]). From this perspective it may seem understandable that Friedman should wish to portray Keynes' theory as subject to the same inability to analyse price.

Analysis of price changes

In line with his initial criticisms of the classical Quantity Theory Keynes analyses changes in prices in relation to changes in the level of output. Since these changes are based on the basic principles of the traditional theory of value, presumably accepted also by Friedman, dispute must then result from differences about how changes in demand for output originate and a misunderstanding of the implications for theoretical analysis of the recognition that the level of output cannot be considered as given. The rejection of Keynes' approach by the new monetarists might then be characterised in terms of their assumptions that (a) since full employment will naturally result from the operation of the real forces of the market in the long run, output can be taken as given, and (b) in the short run the demand for output, and thus the level of nominal income, can be most easily influenced by changes in the quantity of money, given the existence of a stable demand function for money.[18]

Yet, the analysis of *changes* in prices has little to do with these two points of difference. Friedman analyses prices on the assumption that output is given in the long run and reaches the not surprising conclusion that a change in the quantity of money will only affect prices and not quantities, while Keynes reaches this conclusion only when output is constant because the elasticity of output with respect to effective demand is zero. In Keynes' approach, for any other case, both prices and outputs will change, and there are other factors besides the quantity of money which will affect changes in the level of output. Friedman's new monetarism eliminates any possible analysis of price as distinct from output change which is seen to respond only to changes in the quantity of money.

Analysis of price levels

Any basic difference (in addition to the first assumption given above) must then concern not the analysis of price *changes*, but the determinants of the price *level*. Keynes assumes that the level of money wages is the prime determinant of the level of money prices (or, as seen above, that the cost-unit determines prices given the degree of competition) while Friedman maintains that the price level is determined by the quantity of money relative to the level of output. But this difference is simply a result of the misunderstanding of the shift of emphasis from the *Treatise* to the *General Theory*. When the level of output is given independently by the 'real forces' which determine relative prices, the level of prices is determined by the quantity of money; but when the level of output is determined independently of the relative price system the price level is given by the level of money wages and the level of output. Assumption (b) must then be the most crucial point of dispute, not the explanation of either the price level or price change.

Money and monetary production

In addition to the implication for the determination of the level of prices, (as well as the factors determining price changes) of the recognition of the necessity of the determination of the level of output, the approach of the *General Theory* also implied a shift in the way money was considered in the economic system. The emphasis shifted from money as a commodity that was required to facilitate exchange, to be held primarily for

18. A corollary of (a) seems to be Friedman's statement that the level of output is given and constant in the short run as well – a position that Patinkin considers as being as misleading in relation to the Quantity Theory as Friedman's attribution of the assumption of rigid prices is to Keynes' theory (cf. Patinkin, [30], in Gordon [10], p. 117). Patinkin notes that 'the systematic analysis of the short-run variations in output and velocity generated by monetary changes was a major concern of the pre-Keynesian quantity theorists'.

transactions purposes, on to the role of money as a store of value in a system of capitalistic production subject to change and expansion over time. The emphasis thus shifted from exchange to production, and from the identification of the appropriate money aggregate to the conditions required for the existence of a money production economy. These conditions are the subject of the complex chapters 16 and 17 of the *General Theory*.[19]

From this point of view, however, money *per se* loses the central importance that it had in the Quantity Theory. This is a development that it would have been just as hard for a pre-*General Theory* monetary theorist to accept as it was for the new monetarists to accept the monetary nihilism of post-*General Theory* 'Keynesianism'. The difference here is not over the 'systematic analysis of the short-run variations in output. . . .' but the mechanisms that were proposed by the different theories to explain them, i.e. assumption (b) above. For Keynes the 'monetary conditions of production' took precedence over the problem of what should be included in the definition of the stock of money, the factors that determine the level of output took precedence over the factors which determine nominal income independently of its breakdown into changes in prices and output – an important distinction from the point of view of the level of employment but not from the point of view of the stock of money.

19. The inability to incorporate this point of view with the Quantity Theory approach is evident in Friedman's view that Keynes' discussion of the 'essential properties' of money involve the 'empirical characteristics of money' when they are, in fact, irrelevant to that purpose (cf. Friedman, [9], p. 929 in his response to Davidson [3]).

References and Bibliography

1. **Cantillon, R.,** *Essai sur la Nature du Commerce en General*, H. Higgs ed., for the Royal Economic Society. F. Cass, London, 1931.
2. **Davidson, P.,** 'A Keynesian view of the relationship between accumulation, money and the money-wage rate', *Economic Journal*, **79**, 300–23, June 1969.
3. **Davidson, P.,** 'A Keynesian view of Friedman's theoretical framework for monetary analysis', *Journal of Political Economy*, **80**, 864–82, Sept.–Oct., 1972.
4. **Davidson, P.,** *Money and the Real World*. Macmillan, London, 1972.
5. **Eichner, A. S.,** *The Megacorp and Oligopoly*. Cambridge Univ. Press, New York, 1976.
6. **Feiwel, G. R.,** *The Intellectual Capital of Michal Kalecki*. Uni. of Tennessee Press, Knoxville, 1975.
7. **Friedman, M.,** 'A theoretical framework for monetary analysis', *Journal of Political Economy*, **78**, 193–238, Mar.–Apl., 1970.
8. **Friedman, M.,** 'A monetary theory of nominal income', *Journal of Political Economy*, **79**, 323–37, Mar.–Apr., 1971.
9. **Friedman, M.,** 'Comments on the critics', *Journal of Political Economy*, **80**, 906–50, Sept.–Oct., 1972.
10. **Gordon, R. J.,**, (ed.), *Milton Friedman's Monetary Framework*. Univ. of Chicago Press. (Reprints Friedman, [7], [8], [9]; Davidson [3] and Patinkin [30]).
11. **Harrod, R. F.,** *The Trade Cycle*. Oxford Univ. Press, 1936.

12. **Harrod, R. F.,** *Economic Dynamics.* Macmillan, London, 1973.
13. **Hicks, John,** 'Must stimulating demand stimulate inflation?' *Economic Record,* **52,** 409–22, Dec., 1976.
14. **Kahn, R. F.,** 'The relation of home investment to unemployment', *Economic Journal,* **41,** 173–98, June 1931.
15. **Kaldor, N.,** *Causes of the Slow Rate of Economic Growth of the United Kingdom.* Cambridge Univ. Press, 1966.
16. **Kaldor, N.,** 'Conflicts in national economic objectives', *Economic Journal,* **81,** 1–16, Mar., 1971.
17. **Kaldor, N.,** 'Inflation and recession in the world economy', *Economic Journal,* **86,** 703–14, Dec., 1976.
18. **Kalecki, M.,** *Selected Essays on the Dynamics of the Capitalist Economy, 1933–1970.* Cambridge Univ. Press, 2971.
19. **Keynes, J. M.,** *A Tract on Monetary Reform.* Macmillan, London, 1923.
20. **Keynes, J. M.,** *Treatise on Money,* two vols. Macmillan, London, 1930.
21. **Keynes, J. M.,** *The General Theory of Employment, Interest end Money,* Macmillan, London, 1936.
22. **Keynes, J. M.,** 'The policy of government storage of food-stuffs and raw materials', *Economic Journal,* **48,** 449–60, Sept., 1938.
23. **Keynes, J. M.,** 'Relative movements of real wages and output', *Economic Journal,* **49,** 34–51, Mar., 1939.
24. **Keynes, J. M.,** *How to Pay for the War.* Macmillan, London, 1940.
25. **Keynes, J. M.,** 'The objectives of international price stability', *Economic Journal,* **53,** 185–7, June–Sept., 1943.
26. **Keynes, J. M.,** *The Collected Writings of John Maynard Keynes,* XIII, XIV, D. Moggridge, ed., Macmillan for the Royal Economic Society, London, 1973.
27. **Kregel, J. A.,** *The Reconstruction of Political Economy,* 2nd edn., Macmillan, London, 1975.
28. **Marshall, A.,** *Money, Credit and Commerce.* Macmillan, London 1923.
29. **Patinkin, D.,** 'The Chicago tradition, the quantity theory, and Friedman', *Journal of Money, Credit and Banking,* **1,** Feb., 1969.
30. **Patinkin, D.,** 'Friedman on the quantity theory and Keynesian economics', *Journal of Political Economy,* **80,** Sept.–Oct., 1972.
31. **Robinson, Joan,** *Essays in the Theory of Employment.* Macmillan, London, partially reprinted in *Collected Economic Papers,* Vol. IV, Blackwell, Oxford, 1937.
32. **Robinson, Joan,** *Collected Economic Papers,* Vol. I, Blackwell, Oxford, 1951.
33. **Robinson, Joan,** *The Accumulation of Capital,* Macmillan, London, 1956.
34. **Robinson, Joan,** 'Michal Kalecki on the economics of capitalism', *Oxford Bulletin of Economics and Statistics,* Special Issue, Michal Kalecki Memorial Lectures, E. Eshag, ed., **79,** 7–17, Feb., 1977.
35. **Rowthorn, R. E.,** 'What remains of Kaldor's law?', *Economic Journal,* **85,** 10–19, Mar., 1975.
36. **Sylos Labini, P.,** *Oligopoly and Technical Progress,* 2nd edn., Harvard Univ. Press, Cambridge, Mass., 1967.
37. **Samuelson, P.,** *Economics,* McGraw-Hill, New York, 1973.
38. **Weintraub, S.,** *A General Theory of the Price Level, Output, Income Distribution and Economic Growth,* Chilton, Philadelphia, 1959.

Chapter 8

Inflation in communist countries

Alec Nove

There are many communist-ruled countries, and the author's knowledge and time are limited. So, perhaps, is the reader's patience. I shall draw my examples almost exclusively from two countries, the USSR and Poland, but no doubt some interesting variations exist elsewhere. One thinks of China and Cuba, for instance. So this chapter does not pretend to exhaust a complex and large subject.

Let me begin with the institutional characteristics of a Soviet-type economy, and the possible manifestations of inflation within it. In the USSR virtually all prices are fixed by state organs, mostly at the centre, though some by the union republics. The only significant exception is the free peasant market (*kolkhoznyi rynok*), in which food may be sold by those who grow it, at prices usually uncontrolled. There are a few other minor legitimate private transactions: the letting of rooms, private medical practice, tutoring, petty craftsmen or seamstresses. There are also a range of illegitimate or downright illegal transactions. But the overwhelming mass of sales is of goods and services provided by state enterprises (or sold by collective farms to state procurement organs) at official prices.

Almost all manufactured goods are made by state enterprises in accordance with the state plan. The plan specifies not only the quantity of various items that should be produced, but will usually attach customers to specific suppliers by a vast and complex scheme of administered material allocation. Consequently, managers are not free to purchase the bulk of their inputs: they need an allocation certificate, which will generally specify the source of the inputs in question. Therefore, the possession of sums of money does not automatically entitle management to spend it. Indeed all but the pettiest of petty cash must be kept at the State Bank, and the bank is under an obligation to disallow payments which are improper (e.g. for an unauthorized purchase, or at the wrong price).

The bank also is under orders to disallow payments of wages and salaries in excess of the enterprise's or institution's 'wages fund', this being the maximum amount payable to labour. There are centrally determined wage scales applicable to each grade of skill, and also for technical and managerial staffs, with rules for payment of bonuses.

Enterprises sell at prices which normally cover operating costs and leave a profit margin. Most of these profits, plus proceeds of turnover tax, form the largest part of the revenue of the state budget. The budget, as published, shows a small surplus every year. This surplus, and also the increment in savings bank deposits, is added to the State Bank's assets, and these are used on a large scale to issue short-term credits to state enterprises; these credits cover the time-gap between production and receipt of payment from customers, goods in transit, etc. The total volume of short-term credits is planned and limited to avoid financing excess demand. Investment expenditures are tightly controlled by the centre. With minor exceptions they are financed out of budgetary grants, retained profits and the depreciation fund. The total volume of investment, and specific investment projects too, are (or should be) related to the availability of the necessary material and human resources.

Therefore, demand for producers' goods is a function of the output and investment plan, which determines in considerable detail the levels of administratively authorized demand for resources at the officially set prices. It follows that a balanced plan, i.e. one in which inputs are made available for the required outputs, cannot generate excess demand, and so inflationary pressure is excluded. Similarly, since the state plans the output of the consumers' goods industries, fixes retail prices and determines the level of incomes, demand should equal supply; if it does not, the adjustments can be made in prices and in wages, either in total or in specific categories of goods or workers. The institutional power is there, and there is no (legal) countervailing power, such as is constituted in the West by trade unions, farmers' associations, opposition political parties and the like. (However, most of agriculture is in the hands of private smallholders in Poland.) It is not surprising to learn that inflation is a greater problem in the West.

Yet it is also a major problem in the 'East'. We will see why in a moment. But before doing so, let us look at the statistics of prices, concentrating on the past twenty years (see Tables 8.1 and 8.2). (Note different base-years of the two tables. For Table 8.1 note that 1949 (base-year) was the year of exceptionally high postwar prices.)

Table 8.1 USSR: Wholesale prices of industry (excluding turnover tax) (1949=100)

	1955	1965	1970	1975
All industry* of which:	68	70	77	75
Electricity	74	62	83	83
Oil	65	63	89	87
Coal	84	84	152	155
Ferrous metallurgy	60	60	90	90
Chemicals	67	66	66	63
Machinery and metal-working	52	41	39	33
Light industry	80	81	86	93
Food industry	91	137	140	144

Source: [8], p. 23.
Note
*Manufacturing and extractive.

Table 8.2 USSR: retail price index (1940=100)

	1958	1965	1970	1975
All products	141	140	139	139
Food	149	152	153	154
(of which: liquor)	(317)	(258)	(262)	(267)
Non-food	133	126	124	122

Source: As Table 1, and [6]. There is no published index for 1955.

Of course within these averages one finds very wide differences: thus watches have almost halved in price, while vegetable prices have risen by over 20 per cent since 1965. However, these figures give one no ground for speaking of serious price-inflation. True, there were large increases in prices of coal, for instance, but this was due to the impact of higher wages on costs in this very labour-intensive industry. The rise in prices of the food industry's products was due to the (much-needed) increase in prices paid to farmers. The overall rise in wholesale prices of a mere 14 per cent in twenty years would turn any Western observer green with envy. As for the retail price index, this shows a remarkable stability – if the official data are to be accepted. Therefore, it might be said, there is no problem, and this article should end *now*. Indeed it should never have been begun.

Table 8.3 USSR: average wages and salaries (roubles per month)

1955	1965	1970	1975
71·8	96·5	122·0	145·8

Source: [8], p. 546.

Wages have, of course, risen, as the figures in Table 8.3 show. Incomes of collectivized peasants have risen faster. But the volume of goods and services produced and sold to the population has (according to the official indices) kept pace with this increase. It follows that real wages must have risen by an impressive figure since 1965.

The Polish data are given in Table 8.4. Again, there are wide disparities between items: thus meat, bread, macaroni and other basic

Table 8.4 Poland

	1960	1965	1970	1975	1976
Retail prices, goods and services of which:	100	106·3	113·5	128·5	134·4
Food	100·0	102·5	109·2	120·7	126·1
(Free market food)	(100·0)	(101·4)	(109·6)	(150·0)	(179·6)
Liquor	100·0	126·2	145·3	184·8	184·8
Non-food goods	100·0	104·3	107·1	121·1	128·4
Services	100·0	111·9	131·3	146·3	149·5

Source: [10], p. 389 and [5], p. 226.

food items show no price change at all during the entire period, except for the abortive (and brief) attempt to raise some of them in December 1970. There appears to be no published Polish index of industrial wholesale prices.

Money incomes in Poland rose much more rapidly than in the USSR after 1970 (see Table 8.5).

Table 8.5   Poland: average wages and salaries (zloty per month)

1960	1965	1970	1975
1560	1867	2235	3562

Source: [10], p. 109.

Peasant incomes, derived from sales of produce (mainly to the state) from their (privately owned) smallholdings, rose also. So did the total employed: thus total personal incomes (excluding consumption in kind) rose by over 100 per cent from 1970 to 1975 [10, p. 79].

The inflation, except in the most recent years in Poland, seems mild. But the figures cited above conceal certain phenomena of an inflationary kind. These manifest themselves in shortages, queues, grey or black markets, high prices in the legal free markets, unspent or unspendable cash balances in the hands of enterprises or individuals. There are also disguised price increases. Let us first of all examine these phenomena more closely, and then consider their causes and consequences, beginning with the producers' goods (investment goods) sectors.

Here there is one contrast between the USSR and Poland that leaps to the eye. Soviet problems could not be attributed to an unusually rapid rise in the volume of investment, as shown in Table 8.6. In *Poland*, by contrast, the government has proceeded very differently (see Table 8.7) the huge increase after 1970 being very noticeable.

Table 8.6   USSR: total investment in constant prices (milliards of roubles)

1965	1970	1975
57·0	82·0	114·9

Table 8.7   Poland: investment (milliards of zloty, 1971 prices)

1965	1970	1975
154·2	227·7	529·6

Source: [10], p. 123.

In both countries, though not for quite the same reasons, the supply of materials and machines has often fallen short of requirements. In Poland, which relies much more heavily on foreign trade, the shortage shows itself as an excessive payments deficit, which compels cuts in input plans and a sharp downward adjustment in the tempi of investment. This fits into an analysis in terms of a 'political trade cycle': the government tries to go too fast, to adopt over-ambitious plans, then has to jam on the brakes, until enough material and currency reserves are accumulated to start the process over again. Similar trends have been noted in Czechoslovakia [3] and Hungary [1] in previous decades. This, then, is the generation of excess demand by over-taut plans, which require more resources than exist or can be paid for.

The Soviet pattern is not cyclical, but is rather one of chronic, persistent shortage. Year after year one reads of delays in construction for lack of means to complete the work, and of constant worries of managers about the non-receipt of essential inputs, even when these are planned and allocation certificates issued. This is consistent with two hypotheses: either the planned utilization exceeds the total resources available (i.e. there is persistent macro-imbalance between output and inputs), or that the planners fail to match supply and demand in detail, i.e. there are micro-imbalances within possibly balanced aggregate totals. There is a sizeable literature about this whole problem in the Soviet Union, and the most convincing explanation appears to me to be along two mutually reinforcing lines. In the first place, the endeavour to achieve full utilization of resources, in the interests of rapid growth, leaves no spare capacity with which to correct the *inevitable* failures to match supply precisely with requirements. Secondly, from all levels below the centre there emerges an intense pressure for more investment resources for the given sector: an enterprise, an industry, a republic or province or city, the department responsible for artillery, or scientific research, or public health, exert pressure through the state and party machine within which they operate.

Let us now look at how these two factors help to explain the generation of excess demand. Why are micro-imbalances *inevitable*? Because of the overwhelming complexity of centralized planning. One can plan and more or less accurately forecast the total requirements for steel, cement and agricultural machinery (for instance), but it is quite another matter when it comes to ensuring the prompt delivery (at the right date) of constructional steel of a given specification, or of the right size of prefabricated cement blocks, or the required spare parts for a specific combine-harvester, to the factory, construction site or farm that actually needs them. This is but one example of perhaps *the* major problem of Soviet operational planning: the necessity and impossibility of disaggregation. So one can easily encounter a situation in which some resources are unutilized while others are short, creating bottlenecks and delays which have a cumulative effect. A further problem arises over the central allocation of investment funds: the cash that is issued is deliberately limited so as to avoid excess demand in total, but obviously those who administer financial flows must sit in a different office to those officials who allocate materials, who in turn are separated by departmental barriers from those who issue orders to those who produce or construct. It is thus quite possible (indeed it is frequently reported) that those who have the money cannot obtain the materials, while others who could obtain the materials are short of money. A network of unofficial supply agents, expediters ('pushers', *tolkachi*) try to overcome persistent shortages of materials in a variety of semi-legal ways. In sum, no Soviet manager, planner or economist would deny that material procurements are a perpetual source of worry and frustration, leading also to a tendency to hoard materials and to overapply for allocation certificates. Is any of this to be correctly labelled 'inflation', or 'repressed inflation'? This must be a matter of opinion or of definition. But no one doubts that, if prices were freed, many producers' goods would cost more. Indeed, this is advanced as a principal reason for retaining strict control over prices.

Turning now to the pressures for more resources which, of course, exist in all countries, this pressure is reinforced by the fact that capital seems free to the recipient. Again, in part this is universal: thus if my own university obtained the much-needed sums to complete its new library complex, this would be an outright grant. This, however, tends to be so in the USSR also in the more strictly economic sphere. As already noted, the enterprise will either receive grants from the budget or will be allowed to retain profits (for an approved purpose) which would otherwise go to the budget. But it would be wrong to suppose, given the nature of the system, that even a stiff interest rate would make much difference. There is, indeed, a capital charge levied since 1967 (averaging 6%), but prices were altered accordingly, and, since plan fulfilment is measured (*inter alia*) in terms of the gross value of turnover (sales), anything that results in the fixing of a higher price is no disincentive, rather the contrary. The ambitions of ministries, managers and localities manifest themselves not only in overapplication for capital investment authorizations, but also in two other much-documented and much-criticized patterns of behaviour. One is to start as many new projects as possible, because an unfinished project is more likely to attract additional grants from the centre. The other is to underestimate the costs of the project. There is thus a constant battle, or tug-of-war, between the officials pursuing sectional interest and the plan-coordination agencies (above all *Gosplan*), whose job is to cut the coat according to the cloth. Out of all these factors combined there arises an over-taut plan, too many planned demands in relation to resources. Among the scarce resources is labour: in an economy with little or no unemployment, it is often hard to man new factories, a fact which is advanced as one of the explanations for delays in bringing new capacity into operation, thus contributing to shortage of material inputs.

There is one other point to be made, which will have to be made again when we come to consider consumers' goods: the price index in Table 8.1 almost certainly understates the increase in prices. This is best seen by examining the index for machinery and metal-working. Is it likely to show a decline in price between 1965 and 1970, for instance, in the face of substantial increases in the prices of fuel and metal, *and* a 25 per cent increase in wages? This is a sector in which there are many new products, and there are plenty of complaints to the effect that new machines are dearer than the ones they replace. Needless to say, the pricing of new products, and their treatment in computing a price or volume index through time, is a problem for statisticians the world over. 'Accuracy' is out of the question. The reason for suspecting the Soviet index is that there is official pressure to prevent price increases, and therefore a tendency to evade price controls by introducing 'new' products which are just 'new' enough not to be comparable to the old. By contrast, the price index is affected by the (authentic) fall in costs and prices of machines which were new in the base year and have since entered the mass-production stage. The resultant 'deflation' of the price index has as one effect the 'inflation' of the growth rate, which pleases everyone.

Now what of consumers' goods and the citizens' purchasing power? We have seen that wage control in the Soviet Union appears to be more effective than in Poland, at least since 1970. The explanation must be primarily political. In the quinquennium 1966–70 Soviet average wages rose by 26 per cent against an announced planned rise of 20 per cent. In the same five years, the average in Poland rose by 20 per cent. However, the outburst of rioting which began in December 1970 and led to the fall of Gomulka changed the political situation, and this was followed by a policy of all-out growth both of investment and consumption in Poland which, as we have seen, led to a mini-wage-explosion: a rise in money wages in five years by over 60 per cent in 1971–75. Whereas in the USSR the relatively modest plan for a rise by 22 per cent in average wages was actually underfulfilled, the increase being 20 per cent. The institutional means of wage control being similar in the two countries, the difference can only have been due to the will of the political leadership and to pressures from below.

Let us look first at the Soviet case. Here one must note that the underfulfilment of the consumers' goods production plan, and also of the agricultural output plan, was substantial, even according to official statistics. Shortages of many goods can therefore be ascribed to this. These shortages can be shown to have increased in intensity by observing the growing gap (also in Poland, see Table 8.4) between official and free (peasant) market prices for foodstuffs. Soviet statistical annuals have ceased printing a price index for this free market. It can, however, be calculated roughly from two series, one giving the share of the free market in food sales in volume, the other in value (see Table 8.8).

Another way of measuring surplus purchasing power is to look at the growth of savings bank deposits: both for the USSR and Poland these show very large rises (see Table 8.9). Since hire-purchase is poorly developed, and there have been increases in production of such expensive items as cars, and also so-called cooperative housing (which requires large amounts of cash down), the incentive to save has grown, so that the savers will have the cash to put down if and when the car or the

Table 8.8 Share of free market in total trade in food* (%)

	1950	1965	1970	1973	1975
In actual prices of sale	28·7	10·0	8·5	7·9	7·8
At official retail prices	27·6	7·3	5·5	4·8	4·4
Free market prices (official prices =100)	104·0	137·0	154·5	164·5	177·3

Note:
*'Comparable items' (i.e. presumably excluding bread, for instance).
  Sources: [7], p. 652, and [8].

Table 8.9 Total deposits

	1965	1970	1975
USSR (milliard rbles)	18·7	46·6	91·0
Poland (milliard zloty)	51·3	114·8	302·8

Sources: [7], p. 597; [10], p. xlviii).

apartment become available. In Hungary savings greatly increased with greater availability after 1968, of cars and housing [4]. However, one has only to relate the total sums deposited in the savings banks with the total annual turnover of state and cooperative trade (178,000 million roubles in 1974) to see what a large overhang of surplus purchasing power now exists. It helps to explain the readily observable fact, especially in the provinces, of persistent shortages of a wide variety of goods and services. No doubt the psychology of a seller's market, continued with little respite for sixty years, contributes to the tendency to hoard and to rush to buy whatever *might* become hard to find, thus ensuring that it does indeed become hard to find. This cannot be quantified, and some purists would treat the evidence as 'anecdotal'. Others might, with more reason, point out that if this has been a chronic tendency for sixty years, this does not show a tendency to inflation, unless the *degree* of shortage has increased. I have suggested already two reasons for considering that shortages (at the official prices) have grown worse. A further point, again, alas, only to be supported by 'anecdotal' evidence, is the growth of black market transactions: thus, several (unofficial) sources have asserted that, in order to obtain a suite of furniture priced at 1000 roubles one must expend 500 roubles on bribes (and even then, according to one informant, there is no choice as to what actual furniture will arrive! 'We just wait and see'). Under such conditions of frequent non-availability and payments on the side, the official price index may be misleading.

It is misleading for another reason, already referred to earlier in discussing producers' goods, the appearance of new or allegedly new goods at higher prices, while the cheaper brands or varieties vanish. This is particularly apt to happen in the case of manufactures, since new varieties of skirts, suits, television sets, bicycles, watches, are a common occurrence, whereas (say) bread or milk is of standard type and is more proof against evasion of price control. Such price drift is also hard to resist or indeed to detect in catering: if a cheap dish is replaced by a dearer one in a restaurant, this may or may not be an authentic improvement in quality. Note that, throughout the whole range of goods and services, the replacement of an inferior by a *better* model at a higher price is *not* evidence of a rise in the overall level of prices, if the citizen prefers the better model. It is equally evident that *some* of the new products on sale in Soviet shops really are better than those they replace. It is, however, the universal belief that disguised price rises occur. Nor is this just a matter of folk-prejudice or anecdotes: it can be shown quite rigorously that when there is a wide range of choice as to product mix, plus price control, plus plans expressed in terms of gross roubles or zloty, this *must* encourage management to disguise price increases, especially as price increases are usually forbidden.

One is sometimes asked: if the official Soviet index claims an increase of retail prices by zero per cent in fifteen years, what is the 'real', or 'correct' figure? The question is unanswerable, not only by a Western scholar but also (I strongly suspect) by the Soviet Central Statistical Office. It is the equivalent to asking it to provide information on unrecorded transactions which, by definition, are not known to it. (There may, it is true, be instances of disguised increases for which the central government is itself responsible: one example often cited is the disappearance of the cheapest brands of vodka after 1972.) In Poland no secret was made of the existence of this sort of unrecorded price inflation: even officials told this foreigner: 'The official index admits to an increase of (say) 8 per cent, which means roughly 12 per cent' (referring to the year 1975). But there is no pretence that this is anything other than a rough order of magnitude.

Errors due to failure to incorporate micro-variations in consumer demand into production and distribution plans are common and certainly contribute to the widespread shortages. As in the case of producers' goods, one is never quite sure whether what one is seeing is a macro-imbalance (total demand exceeds total supply) or a series of micro-imbalances (with some goods in excess supply while others are short). In the case of Poland, one can assert with confidence that the wage increases in 1971–75, even after allowance for the increase in prices in these years, exceeded any possible increase in supply of consumers' goods and services (unless these were sustained by massive foreign borrowing, which could only be temporary). One has only to refer to Table 8.4 and 8.5 above. But this has not been so obviously the case in the Soviet Union. In any event, excess supply and shortage (which in the case of producers' goods can be a matter of input–output necessity, independent of relative prices) cannot be analysed without reference to the peculiar distortions of the retail prices system, typical of both the USSR and Poland.

In both countries prices tend to be sticky, for two reasons. One is the sheer administrative burden of altering prices, millions of prices, which totally excludes flexible adjustment to ensure the balance between demand and supply. Matters are not helped by the fact that goods in heavy demand, even if retail prices *are* moved upwards, may not be profitable to produce, since industrial wholesale prices are related to cost, and the gap between the wholesale and the retail price is absorbed by turnover tax. The second reason, however, is the conscious price policy of the government. Higher prices are seen as politically dangerous, higher prices of necessities, especially of food, as very dangerous indeed. One has only to recall the effects of two attempts to raise prices of livestock products in Poland: in December 1970 there were riots and the increase had to be rescinded after the removal of Gomulka from the leadership. In June 1976 the party leader, Gierek, survived, but the proposals had to be hastily withdrawn. In the USSR the last increase in the price of (non-luxury) foodstuffs was in 1962.

The effect of such a price policy has been to create major (and predictable) disequilibria between demand and supply of livestock products, especially meat. Meat is, everywhere, a product with a high income-elasticity of demand. Average wages and salaries in the USSR have increased from 1962 to 1975 by 70 per cent and total disposable incomes have increased by more than this (allowing for the increase in the labour force, higher peasant incomes and some tax cuts), let us say by roughly 85 per cent. Output of meat has risen in the same period by 60 per cent. But demand has plainly risen much faster, as Soviet calculations show an income-elasticity of over 1·4. 'Revealed preference' can tell us nothing about demand, when a frustrated customer cannot reveal how she would spend her roubles because what she prefers cannot be obtained.

In Poland the position is equally striking. In just the five years 1971–75 average money wages rose by over 60 per cent, as we have seen. Meat output could not possibly keep pace with demand. (The principal bottleneck is fodder for livestock.) While prices paid to farms have risen to encourage higher output, retail prices have been frozen, and so livestock products now attract some of the highest subsidies known in human history: 19 milliard roubles in the USSR [2] (over $25 billion at the not-unrealistic official exchange rate), and in a speech by Jaroszewicz to the Sejm (Parliament) in June 1976 claimed to be well over 100 milliard zloty in Poland (possibly $5 billion in terms of purchasing power: there are many dollar–zloty exchange rates).

So one has a heavy burden on the budget to subsidize a price at which demand and supply could not possibly balance. Evidently, then, politics as well as the complexities of price control have totally frustrated any attempt at market-clearing retail prices, and both the USSR and Poland are suffering from this. This fear of higher prices and their political consequences did not operate in Stalin's time: prices of essentials were multiplied in the early 1930s, and also in 1946–47. But the Stalin terror is no more.

Space forbids more than a bare mention of other East European countries. They (Poland too) have also had to contend with the dangers of imported inflation, especially in and after 1973. The great stability, accompanied by the least evidence of physical shortage, has been achieved by the GDR, thus showing the two Germanies out in front in both their halves of Europe. In Hungary, where some progress was made towards aligning domestic and world prices, as part of a market-oriented economic reform, skilful demand management kept the rise in prices to quite modest levels: about 2 per cent per annum in 1968–73 [11, p. 23], and this despite the fact that a large number of prices were decontrolled. However, the large increase in world prices after 1972 placed severe burdens on the Hungarian economy, and led to a realignment of prices and wages (including a rise in meat prices by 35 per cent in 1976). One can fairly say that these difficulties were due primarily to external factors over which the Hungarian authorities had no control.

The very high rates of inflation in Yugoslavia, accompanied by high unemployment, raise other important questions, which cannot be pursued here.

So, returning to the USSR and to Poland, what conclusions can one draw from the evidence presented, which may (or may not) help us to understand the causes and cures of inflation?

The following points seem to be sufficiently significant to justify further consideration.

In the first place, allowing for the important institutional differences, it seems clear that inflationary pressures do exist in Soviet-type economies, and that they, too, have to wage a constant struggle to restrain excess demand, a struggle which is not always successful.

Secondly, the causes of this excess certainly include pressures from various social groups, exercised through the party–state machine (e.g. by ministers, generals, regional party secretaries, etc. etc.), but also more 'passively' from below (e.g. threat of riot if prices rise). Those who, in analysing the causes of Western inflation, lay stress on social pressures in a pluralist society should note that these pressures (for more than can be provided) exist also in societies thought to be totalitarian. One can speak in fact of their economies as characterized by a kind of 'centralized pluralism'.

Thirdly, control over incomes in the Soviet Union – but not in Poland after 1970 – seems to have been effective, certainly much more effective than in the West. However, the one effective method of control has been over the total wages bill (the 'wages fund'). With widespread bonus and piece-rate schemes, and the possibility of evasion through promotion and regrading, no control of individual take-home pay could be effectively applied. Chronic shortage of labour in many areas leads to a built-in tendency to overpay labour, and to evade rules designed to counteract this tendency, except the crude rule which specifies how much the total wages bill should be. This rule does, however, cause serious inconvenience to management: necessary tasks requiring the taking-on of extra workers cannot be carried out except after a long and complex procedure for authorization of additional payments.

Fourthly, price control can be seen to present two kinds of difficulties. The first is political: necessary price increases turn out to be a menace to security and order and are thus avoided or, as in Poland, reversed. The second is technical: it is simply impracticable to amend extremely long price schedules, and to collect reliable information upon which such amendments must depend, without creating a multitude of contradictions and anomalies. (Thus, any relationship between demand and scarcity on the one hand and profitability on the other is purely coincidental.) As we have also seen, it is also impossible to prevent disguised price increases via the introduction of 'new' products.

Finally, there is the role of money supply in 'eastern' inflation. Here it is necessary to distinguish, in the Soviet model, between producers' goods and consumers' goods. Producers' goods are in a real sense rationed, demand is 'authorized' by the plan, dependent on allocation certificates. The money flows, especially of short-term credits, are supposed to match the availability of resources, but there are frequent instances when an enterprise bank balance cannot be used because the resources that are needed have not been administratively allocated to this enterprise. Therefore most of the 'inflationary' phenomena in *this* field are due to overambitious plans, often quantitative plans, or to sectoral imbalances, with money supply playing a subordinate role as a causal factor. It is worth noting that attempts to control credits, if accompanied by overambitious obligatory plan targets, have little chance of success. As the work of Podolski [9] shows such attempts in Poland led to the expansion of 'involuntary' suppliers' credits, i.e. delays in payment of debts (though in principle the rules bar the granting of credits by enterprises to each other).

However, in the case of consumers' goods it is possible to speak of excess supply of cash and savings deposits in the hands of the population, though, as has been stressed, it is difficult to distinguish the consequences of 'macro' excess of purchasing power from those of price irrationalities and planning errors and the resultant shortages of many goods (together with excess stores of others).

The USSR and most of its allies seem better able than most Western countries to keep inflation under control. But the methods used to achieve this end, especially the tight control over material allocation and prices, cause much inefficiency through delays and inflexibilities, the discouragement of initiative and so of innovation. Reformers have been proposing a relaxation of these controls, which would have the effect of increasing the scope of inflationary pressures: thus any measure designed to provide an active role for prices within a more market-orientated economy would lead to a sharp rise in prices, *unless*, as in Hungary in 1968–72, monetary and credit policy plus wage controls can eliminate excess demand.

There is no simple solution anywhere.

Addendum

After the paper was written and sent off to the publishers, I read an article by Richard Portes on 'Control of inflation: lessons from East European experience', which appeared in *Economica* in May 1977. Its conclusions differ very considerably from those of the present paper, and are in certain respects surprising in so far as they relate to the USSR. It is certainly arguable that a reasonable balance between the cash incomes of the population and the goods and services available has been achieved in Hungary. This is easy to observe from the absence of queues and black markets. However, it seems totally improper to dismiss the repeated complaints about non-availability of the desired products in the USSR as just anecdotal and to assert that there is no sellers' market! Apart from the plain evidence of the *growing* disparity between official and free-market prices for food, documented above, the evidence of shortage is massive. Hungarians travelling to the Soviet Union and Soviet citizens travelling to Hungary (or Czechoslovakia, or East Germany) never fail to notice the contrast in availability, choice and ease of shopping. Whenever the question of the relaxation of price control is raised in the Soviet Union, one of the most frequently cited arguments against such relaxation is that prices would at once rise. It must be accepted, of course, that a considerable part of the phenomenon of shortage is caused by the mismatching between supply and demand for specific products, rather than by a macro-imbalance between total demand and total supply. One cause for such mismatching is cited in Portes' own article: the remarkable stability of most prices over long periods. One consequence is that when price adjustments are made, they are usually very big, as in the case of petrol and coffee in the Soviet Union in February 1978. Would Portes apply the pejorative term 'anecdotal' to the repeated stories from correspondents and others about visible shortage of both petrol and coffee in the period before the price rise?

Finally, a word on savings bank deposits. I agree that by themselves they do not provide conclusive evidence of supressed inflation, except in the sense that the effort to save to obtain cars and cooperative apartments which are not now available does at least prove that they are not available! However, we have no ground for supposing that savings bank deposits represent the totality, or even a major part of, stocks of money in the hands of the population.

References

1. **Gàcs, J. and Lacko, M.,** 'A Study of Planning Behaviour on the National Economic Level', *Economics of Planning*, **13**, No. 12, 1973.
2. **Glushkov, N.,** *Pravda*, 8.2.1977.
3. **Goldman, J.,** 'Fluctuations and Trends in the Rate of Economic Growth in Some Socialist Countries', *Economics of Planning*, **4**, No. 2, 1964.

230 Perspectives on inflation

4. **Lacko, M.,** 'Consumer Savings and the Supply Situation', *Acta Oeconomica* **15,** (34), 1975.
5. *Maly Rocznik* 1977.
6. *Narodnoye Khozyaistvo,* 1962.
7. *Narodnoye Khozyaistvo,* 1973.
8. *Narodnoye Khozyaistvo,* 1975.
9. **Podolski T.,** *Socialist Banking and Monetary Control,* Cambridge, 1972.
10. *Rocznyk Statistyczne,* 1976.
11. *Statistical Year Book,* Budapest, 1976. (in English).

Notes on contributors

J. D. Byers. Lecturer in Economics, University College, Aberystwyth. Has taught at the University of Southampton where he was associated with the Econometric Model Building Unit. Author of 'The supply of labour' in *Topics of Applied Macroeconomics* edited by D. F. Heathfield, Macmillan, 1975.

S. P. Chakravarty. Lecturer in Economics, University College of North Wales, Bangor. He has worked on the Southampton Econometric Model Building Unit of the UK and has held various postdoctoral research fellowships on both sides of the Atlantic. He has published on input–output economics, hydrogen energy and stability of nonlinear systems.

Victoria Chick. Lecturer in Economics, University College, London. She has been Visiting Associate Professor at the University of California at Berkeley, Visiting Professor at the University of California at Santa Cruz, Visiting Economist with the Reserve Bank of Australia and Visiting Lecturer at the University of Southampton. She has published articles on macroeconomic theory and is the author of *The Theory of Monetary Policy*, revised edition, Basil Blackwell, 1977.

Phyllis Deane. Reader in Economic History in the Faculty of Economics and Politics and Fellow of Newnham College in the University of Cambridge. Author of *The First Industrial Revolution*, Cambridge University Press, 1965, *British Economic Growth 1688–1959* (with W. A. Cole), Cambridge University Press, 1962 and *The Evolution of Economic Ideas* (forthcoming).

David F. Heathfield. Senior Lecturer in Economics at the University of Southampton having previously worked on the Southampton Econometric Model Building Unit. He was Visiting Associate Professor at Washington University, St. Louis, 1973–4. He has published a number of papers and a book on Production and has edited *The Econometric Study of the United Kingdom* (with K. Hilton), Macmillan, 1969, *Topics in Applied Macroeconomics*, Macmillan, 1976 and *The Economics of Co-determination*, Macmillan, 1978.

J. A. Kregel. Senior Lecturer in Economics at the University of Southampton. He has been Visiting Professor at Rutgers University, the Université Catholique de Louvain and the University of Bologna. He has written extensively on the economics of Keynes and is the author of *The Rate of Profit, Distribution and Growth*, Macmillan, 1971, *The Reconstruction of Political Economy*, Macmillan, 1973, second edition, 1975 and *Theory of Capital*, Macmillan, 1976.

George W. McKenzie. Senior Lecturer in Economics at the University of Southampton having previously taught at Washington University, St. Louis. He has published in a number of economic journals and is the author of *The Monetary Theory of International Trade*, Macmillan, 1974 and *The Economics of the Eurocurrency System*, Macmillan, 1976.

Alec Nove. Professor of Economics and Director of the Institute of Soviet and East European Studies at the University of Glasgow. He has been visiting Professor at the Universities of Kansas, Pennsylvania, Columbia and the Catholic University of Chile. Publications include: *The Soviet Economy*, Allen and Unwin, 1968, *The Soviet Economic System*, Allen and Unwin, 1977, *Economic History of the USSR*, Allen Lane 1969, Penguin, 1972, *Stalinism and After*, Allen and Unwin, 1975, *Efficiency Criteria for Nationalised Industries*, Allen and Unwin, 1973.

Index